A7

Socialism
for a
Sceptical Age

Socialism
for a
Sceptical Age

Ralph Miliband

VERSO

London · New York

Copyright © Ralph Miliband 1994

The right of Ralph Miliband to be identified as
author of this work has been asserted in accordance with the
Copyright, Designs and Patents Act 1988.

First published in USA by Verso 1995
This edition © Verso 1995

First published in UK by Polity Press in association with
Blackwell Publishers 1994

All rights reserved

Verso
UK: 6 Meard Street, London W1V 3HR
USA: 29 West 35th Street, New York, NY 10001–2291

Verso is the imprint of New Left Books

ISBN 1 85984 947 4
ISBN 1 85984 057 4 (pbk)

Library of Congress Cataloging-in-Publication Data
A catalog record for this book is available from the Library
of Congress

Typeset in 9 on 10 pt Sabon by Graphicraft
Printed in Great Britain by Hartnolls Ltd., Bodmin, Cornwall

To Marion

It must be considered that there is nothing more difficult to carry out, nor more doubtful of success, nor more dangerous to handle, than to initiate a new order of things. For the reformer has enemies in all those who profit by the old order, and only lukewarm defenders in all those who would profit by the new order, this lukewarmness arising partly from fear of their adversaries, who have the laws in their favour; and partly from the uncredulity of mankind, who do not truly believe in anything until they have had actual experience of it.

Machiavelli, *The Prince*

Contents

Acknowledgements

I am very grateful to the following friends who made detailed and very useful criticisms of an earlier version of the book: Ted Honderich, Andrew Glyn, John Griffith, Jane O'Grady, Leo Panitch and John Saville. It also gives me great pleasure to acknowledge the very helpful (and stringent) criticisms and suggestions I have had from David and Edward Miliband. The book owes much to the advice I have received, even if I have not always followed it. Given the controversial nature of the book, it may be particularly necessary to say that I alone am responsible for its contents. My greatest debt, as always, is to Marion Kozak, for her unfailing support and her critical reading of the text. The dedication of the book to her is a very small token of all that I owe her.

R. M.

Foreword

Ralph Miliband completed this book in January 1994. He saw the proofs in hospital in May 1994, but his death in the same month means that he did not live to see it published. He was, as we are, grateful to Ellen Meiksins Wood for stepping in to check the proofs against the original manuscript.

The book tackles many of the central issues and problems with which Ralph Miliband was concerned during his life. It is, however, an argument for fundamental social and economic change stretching well beyond one lifetime. If it succeeds in stimulating further debate about the nature of such change, and how to achieve it, it will serve the twin purposes of political and scholarly engagement for which it was intended.

Nothing can make up for the loss we feel, but it is some comfort that the ideas developed by Ralph Miliband in this book and elsewhere will live on.

Marion Kozak
David Miliband
Edward Miliband

July 1994

Introduction

This book is based on two distinct propositions. The first is that capitalism now constitutes a massive obstacle to the resolution of the evils which its own development has produced. The second is that there is a socialist alternative to capitalism which makes possible the resolution of these problems.

These propositions are distinct because whatever may be said against capitalism, it does not inevitably follow that there is a desirable alternative to it. Even its most ardent defenders do not deny that capitalism has failings; but they also insist that these are not inherent, and that they are remediable within the framework of the system. In any case, it is also argued, capitalism with all its defects is infinitely preferable to any socialist alternative that could ever be. On this view, in Francis Fukuyama's words, capitalism, or rather liberal capitalism, represents 'the end point of mankind's ideological evolution', and 'the final form of human government'.[1]

People who believe this readily accept that 'socialism', in a mild social democratic version, remains, and will long continue to be, part of the political scene of capitalist societies, and that it may even become, if it is not already, a stronger current of thought than laissez-faire capitalism. But mild social democracy is not, in practice, an alternative to capitalism, but a certain kind of adaptation to it. I take socialism, without inverted commas, to mean on the contrary

[1] F. Fukuyama, *The End of History and the Last Man* (Hamish Hamilton, London, 1992), p. xiii.

a fundamental recasting of the social order. It is this socialism which is now commonly declared to be an obsolete construct, to be relegated to the crowded museum of visionary projects which have proliferated through the ages: to cling to that project is taken to demonstrate a lamentable lack of realism.

I believe this view to be false, and that socialist democracy is a feasible and desirable alternative to capitalism and capitalist democracy. I cannot *prove* this, since the proof has to be the construction of this alternative, which remains a task to be accomplished. But the absence of proof, in the form of a socialist society clearly superior to capitalist ones, as was at one time claimed to exist in the Soviet Union and other Communist societies, does not itself prove anything. To believe that such absence of proof is conclusive amounts to saying that anything much better than what is now available is quite beyond the reach of humankind. Such fetishism of the here and now is naive.

Even though it is not possible to prove that a desirable alternative to capitalism and capitalist democracy is possible, it is at least possible to present a reasonable argument for it. This is what I seek to do here, on the basis of a reassessment of the socialist enterprise in the light of the experiences which have affected (and afflicted) socialism in this century; and in the light also of the vast changes which have occurred in capitalism and in the world at large in the decades since World War II, and particularly in recent years.

I started work on this book in 1989, but I had to stop working on it from the beginning of 1991 to the spring of 1992. Those were of course exceptionally dramatic years; and I am very conscious that, in one way and another, they have had a deep influence on my thinking about socialism. Over a period stretching over four decades, I have discussed in various writings some of the themes which are to be found in this book. But I believe that, taken as a whole, the book offers perspectives which go well beyond these themes, and which reflect something of the thinking to which the developments of recent years have led me. In this sense, much of the text is based on a questioning of the ideas I have held over the years, and a response to that questioning. I have throughout been extremely concerned to move away from over-familiar formulations (my own as well as those of others) and to undertake a genuine reappraisal of socialism, and of the ways in which its prospects might be advanced. In the course of doing this, I have become more conscious than ever before of the vast problems – some old, some new – which are posed by the socialist enterprise. I do not pretend to have solved these problems, because they cannot be solved in words, only in practice. In other words, I offer no blueprint of the socialist alternative, all neat and tidy. Rather than engage in such an exercise, I have tried to indicate what, in my view, socialism should now be taken to mean, what its problems are, and how they might be tackled.

I am particularly concerned in this book with what Alec Nove has called 'feasible socialism'. He meant by this a socialism 'which might be achieved within the lifetime of a child already conceived'.[2] For my part, I think of socialism as a new social order, whose realization is a process stretching over many generations, and which may never be fully 'achieved'. Socialism, that is to say, involves a permanent striving to advance the goals that define it.

I should say something in this introduction about my use of terms. What I mean by socialism will be discussed in the second chapter, and in later chapters as well, but I may say here that I understand it to involve two fundamental and intertwined objectives – democratization far beyond anything which capitalist democracy can afford; and egalitarianism, that is to say the radical attenuation of the immense inequalities of every kind which are part of capitalist democracy; and to these must be added another objective, which I will argue to be an essential means to the implementation of the other two, namely the socialization of a predominant part of the means of economic activity.

I use 'the Left' to denote a large number of people, of course including socialists, but also many more who might be reluctant to accept the socialist label, or who would reject it altogether. 'Progressive' might be used to designate such people – people, that is, who seek the reform of various aspects of the social order in democratic and egalitarian directions. The same designation also applies to the men and women who form part of the 'labour movement', and of many 'new social movements' as well. All such people may be taken to be on the left or progressive side of the ideological and political spectrum, though at different points.

[2] A. Nove, *The Economics of Feasible Socialism* (George Allen and Unwin, London, 1983), p. ix.

'Radical reform' as used here denotes measures of reform which are intended to make a serious indent into one or other aspect of the social order, again in democratic and egalitarian directions. On this view, movements seeking the end of discrimination on such grounds as race and gender are also clearly involved in the business of radical reform. I should add that, even though the book makes a good many general recommendations for the advancement of socialist goals, it does not offer specific proposals in regard to a vast range of issues which must obviously be of primary concern to socialists – health, education, transport, housing, the environment, social benefits, child care, taxation, penal reform, and so on: the list could be extended indefinitely. Socialist policies in regard to all such issues clearly do need to be articulated. But doing this was not my intention in writing this book, and the task lies in any case well beyond my means.

'Revolution' and 'revolutionary' are ambiguous terms, for they denote two different concepts. On the one hand, they denote an accumulation of radical reforms so substantial and sustained as to bring about a revolutionary transformation of the social order. This was the perspective of social democracy before 1914, so that its 'reformism' could be said to have a revolutionary charge, in the above sense of the word. On the other hand, 'revolution' and 'revolutionary' are commonly understood to involve the overthrow of the existing state as well as the transformation of the social order. This perspective does not reject the struggle for reform, but sees it as a preparation for a seizure of power based on an insurrectionary popular upheaval. Both perspectives will be given critical attention in the following pages.

The denotation 'Communism' (with a capital C) refers to the regime that came into being in Russia in October 1917 and in other countries after 1945. Communism in this meaning has, I believe, nothing to do with what Marx meant by communism, a far-distant state of society marked by abundance, equality and harmony, a very long way beyond socialism.

Readers will find references to Marx and other figures of 'classical Marxism' at various points of the text. The reason for this is that the kind of reappraisal of socialism which is undertaken here demands an engagement with Marxism. Such an engagement involves an acknowledgement of what remains of enduring importance in classical Marxism – and there is a lot more of this than is currently said; but it also involves a move away from some of its propositions.

Either way, I believe that Marxism has to be taken as a major point of reference in the discussion of socialism.

The focus of the book is on advanced capitalist countries, though I discuss in chapter 1 the impact which Western imperialism has had on the rest of the world, and in chapter 7 the prospects for ex-Communist countries and countries of the 'third world'. The questions I discuss in the book are also relevant to these countries: socialist values are universal, but the problems which their advancement poses present themselves differently in these countries, given their different histories and experiences. To deal adequately with these problems and possibilities in ex-Communist countries and the 'third world' would require another book, which I am not competent to write.

In chapter 1, I discuss the main items in the indictment that can be drawn up against capitalism, and I seek, on the basis of that indictment, to answer the question 'Why not capitalism?'. In chapter 2, I discuss the meaning of socialism and, in doing so, suggest how fundamentally different, in this meaning, it is from Communism. The next two chapters elaborate the main propositions advanced in chapters 1 and 2. Chapter 3 discusses a question which has received less attention than its importance warrants, namely the nature of the institutional reforms which would give substance to socialist democracy; and it also suggests some other fundamental reforms which the establishment of such a regime would require. Chapter 4 deals with the economic reforms which would provide the essential 'base' for the transition from capitalist to socialist democracy; and it also discusses the problems which these reforms would pose in the context of an ever more global capitalism. Chapters 5 and 6 are concerned with the crucial question of implementation. Chapter 5 takes up the question of what support might reasonably be expected for the reforms proposed in previous chapters, and what organizations and strategies would be most likely to further the process. Chapter 6 discusses the problems which would confront a socialist government; and it outlines the ways in which such as a government would have to cope with these problems. Finally, chapter 7 discusses what prospects there are for socialist aspirations to gain a far greater measure of support in different parts of the world than they now have.

Throughout, my concern has been to open a discussion on themes which badly need detailed exploration, and which the present climate of pessimism on the Left about the possibility of fundamental change tends to discourage. The pessimism is understandable, but I think it is overdone. I will myself argue that the kind of fundamental change which socialism implies should not be taken to mean that this will usher in a reign of perfect harmony. I take a much less 'utopian' view of what is possible, even in the long run; and I also think that even a rather more sober version of socialism is not likely to see the light of day for a long time to come. But if socialism *is* taken to involve a permanent striving to advance its goals, then the outlook, for reasons to be discussed presently, is not nearly as bleak as is commonly made out; and now is as good a time as any to prepare the ground, not least by reasoned argument, for advances to come.

1

The Case Against Capitalism

The first question socialists have to answer is what it is about capitalism which leads them to strive for a radical alternative to it. Any such alternative, most socialists readily acknowledge nowadays, is fraught with great uncertainties and unresolved problems; and capitalism today is obviously not what it was in the mid-nineteenth century, when Marx was beginning to labour on what eventually became *Capital*, published in 1867. Capitalism since then has produced a vast range of improvements in the daily lives of wage-earners; and it has shown itself to be amenable to reforms of many kinds, undreamt of a hundred years ago. Marx could have had no inkling of the degree of 'social democratization' which has occurred in advanced capitalist countries. From the last decades of the nineteenth century onwards, 'mass politics' and the growth of labour movements have compelled governments, whatever their own inclinations, to make concessions to the working class in many areas, which have resulted in the creation of a wide range of entitlements. Capitalist countries greatly differ in the nature, level and substance of these entitlements: Swedish capitalism is very different in this respect from American or Japanese capitalism, as are West European countries from each other. But nowhere in advanced capitalist countries have workers and their families failed to register important advances, particularly in the decades following World War II, the

golden age of capitalism in the twentieth century. In an article in
New Left Review in 1984, the Swedish sociologist Göran Therborn
thus argued that 'in the 1960s and 1970s', 'advanced capitalism
underwent a silent yet major transformation, the full economic, social
and political range and impact of which remains to be explored.' He
labelled this transformation 'welfare state capitalism', and noted
that under it, 'a growing part of people's incomes is determined by
political rules and rights, and that the routine activities of the state
are increasingly devoted to regulation and provision of social security, health and social care and education.' 'In advanced capitalist
countries today, between a fifth and one third of all household
income derives from public revenue and not from property or labour
for private or public capital.'[1] Two other writers have also suggested
that, by the late sixties, 'the social democratic paradigm of commitment to political liberalism, the welfare state, the mixed economy
managed on Keynesian principles, and the gradual transformation of
society in an egalitarian direction seemed more likely than its rivals
to provide the basis for a widely held consensus.'[2]

This proved to be much too complacent. Such consensus as there
had been between conservative and social democratic parties on
economic and social issues began to erode with the end of the post-
war boom years, and the trend, from the 1970s onwards, was
towards an attack on public expenditure for public and welfare
services and towards the curtailment of entitlements. But even the
governments most determined to reduce the level of public provision,
as in Britain and the United States, were only partially successful in
their endeavours. The 'welfare state' has been steadily eroded, but it
has not been, and cannot be, altogether destroyed. 'Welfare state
capitalism' is a mean and grudging business, and leaves in existence

---

[1]   G. Therborn, 'The prospects of labour and the transformation of advanced
capitalism', *New Left Review*, 145 (May–June 1984), pp. 25, 26, 27. In the
same vein, an American author notes for the United States that 'by 1980, 36
million Americans received monthly Social Security checks. Benefits were received by 22 million from Medicaid, 28 million from Medicare, 18 million from
foodstamps, 15 million from Veterans programs, and 11 million from Aid to
Families and Dependent Children'. 'It has been estimated', the author adds,
'that perhaps half of the US population depends in whole or in part on federal
aid in one form or another': C. Wolf Jr, *Markets or Governments: choosing
between imperfect alternatives* (MIT Press, Cambridge, Mass., 1988), p. 44.
[2]   W. E. Patterson and A. N. Thomas, *The Future of Social Democracy*
(Clarendon Press, Oxford, 1986), p. v.

vast areas of bitter deprivation; but it is now a part of capitalist reality which it would be difficult and dangerous to subvert altogether. Beyond a certain point, slashing entitlements produces electoral retribution or social disorder, or both.

In the light of this evolution, and despite all its limitations, is it reasonable to seek the replacement of capitalism by an entirely different system? Is it not much more sensible to press for more reforms within the present system, and thus to achieve a capitalism with a more human face? If socialism is indeed taken to be a far-distant prospect, or a proven illusion, why not concentrate on the struggle for such advances as can be achieved, and forget an idea, a vision, a utopia which is now widely discredited; and is it not possible, even likely, that these advances will in time further transform capitalism in the desired directions? More generally, are we not now at a remarkable moment in history where capitalism has so changed, and has thereby so changed the perspectives and expectations of people, that the notion of a socialist alternative is an increasingly irrelevant eccentricity?

Such siren songs have an undoubted appeal to many people on the Left nowadays.[3] But there are cogent reasons for resisting them. For, it will be argued here, piecemeal reform is not sufficient to cure the fundamental evils of the system; and the abandonment of the radically transformative perspective which socialism represents also has a profound influence on the nature and scope of reform itself. The history of reform under capitalism shows it to have been a very partial response to specific 'problems', and to have remained constrained by the logic of capital. Far from seeking to achieve radical cures, conservative governments have viewed reform as a means of preventing radical transformation from occurring by buying social peace with concessions. But even where reforms have been undertaken by social democratic governments, they have not resulted in the abolition of the essential features of capitalism. Nor is this remarkable, since such abolition was seldom what was intended. None of this is to denigrate the struggle for reform, or what that struggle

---

[3] The songs are not, however, new. In 1952, C. A. R. Crosland was already writing that 'by 1951 Britain had, in all essentials, ceased to be a capitalist country': 'The transition from capitalism', in *New Fabian Essays*, ed. R. H. S. Crossman (J. M. Dent, London, 1970 edition), p. 42. The arguments in that essay were elaborated in *The Future of Socialism* (Jonathan Cope, London, 1956), which became the bible of Labour 'revisionism'.

has achieved; it is only to say that, from a socialist perspective, what is proposed by way of reform needs to be inscribed in a radical transformative project, and judged *both* in terms of the improvements it achieves, *and also* in terms of its contribution to the advancement of that project.

Of course, the limited nature of the reforms which have been achieved in a capitalist-dominated context is not sufficient ground to condemn capitalism. Nor does it by itself make the case for a socialist alternative. What is required is that an answer be given to the question 'What is fundamentally wrong with capitalism?', and also that a case be made for a socialist alternative to it. I am concerned in this chapter with the first question, and I defend in the following chapters the proposition that an altogether different and more desirable system is possible.

First, the question 'Why not capitalism?' rests on a combination of economic, social, political and moral factors, all closely interlinked. Secondly, and crucially, there is the argument that the items in the indictment of capitalism and of the social order in which it is embedded are inherent to the system, however real the improvements of which it is capable. This is why the notion of a capitalism with a human face is such a problematic one. It is certainly possible to lessen the system's grossest abuses; but it is not possible to eradicate its essential inhumanity. To do this requires a different system, moved by a different dynamic.

Definitions of capitalism very, but it is best conceived as a system in which at least the predominant part of the means of economic activity – industrial, commercial, financial, and those relating to communications – are under private ownership and control; and in which the primary dynamic of that activity, overwhelmingly stronger than any other, is the extraction of private profit from formally independent wage-earners. In this sense, capitalism is more firmly embedded in the social order than it ever was, notwithstanding all the transformations which it has undergone over the years. Market relations are insistently praised as the most desirable form of individual and social interaction; and there has never been a time when commercialization has more thoroughly come to pervade all spheres of life.

The distinction between capitalism and the social order is, however, of great importance. Capitalism is a mode of production and its pervasiveness does make it proper to speak of a capitalist social order. But 'the social order' is nevertheless a much more comprehensive denotation of a vast complex of institutions in society which are the product of a long historical evolution. Gramsci once said that, in Russia, 'the state was everything, civil society was primordial and gelatinous'; whereas in the West, 'the state was only an outer ditch, behind which there stood a powerful system of fortresses and earthworks.'[4] But no society, however 'primordial', is really 'gelatinous': in all societies, there are 'fortresses and earthworks', which deeply affect their character.[5] In all of them, there are also enduring and diverse currents of thought, sentiment, and practices, and some of them at least constitute important sources of resistance to the domination of society by the imperatives and values of capitalism – for instance, resistance emanating from labour and socialist movements, from social movements based on race, ethnicity, gender, fighting against super-exploitation; and resistance to capitalist values and practices also derives from religious or traditional modes of thought. Hegemony, in Gramsci's sense, is usually taken to mean the capacity of ruling classes to instil their values into subordinate classes and to turn these values into the 'common sense of the epoch'. By now, hegemony has acquired an additional meaning: it must also be taken to mean the capacity of ruling classes to persuade subordinate ones that, whatever they may think of the social order, and however much they may be alienated from it, there is no alternative to it. Hegemony depends not so much on consent as on resignation.

Despite the reality of opposition forces directed against it, capitalist domination, even though qualified, is a reality. This being so, what, in socialist terms, are the main items of the indictment to be mounted against it and against the social order which it dominates?

2

A very large item in the indictment of capitalism relates, paradoxically, to its extraordinary success as a productive system. It is often recalled nowadays by the defenders of capitalism that Marx and

---

[4]   A. Gramsci, *Selections from the Prison Notebooks*, ed. Quintin Hoare and Geoffrey Nowell Smith (Lawrence and Wishart, London, 1971), p. 238.
[5]   On which, see e.g. J. S. Migdal, *Strong Societies and Weak States* (Princeton University Press, Princeton, N.J., 1988).

Engels, in the *Communist Manifesto* of all places, paid glowing tribute to capitalism's productive and innovative capacity;[6] but prescient though this was at a time when industrial capitalism was still in its early stages, they could not have imagined how extraordinarily powerful and sustained its dynamic would prove to be. Far from 'collapsing' under the weight of its own contradictions, capitalism has constantly found new sources of vigour and renewal. If it is true, as Marx said, that 'no social order ever perishes before all the productive forces for which there is room in it have developed,'[7] capitalism, however crisis-laden, seems assured of a fairly long lease of life.

In the same preface, Marx wrote that 'at a certain stage of their development, the material productive forces of society come in conflict with the existing relations of production . . . From forms of development of the productive forces these relations turn into their fetters.'[8] The 'fetters' proved to be a lot less inimical to the productive process than he thought. Even so, the fatal flaw in capitalism's immense productive capacity is that it is unable to ensure the beneficent use of the resources which it has generated and continues to generate. The discrepancy between the promise which the development of the forces of production holds and the daily reality which wage-earners confront remains fundamental. Capitalism has created for humankind, for the first time ever, the possibility of assuring, minimally, a materially secure and morally decent life for all inhabitants of the planet; but it is incapable, by its very nature and purpose, of turning this marvellous promise into reality. Capitalism is above all about private profit; and this, for all the proclamations to the contrary, is not compatible with a good life for all. For capitalism is essentially driven by the *micro-rationality* of the firm, not by the

---

[6] 'The bourgeoisie cannot exist without constantly revolutionising the instruments of production, and thereby the relations of production, and with them the whole relations of society . . . Constant revolutionising of production, uninterrupted disturbance of all social conditions, everlasting uncertainty and agitation distinguish the bourgeois epoch from all earlier ones.' K. Marx and F. Engels, *Manifesto of the Communist Party*, in *Collected Works* (Lawrence and Wishart, London, 1980), vol. 16, p. 469. There is much else in the same vein in the *Manifesto*.
[7] Preface to *A Contribution to the Critique of Political Economy* (1859), in *Selected Works* (Foreign Languages Publishing House, Moscow, 1950), vol. I, p. 329.
[8] Ibid., p. 329.

macro-rationality required by society. The improvements in the condition of life of the majority to which the development of the productive forces of capitalism has made a crucial contribution are real enough; but it is by now only the more extreme devotees of laissez-faire who argue that the two forms of rationality necessarily coincide. On the contrary, the development of the productive forces has also been accompanied by great social evils, most of them precisely due to the dynamic of private enterprise, which have compelled the state to intervene in order to alleviate them;[9] and the state's capacity to do so is itself impaired by the capitalist context in which it (very willingly) functions.

One obvious token of the incompatibility between capitalism and what I have called a materially secure and morally decent life for all is the continued existence, even in the richest capitalist countries, of a substantial population steeped in dire poverty and degradation. J. K. Galbraith prophesied in *The Affluent Society*, first published in 1958, that poverty in the rich societies of the West would soon become a residual, disappearing phenomenon. But poverty, deprivation, preventable disease, homelessness, squalor and despair have remained a blight for millions of people in these societies, with no sign that it can be eliminated within the confines of a system mainly geared to the pursuit of private profit. On the contrary, conditions for substantial minorities in 'affluent societies' have got worse rather than better in recent decades, and been made all the more bitter by the shrill celebration of a 'consumer society' from which they are largely excluded. These conditions are a fertile ground for the growth of drug addiction and crime as an increasingly prevalent way of life for substantial numbers of people;[10] and the same conditions nurture

---

[9] The point is suggested by Guillermo O'Donnell, who describes the state in *Bureaucratic Authoritarianism* as that institution which 'can transcend the micro economic rationality on the basis of which even the largest economic units act', and which 'may be capable of restoring the general conditions for the normal functioning of society *qua* capitalist': G. O'Donnell, *Bureaucratic Authoritarianism* (University of California Press, Berkeley, Los Angeles, London, 1988), p. 22.

[10] Thus, Douglas Hay notes that, according to Home Office statistics for 1985, 'in Britain, almost one-third of all young men, *mostly the poorest*, now have serious criminal convictions': D. Hay, 'Time, inequality, and law's violence', in *Law's Violence*, eds A. Sarat and T. R. Kearns (University of Michigan Press, Ann Arbor, 1992), p. 160, my emphasis. 'In the United States', he also notes, 'nearly one-fourth of African-American males in their twenties were actually in jail, on parole, or on probation in 1990' (ibid., p. 160).

pathologies such as racism, antisemitism and xenophobia, and encourage a search for scapegoats which always finds a target. While apologists celebrate the virtues and triumphs of capitalism, ominous signs appear of the recrudescence of ethnic and national racism among young men and women bred in hopelessness and disaffection, and whose prospects in life are utterly dismal.

The deprivations suffered by the poor in the societies of advanced capitalism, bitter though they are, nevertheless constitute 'affluence' when compared with the conditions in which the majority of the people of the 'developing world' are condemned to live and die. But this does not detract from the reality of deprivation for masses of people in the countries of advanced capitalism.

Furthermore, it is essential if the nature of capitalism is to be understood not to focus only on the existence in 'affluent' societies of vast pools of acute deprivation, important though this is. In these countries, the idea has gained much ground that wage-earners, far from being in any way deprived, have, all things considered, been doing remarkably well. This is based, for wage-earners in employment, on improvements in the conditions of daily life; on better housing and home ownership; on more disposable income, with wives as well as husbands contributing to the family income; on the access to consumer durables which wage-earners have enjoyed since World War II; on such things as foreign holidays and other amenities; on the achievement of better conditions at work; and so on.

This, however, leaves out of account some crucial facts about the condition of wage-earners: the fact that they are never safe from unemployment, with all the deprivations and traumas this entails; that they have to wage a constant struggle to maintain, let alone improve, their level of income and conditions of work; that vast numbers of them, particularly women, work for dismally low wages, often in appalling conditions; that relations of production remain profoundly undemocratic; and that the social and collective services on which much of their standard of living depends are inadequate on many counts. In this respect, the trend in recent years has been highly regressive: in many advanced capitalist countries, a two-tier system of provision is being strengthened by the shortcomings of public services. Provision in the first tier is dependent on ability to pay for privatized services. The second tier, generally inferior to the first, is what remains for the majority which cannot afford these services.

There are marked differences between capitalist countries in all these respects. But for all the talk of the 'affluent' working class and the devaluation of the importance of class, class location remains a primary source of deep inequalities in relation to work, income, housing, education, opportunities and much else that defines ways of living. There is a vast gap – truly staggering at the extremes – between the condition of the majority of the population on the one hand and of members of the middle and upper classes on the other. Even Sweden, so much more socially advanced than other capitalist countries, and described by one writer as 'closer than any other capitalist nation to the social democratic ideal of full employment, social security and income parity',[11] remains a class society, with great inequalities in the distribution of wealth, power and opportunities. A simple proof of the point is that members of the middle and upper classes everywhere would quite rightly find utterly catastrophic their descent – and it would be a descent – to the condition of even the most favoured wage-earners. Socialism is about achieving an ascent which would drastically reduce the gap and deprive remaining inequalities of the invidious and divisive character they now have. This does not mean the imposition of a dull uniformity in the ways life is lived: on the contrary, it means the creation of societies in which a rough equality of condition is allied to a genuine diversity – a diversity made possible by the flowering of capacities now stifled in the majority by a deeply unfavourable context.

A different area where the discrepancy between the micro-rationality of the firm and the requirements of society is blatant and laden with dramatic consequences is the environment. The nature of the system compels those who run it to treat such protection as being, in relation to their firm, as at best of secondary importance. As individuals, men and women in charge of capitalist firms may be as concerned with ecological protection as anyone else; as owners and controllers of their firms, their concern is greatly inhibited, notwithstanding their own intentions; and governments too, despite their proclamations, are also inhibited by the economic and political obstacles they face in dealing effectively with the ecological vandalism which the pursuit of private profit generates.

[11] F. W. Scharpf, *Crisis and Choice in European Social Democracy* (Sage, London, 1991), p. 92.

3

Capitalism as a mode of production is of crucial importance in shaping the social structure of the societies it dominates. It perpetuates a division of society between a relatively small dominant class on the one hand, and subordinate classes which constitute the vast majority of the population on the other.[12] This division was common to most previous modes of production, but capitalism, far from obliterating it, perpetuates it in its own particular ways. Nor is this rendered any less true by the degree of social mobility which distinguishes capitalism from earlier modes of production. As will be argued later, access to positions of power by members of subordinate classes does not change the fact of domination: it only changes its personnel.

At the upper levels of the social pyramid is to be found that part of the dominant class which, to use C. Wright Mills's term, constitutes its power elite. These are the people who own or control the 'strategic heights' of the economy; who control the central state apparatus; and who own and control the main means of communication in the private sector, or control those means of communication which are in the public sector. The power elite is, so to speak, the 'vanguard' of the dominant class: it is largely recruited from that class, and members of the power elite return to it as a result of resignation or retirement. The (much larger) part of the dominant class which is not the power elite makes up a business and professional bourgeoisie which, although less powerful than the power elite, does nevertheless possess a great deal of power and influence. It may be said that there is bound, in all societies, to be something like a power elite. The point, which will also be argued at length in later chapters, is that the power elite in capitalist societies is to a very remarkable degree free from effective democratic control and thus constitutes something of an oligarchy only partially tempered by democratic forms.

It should be said at once that neither the power elite nor the rest of the dominant class constitutes a united, cohesive class, in any

[12]   This section draws heavily on the more detailed analysis of the class structure of capitalist countries which is to be found in R. Miliband, *Divided Societies: class struggle in contemporary capitalism* (Clarendon Press, Oxford, 1989).

economic, social, political or cultural terms. As in any other such class, there are innumerable divisions to be found in it, often on matters of great importance. In normal circumstances, however, what divides the dominant class is rather less important than what unites it, namely the determination of most of its members to maintain and strengthen the existing social order, in the name of the national interest, or freedom, or democracy, or anything else that may at any given time serve as a means of legitimation. These legitimating notions must not be taken to be purely manipulative devices. On the contrary, they are deeply believed in, and also serve the crucial purpose of self-legitimation. Self-righteousness is an essential ingredient in the exercise of power; and it is quite compatible with the habitual manipulation of opinion, the perversion of truth, and the abuse of power. Indeed, the belief that reprehensible means serve higher ends provides its own justification for their use.

The determination to maintain and strengthen the social order does not imply the rejection of all reforms and concessions. Conservatism has always been divided between those people who accepted, reluctantly or not, the need to make concessions as a means of averting or reducing the discontent produced by intolerable conditions, and die-hards who set their face against it because they feared that reform would only breed further demands.

But when all such divisive factors have been taken into account, there remains a powerful unifying bond based upon common class privilege and the fact that members of the dominant class enjoy larger (often staggeringly larger) incomes than the vast majority of the population and own a wholly disproportionate amount of wealth, which is itself an important source of income. It is a matter of fundamental significance that, in Britain, 10 per cent of the population owned, in 1993, 50 per cent of all wealth, and that 25 per cent owned 71 per cent. In other words, 75 per cent of the population had to make do with 29 per cent of the remaining wealth.[13] The same kind of disproportion in regard to wealth is to be found in all capitalist countries.

The relationship of the holders of corporate power to the holders of state power is particularly important. That relationship is by no

---

[13] Inland Revenue Statistics 1993, in *The Justice Gap* (Institute for Public Policy Research, for the Commission on Social Justice, London, 1993), p. 47. The figures do not include occupational or state pension rights.

means smooth and harmonious. But both sides, for all their many differences and disagreements, are involved in a solid partnership. The executive power of the state often acts quite autonomously, on matters of the greatest importance, and without reference to its corporate partner. Ministers may in fact have little sympathy for business and business people, and be contemptuous of their limited horizons; and business people for their part are often contemptuous of politicians who, in an American formulation, have never had to meet a payroll. The concern of ministers may be for such lofty matters as the national interest and national security. But whatever these concerns may be, their fulfilment depends to a crucial degree on the health of the economy; and, in capitalist economies, this in turn is largely influenced by 'business confidence', that is to say by the confidence that the 'business community', at home and also abroad, has in the government. The cultivation of that confidence has been a compelling, even a determinant factor in the policies and actions of governments. In other words, the partnership is one where the corporate partner is able to exercise a major influence on its state partner, simply by virtue of its economic power.[14] The remarkable fact is how seldom the partnership has run a really serious risk of being dissolved because of the actions of governments. What happens where this does occur will be discussed in chapter 6.

The subordinate classes in capitalist societies are constituted by two different elements: a working or wage-earning class which makes up the great majority of the population of capitalist countries; and a lower middle class or petty bourgeoisie, itself divided between a small business and self-employed artisan stratum and a sub-professional, sub-managerial, supervisory stratum, comprising school teachers, social workers, civil servants and local government officers at the lower levels of the administrative structure, and many other people in a variety of occupations. These are the people who have some fairly small degree of power and responsibility in the operation of the mechanisms which help to ensure the daily reproduction of the social order.

[14] While this situation applies in capitalist democratic regimes, it is reversed in some authoritarian regimes, where a 'developmental state', as in South Korea and Taiwan, is able to exercise a decisive influence on business: the partnership endures, but on the state's terms. For some further remarks on this topic, see chapter 6.

Members of the wage-earning class all share, though unequally, certain key characteristics. *First*, they wholly or mainly depend on the sale of their labour power for their income, or on one form or another of state help. *Secondly*, the level of that income places wage-earners and beneficiaries of state help in the lower and lowest levels of the income scale. It is easy to point to some cases where skilled workers enjoy high wages. But even their wages can hardly be compared with the salaries paid to most members of the business or professional bourgeoisie. *Thirdly*, wage-earners have the least individual power and influence at their place of work or in society at large. Collectively, the working class has a formidable degree of potential power, as is evident on the occasions – for instance, a major or general strike – when that power is exercised. But this is an altogether different matter.

Apart from divisions based on gender, race, ethnicity, nationality and religion, recent developments in the productive process have strengthened an age-old division between a minority of skilled workers, with far better wages and conditions of work, and a growing army of workers employed in low-level jobs, often on a casual and part-time basis, without employment protection or the benefits enjoyed by the minority. This division has serious implications for trade union organization and the politics of labour, but neither this, nor other divisions in the working class, invalidates the fact that it remains, in objective terms, a majority of the population: the question, to be considered later, is under what conditions it may, despite its divisions, turn into a reasonably coherent political majority.

To say that the working class still constitutes the vast majority of the population of capitalist countries runs counter nowadays to prevailing opinion. For is not 'the working class' a notion that has had its day? Are we not all working-class now? Or, even better, middle-class? Or even working middle-class? In the United States, 'working-class' has been all but expunged from the political vocabulary: there are the very rich at the top, the very poor at the bottom, and everybody else is 'middle-class', whether well-to-do lawyers and doctors or factory workers and shopkeepers. Another such obfuscating notion which has gained currency in recent years is that these societies are divided on a 'two-thirds, one-third' basis, meaning that whereas one-third is doing badly or very badly, two-thirds are doing well or very well. This too obscures the real divison, which is that between the middle and upper class on the one hand and the class of wage-earners and members of the lower middle class on the other. The divisions which are to be found within this subordinate population, as noted, are very far from negligible, and have profound political consequences. But in relation to power, influence, income, wealth and style of life, they are less deep than the divisions between the people who occupy the upper levels of the social pyramid and those located at its lower ends. The lower middle class may well perceive itself to be very far removed from wage-earners; and the perception is in some ways correct, particularly in regard to unskilled labourers, not to speak of people on the margin of society. But on the criteria just noted, as distinct from the perceptions people may have of their status, the gap between the lower middle class and the middle and upper class remains very great.

The convenient obliteration of the working class in the language of politics does not correspond to reality. The industrial working class in advanced capitalist countries is certainly much less numerous than it used to be; but clerical, service and many other employees are wage-workers and part of the working class, whether they think of themselves as such or not. On the other hand, the term 'working-class' is commonly taken to denote the 'old', 'traditional', industrial working class, so that 'the wage-earning' class, though awkward-sounding, is probably a better term to use. As Alex Callinicos notes,

> despite the long dole queues of the 1970s and 1980s, usually some nine tenths of the population of working age in the Western economies are in some kind of employment, in most cases as wage-earners. The fact that manual industrial workers no longer form the majority of wage-labourers does not of itself imply the beginning of the end of the 'work-based society'. Wage-labour has if anything become a more pervasive feature of social experience in the past half century, with the decline of peasant agriculture and the growing involvement of women in the labour-market.[15]

Taken together, industrial, clerical and service workers, with their dependents, do constitute the majority of the population of capitalist countries; and that majority is further increased by a poverty-stricken 'underclass', mainly recruited, so to speak, from the ranks of the working class.

---

[15]   A. Callinicos, *Against Postmodernism: a Marxist critique* (Polity Press, Cambridge, 1989), p. 127.

4

The deep inequalities between the wage-earning population and the dominant class, and the constant reproduction of these inequalities, are not alone at issue. For these classes do not merely co-exist. They also relate to each other; and the relationship under capitalism is inherently one of opposed interests. This is so for reasons which are intrinsic to the system. The site where this opposition most commonly occurs is in the process of production, in the relationship between employers and wage-earners. The former are driven, by the inexorable laws of competition, to seek to extract the greatest possible surplus from their workers, within the constraints dictated by the specific historical circumstances which influence relations of production; whereas workers seek to improve as far as they can their wages, hours and conditions. The conflicts which these contradictory interests produce may be attenuated and routinized; and conflict is compatible with a great deal of cooperation on the part of workers at the point of production – such cooperation, however grudging, is essential if the process of production is not to be fatally impaired. Nevertheless, conflict remains an endemic part of the system.

Moreover, it is not confined to disputes between capital and labour over wages, conditions and hours. Larger matters affecting the different classes are constantly at issue – matters relating to wage-earners' rights in the process of production; trade union rights, including the conditions surrounding strike action; civic and political rights in general; the level and scope of social and collective services; the incidence of taxation; the regulation of business; and so on. On all such issues, conservative forces are involved in a permanent contest with labour movements, left parties and various other groupings pressing against the existing structures of power and privilege. The pressure greatly varies in intensity according to place and circumstances; but it can never be wholly subdued, and episodically erupts in major confrontations. It also needs to be said that 'conservative forces' here include the state itself. In relation to capital and labour, the capitalist state is not in the least neutral. It always proclaims itself to be such, and to be solely guided by its concern for the 'national interest'. But those who run the state tend to find that the 'national interest' and the interests of capital coincide, and act accordingly, particularly when serious conflict erupts.

Much in recent years has been made of the fact that some of the most acute conflicts in capitalist societies have not been directly concerned with the antagonism between capital and labour, but have had their source in gender oppression and discrimination, in racism, or in ethnic or religious differences; in the discontents of youth; and in the concerns of an endless variety of pressure groups. Moreover, many such conflicts have been of an 'intra-class' character and involved workers against workers, divided on the basis of gender, race, religion, ethnicity and so on. But it is not to fall into a sinful 'economic reductionism' to argue that one of the main causes of intra-class conflicts among wage-earners, involving race or gender or ethnicity or religion, is the insecurity, and the fear of competition for jobs at lower wages from women, immigrant workers and others, which is felt by male, white workers in societies one of whose distinguishing characteristics *is* insecurity of employment and the constant struggle to maintain or improve conditions of work. Still, it is true that many intra-class conflicts are only very distantly related to economic causes, or are not related to them at all, and appear to have a life of their own, fuelled by rationalizations about the negative traits of feared and despised groups. The existence of such sentiments produces the facile view that the hatreds which are at work are 'innate' to the human condition, or, in relation to sexism and racism, at least to the white or male condition. It is much more reasonable to see these hatreds as the product of a search for scapegoats to explain and avenge the multiple insecurities and alienations which are inscribed in societies that cannot provide a secure and satisfying life for their populations.

In discussing these conflicts, there is always a strong tendency to concentrate exclusively on the pressures which emanate from below, and to think of class struggle as a one-way process, as something in which wage-earners alone engage. This is a great mistake, simply because at least as important is pressure from above, in other words the constant concern of members of the power elite and the dominant class in general, *and* their allies in the subordinate classes, to maintain and defend the existing social order and all that goes with it. This pressure is much more constant and determined than that of wage-earners, and it crucially affects every aspect of social life. For it is applied in all walks of life and is based on a common belief that the existing social order, while not perfect, is the best that can be had in a very imperfect world, and must therefore be defended against all attempts to modify it in egalitarian and democratic directions. Those involved may differ over the strategies to be employed for the purpose, with a division, as noted earlier, between 'hardline' conservatism of various sorts and moderate conservatism, whose concern is to blunt whenever possible the edges of social conflict. Neither side is frozen in its position – reactionaries may bend to necessity and engage in reform, and moderate conservatives may become very immoderate under the pressure of circumstances. The division is nevertheless real; yet it should not obscure the reality of pressure from above.

It is worth dwelling on this, because politics is largely constituted by the permanent struggle, now more acute, now less, between dominant and subordinate classes. That struggle assumes a great variety of forms and is greatly obfuscated by the daily ebb and flow of political life, by jockeying for position and power between politicians, by an accumulation of events, scandals and misdemeanours involving people in high places, all of which is greedily seized on by the press and seems to be altogether removed from larger questions about the nature of the social order. Yet, beneath this bewildering kaleidoscope, there is a pattern, determined on the one hand by pressure and struggle from below against various forms of domination, discrimination, exclusion and enhanced exploitation, and on the other by pressure and struggle from above for the maintenance of the social order of which these features are an intrinsic part.

Of course, this is not how the protagonists themselves necessarily see politics and political life. What they do tends to be clothed in language which may help to conceal the fact that the purposes at hand have larger implications than is often proclaimed. But ultimately, these activities do relate to the nature of the social order: whether to defend it, and if so how, or whether to change it, and if so how radically. It is no exaggeration to say that the reality of political life, including its most important aspects as expressed through currents of thought and a great variety of institutions, cannot be understood without reference to these contradictory purposes.

Class societies cannot overcome this struggle. As noted earlier, it has proved possible for these societies to achieve a routinization of conflict, meaning the accommodation of subordinate classes to their location in the social order, at the price of certain (often significant) concessions. But such routinization is not stable; and even where it endures, and acute conflict is avoided, it is impossible for such societies to achieve real harmony, and to become communities in reality as well as rhetoric.

5

One of the proudest boasts of developed capitalist regimes concerns their democratic nature; and defenders of the system have insisted on the intimate link there is between capitalism, freedom and democracy.[16] Here too, Communist regimes have served a very useful purpose in appearing to justify the claim that 'socialism' was the enemy of democracy and freedom, and that 'free enterprise' is their only guarantee.

In looking at this claim, it may be noted, to begin with, that capitalism, for most of its history, was not associated with democracy in any sense at all; and that most of the conservative and liberal defenders of the system were utterly determined to *oppose* the advancement of democratic forms, notably the extension of the suffrage, but many other democratic advances as well. Capitalism did require certain freedoms in order to develop, and is historically linked with bourgeois demands for these freedoms, for the curbing of absolutism and the protection of individuals, particularly propertied individuals, from the exactions of the state. But valuable though this was, the freedoms that were gained left the bulk of the population in conditions of harsh economic, social and political subjection; and such democracy as was obtained was mainly democracy for property owners and excluded from its ambit the great majority which had no 'stake in the country'. The enlargement of democracy and freedom was largely the result of stubborn pressure from various sources, notably labour and left movements, against the dominant forces of property and privilege, with help from members of the dominant class fearful of the consequences of continued opposition to such enlargement. With the growth of labour movements and working-class parties in the last decades of the nineteenth century, it became more difficult to sustain the exclusion of the majority from political citizenship, and an extended suffrage was grudgingly

[16] See, for instance, among many other texts, P. Berger, *The Capitalist Revolution: fifty propositions about prosperity, equality and liberty* (Gower, Aldershot, 1987), and M. Friedman, *Capitalism and Freedom* (University of Chicago Press, Chicago and London, 1962).

conceded, first to more male voters, and ultimately, well into the twentieth century, to women voters. It is well to recall, however, how strongly such (very limited) democratization was resisted by entrenched privilege throughout Europe (and in different ways also in the United States); and how the mechanisms of the state apparatus were used to guard against the dangers to that entrenched privilege (both aristocratic and bourgeois) represented by the extension of democratic forms.

It is in the light of this steadfast resistance that must be viewed one of the most remarkable acts of appropriation which conservatism has ever performed, namely the insistence of its upholders in the twentieth century that *they* were the most ardent defenders of democracy.

What made it possible for them to advance the claim was the narrow meaning they attributed to democracy, which they defined as the competition between political elites for power to be achieved on the basis of popular support as expressed in competitive elections. In *Capitalism, Socialism and Democracy*, first published in the United States in 1942 and destined to have considerable influence on the subsequent discussion of the meaning of democracy, Joseph Schumpeter thus defined democracy as an 'institutional arrangement for arriving at political decisions in which individuals acquire the power to decide by means of a competitive struggle for the people's vote'.[17] Anything beyond this by way of popular decision-making was deemed to be undesirable and dangerous, a view endorsed by a wide range of theorists of democracy in the fifties and beyond.[18] To this could be added a range of (qualified) political and civic rights traditionally associated with liberalism.

If, however, democracy is taken to mean that 'ordinary people' have real power in all the areas of life where decisions that concern them are to be made, the idea that capitalist societies are democratic belongs to the mythology of politics, not to its reality. Capitalist democracy means that democratic forms exist which make possible

[17] J. A. Schumpeter, *Capitalism, Socialism and Democracy* (George Allen and Unwin, London, 1943), p. 269.
[18] For a useful review of the literature up to the early sixties, see L. Davis, 'The cost of realism: contemporary restatements of democracy', *The Western Political Quarterly*, XVII, 1 (March 1964). See also C. Pateman, *Participation and Democratic Theory* (Cambridge University Press, Cambridge, 1970), chapter 1.

a certain amount of pressure on governments and the state; and that it also allows for the removal of elected officials, including the removal of governments from office. This is by no means to be undervalued. So too does capitalist democracy make possible on rare occasions the election of governments which seek radical reform.

There are many countries across the world where democratic forms are notionally in place, but where the processes and procedures which they entail are turned into a sham, with rigged elections and cowed oppositions. Such elections belong to the realm of public relations, and have mainly been held to gain the support of the United States, concerned as it is that countries which seek aid should have 'democratic' credentials.[19] Even so, the coming into being of 'democratic' regimes in place of dictatorships is obviously a welcome improvement. But the improvement is nevertheless limited; for here is an instance where changes in the political system leave in place an oppressive social order, which political changes such as elections do not greatly affect, or do not affect at all, and are not intended to.

Where capitalist democracy has had a fairly long history, on the other hand, and where it is strongly supported from below, democratic forms can be much more significant. But it is just as well to note that while elections do involve a great turnover of political personnel, and often lead to a turnover of administrative personnel as well, the difference this makes in regard to *policy* is usually much less spectacular than the rhetoric of parties in election campaigns suggests. Professor Edmund Morgan notes that the participation in politics which elections involved in colonial America was 'a safety valve, an interlude when the humble could feel a power otherwise denied them, a power that was only half-illusory. And it was also a legitimising ritual, a rite by which the populace renewed their consent to an oligarchical power structure.'[20] This could well be said for elections in the United States today and in other capitalist democracies as well, with the important qualification that elections may sometimes make a real difference.

Nor should another facet of capitalism, which greatly undermines its democratic pretensions, be left out of account. For 'free enterprise' enables the controllers of corporate power to make decisions

[19] On this, see e.g. E. S. Herman and F. Brodhead, *Demonstration Elections: U.S. staged elections in the Dominican Republic, Vietnam and El Salvador* (South End Press, Boston, 1984).

[20] E. Morgan, *Inventing the People: the rise of popular sovereignty in England and America* (W.W. Norton, London and New York, 1988), p. 206.

which are of vital importance to local, regional and national life, and which also very often have great international repercussions as well, without any reference to the people affected by these decisions.[21] Among other things, this means that workers find themselves working for a new employer, as a result of a takeover about whose conditions they have had little or no say. The point extends to all areas in which corporate power is exercised: in regard to major decisions, the consultation of wage-earners, where it occurs at all, amounts to very little.

Controllers of economic power have to work within the constraints set by the state, and they also have to pay some heed to external opinion, which is why public relations have become a major industry. But these constraints to which corporate power is subjected are usually loose enough to allow a remarkable amount of elbow room and autonomy to people who, it should be remembered, are required by their position to have as their over-riding concern the highest rate of return for the firms they control, with any other concern playing, at best, a subsidiary role in their decisions. The growth of multinational corporations makes matters worse: for they have even less concern for the interests of the city, region or country in which they are located.

Democracy has no access to corporate boardrooms. Nor does it have much of a presence in the productive process in general. Experiments in worker 'participation' in that process are legion, but this does not detract from the fact that relations of production in capitalism remain heavily authoritarian in character, with managerial prerogatives strongly protected and exercised. In other words, a large sphere of life, of crucial importance to everybody, is firmly dominated by a small minority of people who are, so long as they remain within the law, accountable only to their shareholders; and shareholders are for the most part content to let directors and executives get on with it so long as profits are adequately maintained.

There is another feature of capitalist democracy which needs to be

---

[21] As I. Katznelson and M. Kesselman note, 'many issues of manifestly public concern, such as where new automobile or computer plants will be built, are decided privately. The principle of majority rule, the very center-piece of representative democracy, thus applies only to a limited sphere of questions and decisions': I. Katznelson and M. Kesselman, *The Politics of Power: a critical introduction to American government* (Harcourt Brace Jovanovic, New York, 1987), p. 7. The reference is to the United States, but, in one degree or another, the point applies to the whole capitalist world.

noted. This is that the rights which it proclaims are permanently under threat, if not of outright abrogation, at least of erosion. People in power, in class societies where conflict is endemic, are likely to find these rights to be something of a nuisance and an impediment to their purposes, and are driven, particularly in times when conflict assumes acute forms, to try and reduce their substance and scope. The most obvious example is the degree to which the right to strike is circumscribed in capitalist democracies. These regimes have a strong authoritarian side, which is parallel to, and more or less compatible with, their democratic forms, but is also permanently at odds with them. That authoritarian side also finds many practical expressions in daily life: in the bureaucratic callousness with which the recipients of state relief are treated; in the treatment of immigrant workers; in the exercise of police brutality and its denial or exoneration by ministers and judges; in the abominable conditions of prison life in most countries; and so on. It may well be said that capitalist democracies are less viciously cruel than authoritarian regimes; and in a world full of the most cruel regimes, this too is greatly to be valued. But the fact that capitalist democracies have a far better record in relation to political and civic rights than authoritarian regimes should not obscure the injustices which are part of the daily life of so many of the poorer people in these societies. It is possible to shrug one's shoulders and say that what is attributed to a capitalist social order is bound to be true of *any* social order and that the best that may be hoped for is the attenuation of gross and manifest evils. Socialists for their part do not accept this and believe that it is possible, given the right context, to do a lot better than that.

6

What has been said so far must be related to a feature of capitalism which is central to it, yet which is nowadays so much taken for granted as to escape notice. This is the fact that capitalism is a system based on wage-labour. Wage-labour is work performed for a wage in the service of a private employer who is entitled, by virtue of his or her ownership or control of the means of production, to appropriate and dispose of the surplus produced by the workers in his or her employment. Employers are constrained by various pressures which limit their freedom to deal with their workers as they will, or to dispose as they will of the surplus that has been extracted. But this only qualifies their right both to extract a surplus and to dispose of it as they think fit. So deeply has the ethos of capitalism penetrated every aspect of the life and thought of capitalist societies that this form of appropriation is hardly questioned at all nowadays, and is generally taken to be 'natural'. So was slave labour thought to be 'natural' in ancient times. As W. G. Runciman notes, 'specialists of all schools are agreed that its [slavery's] legitimacy was never seriously questioned in the Ancient World and that the advent of Christianity, though it may have helped to incline some individual slaveowners to manumit their slaves out of piety, made little or no difference to the way in which the institution was viewed.'[22] What criticism there was concerned the way in which slaves were treated. Slave labour is not wage-labour. The point, however, is that wage-labour is a social relationship which, in a socialist perspective, is morally abhorrent, because it is based on exploitation and is, as such, a process which requires subordination. Nor is it rendered much less abhorrent by the fact that the conditions of the majority of wage-earners have greatly improved over time. For reform, however valuable, only qualifies but does not abolish the exploitation that characterizes the capitalist mode of production and the domination which exploitation demands. Socialism postulates that an altogether different economic system will in due course come to replace capitalism, and that this economic system will be based on the principle that no person should work for the private enrichment of another and under conditions of enforced subordination; and wage-labour, as defined here, will then be taken to be as morally repugnant as slavery or serfdom are now viewed as being.[23] When this comes to pass, people will find it remarkable that, as in the case of slavery in the Ancient World, so little should have been made of the fact of wage-labour by liberal and left-inclined theorists concerned with equality, justice, fairness, democracy, citizenship and the like, not to speak of conservative theorists. A very good example of this

[22] W. G. Runciman, *A Treatise on Social Theory* (Cambridge University Press, Cambridge, 1989), vol. II, p. 133.
[23] In *Value, Price and Profit* (1865), Marx writes that 'instead of the *conservative* motto "*A fair day's wage for a fair day's work!*" they [the working class] ought to inscribe on their banner the *revolutionary* watchword "*Abolition of the wages system!*"': in Marx and Engels, *Collected Works*, vol. 20, p. 149, emphasis in text.

neglect is provided by the vast industry which has grown around John Rawls's *A Theory of Justice* (1971). His 'communitarian' critics have rightly reproached him for abstracting the individual from the social order.[24] But their own work does very little to clarify the class nature of the social order and the degree to which it rests on exploitation and domination.

It may well be objected that the public ownership of the means of production does not by itself do away with wage-labour, in so far as the controllers of these means may well derive private enrichment from their control, and because it may even create conditions of harsher exploitation and domination than prevail under private ownership. Communist experience has amply demonstrated how real is the danger of what might be called bureaucratic exploitation as distinct from exploitation based on capitalist ownership.

The objection, however, misses a crucial difference between private and public ownership. This is that the exploitation which occurs under public ownership is a *deformation*, in so far as public ownership does not rest on and require exploitation, and provides at least the basis for the cooperative association of the producers, under conditions of democratic control, and with differential rewards kept within agreed bounds. By contrast, the whole of economic activity under private ownership *is* exploitation and makes no sense if it is not to result in the private enrichment of the owners and controllers of the means of that activity. Socialization offers the promise and the possibility of realizing the abolition of wage-labour: such an eventuality is rigorously precluded by the very nature of capitalism.

There is one form of extraction which is inevitable even under the best mode of social ownership: this is the extraction which society wrests from the producers by way of help for the non-producers – the young, the old, the sick, the disabled, the unemployed and others. This is an inevitable form of extraction which occurs in any society; and it is clear that the producers themselves do directly or

---

[24] See e.g. Michael J. Sandel, *Liberalism and the Limits of Justice* (Cambridge University Press, Cambridge, 1982), and Michael Walzer, *Spheres of Justice* (Robertson, Oxford, 1983). Rawl's recent revision of *A Theory of Justice*, entitled *Political Liberalism* (Columbia University Press, New York, 1993), does nothing to remedy the neglect of social context which marred the earlier work: a token of this is that the index to the book has no entry for 'capitalism' or 'class'.

indirectly benefit from it. For producers were children once, and enjoyed the benefits of such extraction, have children of their own, get sick or unemployed, grow old. So too do they benefit from collective services which are paid for from the surplus. Much in this respect depends on how democratic is the process whereby decisions in this field are made. But this levy on the producers, even in a democratic and egalitarian context, is likely to remain a source of tension between producers and non-producers, because of the tax burdens which it involves. Indeed, it is quite likely to grow with the increase in the number of old people.

7

Dominant classes rely, at least in part, on their control of the main means of communication and persuasion. There is no question about the existence of that control in capitalist societies, by capitalists in the private sector or by officials in the public one. The question that does arise, however, is what this control actually means in capitalist democracies. For whereas all means of communication were under close control in Communist regimes, and were expected to conform to the official view on most issues, with dissent severely penalized, there prevails in capitalist democracies an extraordinary diversity in the production and dissemination of ideas of every conceivable sort. What then, given such diversity, does control actually mean?

It means that in some areas, in which ideology and politics are directly and obviously involved, views which jar sharply with those of the controllers of the means of communication, whether private or public – in other words, views strongly at odds with conventional ones – will have some difficulty, to put it no higher, in getting a fair hearing. This, it should be emphasized, is not to say that all such views will be suppressed. That is certainly not so; and there are in any case alternative 'minority' channels of expression for them. The point is rather that views which the controllers of the main means of communication find deeply obnoxious will have to run an obstacle course, which some survive, in a more or less battered condition, and others do not.

But are not the means of communication full of sharp criticism, and are they not marked by a thoroughgoing iconoclasm, from which nothing, however elevated or hallowed, is safe? The answer is a mixed one. For anything to the left of social democracy is very poorly represented in the mainstream media, and hardly represented at all in the United States. The spectrum extends much further on the Right. Views which proceed from openly fascist positions, and virulently explicit racism, are nowadays shunned by the media; but reactionary views on many issues are entirely acceptable, not sur- prisingly, since they closely correspond to the views and inclinations of many of the controllers themselves. The criticism and iconoclasm which are to be found in the mass media take the form of attacks on the failings of individual politicians or other power holders, or on other exalted figures. Nor does criticism spare conservative gov- ernments and parties. Much of this proceeds from a spurious and demagogic 'populism' much favoured by reactionary tabloids. Nevertheless, the role of the press as a critical voice should not be under-estimated; but neither should its limits be overlooked. One reason for its limits, of great importance, is that the people who actually produce and disseminate the products are themselves sub- ject to one of the most effective forms of censorship – self-censorship. The people concerned generally *know* what is likely to produce problems with their bosses; and they will for the most part try to avoid these problems. In some cases, they may resist the temptation to opt for a quiet life; but this is to invite serious trouble.

There is nothing very remarkable in all this. Dominant classes always and naturally seek to limit the spread of ideas which chal- lenge and appear to threaten their predominance. Government regu- lation does something to redress the balance, but it would be naive to expect this to remove the strong bias towards conformity which marks mass communications. What *is* remarkable, however, is that the existence of a huge private sector in this realm of communications should be so readily taken to be right and proper, and as being compatible with democracy – indeed as being essential to it. The people who control the public sector of communications also engage in the censorship of unpalatable ideas, either on their own account, or because of external pressures from people with power; but they are at least to some degree accountable. The people who control the private sector are mostly accountable to their major shareholders, who are not likely to pine for the representation of radical views.

It is surely a state of affairs to be questioned that a press mogul should be able to exercise control, if he or she is so inclined, over what views are expressed in his or her newspapers, for no other reason than that he or she had the money to buy these newspapers, or inherited them. The same is true for other means of communication, for instance radio and television under private ownership and control, and the cinema, which remains a powerful means of persuasion. Nor is the situation any better when the control is exercised by banks, insurance companies and other financial institutions. This control confers a considerable degree of power in the shaping of the national culture, indeed in the shaping of a growingly international culture. Most of the tabloid press in Britain, with its sustained, virulent and, at election time, hysterical vilification of the Left, exemplifies well how far political pollution can go. One author notes that 'each year it is more likely that the American citizen who turns on any medium – newspapers, magazines, radio or television, books, movies, cable, recordings, video cassettes – will receive information, ideas or entertainment controlled by the same handful of corporations, whether it is daily news, a cable entertainment program, or a textbook.'[25] The same goes for the media under private control in all capitalist countries. There is nothing 'democratic' about this; and it is not far-fetched to think that the power which such private ownership and control allows will, in time, come to be as unacceptable as the capacity of small groups of men to raise armed bands and to conduct assaults on chosen targets now is. 'Freedom of the press' is now exclusively taken to mean freedom of the press from control by government. Under present arrangements, however, it also and crucially means the freedom of media and other communications moguls to inject their (conservative) predilections and prejudices into the means of communication under their control.

Owners and controllers of private means of communication are much given to protesting that they are not concerned with 'politics', and that their purpose is making money, entertaining the public, spreading knowledge, educating the masses and so on. But it is naive or hypocritical to claim that all such purposes are incompatible with the advancement of political views. In any case, the controllers of the means of communication are only indifferent to politics so long as the politics advanced do not greatly deviate from their own positions. Where this does occur, owners and controllers quickly discover a keen interest in politics.

[25] B. H. Bagdikian, *The Media Monopoly* (Beacon Press, Boston, 1990, 3rd edn), p. ix.

The issue, however, is not only the ability of private and public controllers to marginalize what they take to be subversive ideas. Perhaps even more important is the extent to which, in deeply divided societies where great disparities of power and privilege are in permanent contradiction with the rhetoric of democracy, the media will inevitably be used to obscure, blur and deny that contradiction. One of the main functions of the media, in such societies, is to help in the struggle which must be waged by people in power to win the hearts and minds of the majority. In the waging of that struggle, the manipulation and distortion of information, the suppression of incovenient facts, the fabrication of useful myths, and plain lying by private and public agencies are all 'structurally' part of the control of the means of communication. The struggle is not completely successful: people do often resist the brainwashing to which they are subjected. The point is that the struggle is waged, and has to be waged; and the greater the distance between rhetoric and reality, the more determined is the endeavour to deny it. Capitalist democracy, I have suggested, is itself a contradiction in terms; one of the consequences of that contradiction is a manipulative and deceitful use of the means of communication as a means of defending the social order.

8

There is one aspect of capitalism which has not so far been discussed, yet which is of fundamental importance: this is its global reach and the international implications of that reach. How far, in the perspective of the present chapter, can the international record of capitalism be added to all the other items of its indictment?

'World trade and the world market', Marx noted in *Capital*, 'date from the sixteenth century, and from then on the modern history of capital starts to unfold.'[26] With the sixteenth century, there begin the plunder and the genocide which attended the conquest of North and South America, followed by the plunder and subjugation of Africa and most of Asia, as a fitting accompaniment of capitalism's global vocation. Ever since then, by far the most important feature of world history has been the merciless exploitation by Western powers of the rest of the world. At the end of the seventeenth century, Paul Bairoch observes, 'it is very likely that the average standard of living

[26]   K. Marx, *Capital* (Penguin, London, 1976), vol. I, p. 247.

of Europe taken as a whole was equal to, or a little lower than, that of the rest of the World.'[27] The subsequent abyss that came to be known as the North–South divide was not an act of God: it was the direct result of the subjugation of the 'South' by the 'North'. Related to that subjugation was the rivalry of major capitalist powers for imperialist advantage. In the epoch of the Second International – the quarter of a century preceding the outbreak of World War I – the view was commonly held among socialists that capitalism made for war. The search for territory, markets, raw materials and cheap labour produced an imperialist competition between nations, and led in turn to international tension and crisis, and ultimately to war.

As an explanation of the causes of World War I, this is obviously much too simple, for it ignores the political purposes which moved dynastic rulers, presidents and ministers. All the same, the link between imperialist competition and war is very strong, and so is the link between capitalist interests and state purposes. To see why this is so, we must return to the complex relationship between the concerns of power holders in the state and those of their counterparts in the economy. The point was made earlier in this chapter that power holders in the state may be concerned with what they take to be the national interest, national security or whatever; but that the service of the national interest depends in a very large measure on the health of the economy. In the years preceding World War I, the governments of some major European countries, notably Britain, France and Germany, were engaged in an imperialist competition that had many sources.[28] But one of them, of the greatest importance, was the striving for economic advantage; and imperialist competition inevitably involved the service of capitalist interests. That competition required governments to support, defend and enhance these interests at home and abroad; and this was in any case demanded by powerful capitalist lobbies with a ready access to the seats of political power. Also, the congruence between the purposes of politicians and those of powerful capitalists was greatly strengthened by the personal ties which bound them together, to the point where speaking here of wholly distinct spheres is misleading.

[27] P. Bairoch, 'Historical roots of economic under-development: myths and realities', in *Imperialism and After: continuities and discontinuities*, eds W. J. Mommsen and J. Osterhammel (German Historical Institute, London, 1986), p. 194.
[28] On this, see e.g. A. J. Mayer, *The Persistence of the Old Regime: Europe to the Great War* (Pantheon Books, New York, 1981).

In this realm of international relations, the notion of partnership is particularly apposite: history does not record capitalist opposition to preparations for war, or to war itself – if anything, the reverse.

In the case of World War II, it is obvious that Hitler's expansionist ambitions were based on many different impulses, of which the service of capitalist interests was of the least importance. But here too, the fulfilment of Hitler's ambitions did involve a close partnership between the Nazi state and German business; and it is a partnership into which German business very readily entered, in which it greatly prospered, and which endured to the end of the Nazi regime. Business was throughout deeply implicated with the Nazis, and found no difficulty in supporting what the Nazis were doing, least of all in employing the slave labour with which the regime supplied it in the war. All this, however, is history; but before leaving it behind us, it is just as well to remember how closely capitalist interests have been involved in state policies which have resulted in the violent death of millions upon millions of innocent men, women and children.

It is unfortunately not true that the absence of these interests is a guarantee of peace. War has been waged by the Communist regimes of China and Vietnam against each other; and the Soviet Union and China came close to war in the late sixties. War has also been waged by regimes in the 'third world' where capitalist interests were minimal or non-existent. What this means is that war is the ultimate means whereby power holders seek to achieve their own purposes, even where there are no interests beyond these purposes to be served. But this does not undermine the point that the service of capitalist interests in the countries of developed capitalism, in the pursuit of imperialist competition, has played an important, even a crucial, part in fostering policies and actions which made for war.

The question, however, is how relevant this has remained in the epoch following World War II. For while competition between developed capitalist states has endured since then, it has also been accompanied, and even overshadowed, by a high degree of cooperation between them. At no point since 1945 has there been the slightest threat of war between any of them. It is quite likely that the 'new world order', following the disintegration of the Soviet Union, the decline of American economic hegemony and the emergence of Germany as a dominant power in Europe and of Japan in Asia, will engender new international tensions; but it seems extremely unlikely that this could produce armed conflict between any of these powers.

This does not, however, settle the question of the relationship of capitalism to international conflict. Competition between the major capitalist powers has been peaceful since 1945; but the world has been the terrain of an international conflict of a different sort, namely the conflict between the United States and its allies on the one hand, and 'Communism' on the other.

Before turning to this, it is worth recalling how murderous was the conflict which opposed colonial powers, notably France, to movements of colonial liberation in the years following World War II. Again, the defence of capitalist interests cannot by itself explain the waging of a struggle by colonial powers which, in the case of France in Algeria, cost the lives of up to a million Algerians. Even so, the defence of these interests, of course in the name of 'the national interest' and the struggle against 'Communism', was of great importance in the waging of colonial wars. The same point applies to the wars waged by other colonial powers after World War II.

What was called the Cold War was always a misnomer for a rather different and larger enterprise undertaken from 1945 onwards (indeed during the war itself)[29] by the United States and its allies. The Cold War was ostensibly waged to contain and repel what were proclaimed to be the expansionist ambitions of the Soviet Union and the threat these posed to the whole world. The notion that there was such a threat, at least as lethal as Nazi expansionism, came to be part of a conventional wisdom which dominated the political culture of the whole capitalist world until the late eighties; and rejection of that notion also came to be seen as a sign of dangerous complacency, wilful blindness, subversive sympathies or treacherous allegiances. It is only since the disintegration of the Soviet Union that the notion of an implacable Soviet will to territorial expansion, akin to the Nazi one, which was supposed to be at the heart of all Soviet policies, has ceased to be taken as a truth too obvious to be questioned.[30]

[29] See e.g. G. Kolko, *The Politics of War* (Pantheon Books, New York, 1968, 1990).
[30] In his autobiography, *The Time of My Life* (Penguin, London, 1990), Denis (now Lord) Healey, in a chapter entitled 'Cold Warrior', writes that 'like most Western observers at this time [i.e. the post-war years], I believed that Stalin's behaviour showed he was bent on the military conquest of Western Europe. I now think we were all mistaken' (p. 101). But there were many people in the Labour Party, who were not Communists, and who were not mistaken; and some who were not mistaken, for instance Konni Zilliacus, MP, were expelled from the Party for not toeing the line.

The belief in the existence of that threat was fed from many
sources: by the non sequitur that, since the Soviet Union was a
repressive dictatorship, it must also be expansionist; by Soviet control of Eastern Europe and Soviet interventions in Hungary in 1956,
in Czechoslovakia in 1968, and in Afghanistan in 1979; by the view
that any move by Communists anywhere, and any movement of
radical reform, were part of a carefully laid Soviet plan for world
domination; and so on ad infinitum.[31] In fact, Soviet interventions
had nothing to do with alleged expansionist ambitions but were the
product of a misconceived concern for 'national security' in a hostile
world. In the two cases where the United States actually went to
war with Communist regimes, in Korea and Vietnam, the Soviet
Union was conspicuous by its prudent absence from the scene. Nor
did movements of reform anywhere owe their being to the Soviet
Union: what the Soviet Union and other Communist countries did
was to extend economic, technical and military help to various regimes
and movements, in the hope of gaining allies in the contest with the
United States. The real aim of the Cold War, as waged by the United
States and its allies and clients, was throughout to defend regimes of
'free enterprise' against revolutionary challenge in some countries,
but much more commonly against pressure for radical reform anywhere. There were no doubt many people, including vast numbers
of Western intellectuals, who did believe and proclaim that the struggle
was against Soviet totalitarianism and for the defence of freedom,
democracy and so forth. But the reality showed otherwise. It is
worth noting in this connection how great was the dereliction of
political commentators, academic analysts and Cold War liberals in
helping politicians to foster the myth of Soviet expansionism. Left
writers have often been traduced for their indulgence towards the
Soviet Union and Stalinism; and there was indeed among many of
them a will to believe which dimmed or obliterated their critical
faculties and made them defend the indefensible, or at least close
their eyes to it. But their default is well matched by the eager collaboration of vast numbers of intellectuals and commentators in the
propagation of the obfuscations and lies which were an indispensable part of the Cold War. This willing and unscrupulous collaboration

---

[31] For an analysis of the uses that were made of the 'Soviet threat' in the
United States, see e.g. A. Wolfe, *The Rise and Fall of the 'Soviet Threat'*
(Institute for Policy Studies, Washington, D.C., 1979).

by intellectuals and others has been amply documented, by no one more so than by that most admirable dissident American intellectual, Noam Chomsky.[32]

Although there was no threat of Soviet expansionism or of Communist revolution in Western Europe, let alone the United States, there did exist the real threat of a serious challenge to existing structures of power and privilege in many countries, most notably in the 'third world', linked, in many cases, to the striving for freedom from subjection to Western hegemony. All such movements incurred the implacable hostility of the United States; and regimes issuing from them were exposed to economic and political destabilization, and, where this did not avail, to military intervention.

There is a crucial dimension of this crusade which must not be overlooked. This is the fact that American interventionism was intended to support regimes upon whose pliability in economic and political terms it could fully rely; and if this involved support for repressive regimes with an abominable record in human rights, this was cheerfully accepted in the name of the struggle against 'Communism'. Where governments to which the United States objected came to power, support was extended to defeated reactionary forces and movements, in the hope that this would bring about their return to power, however terrible the consequences might be for the mass of the people. Country after country in the 'third world' was thus condemned by a succession of American presidents to great suffering at the hands of reactionary and tyrannical regimes enjoying the financial and military support of the United States. Examples of such interventionism are legion – in Greece, where Britain preceded the United States in ensuring the victory of an exceptionally reactionary Right against a coalition of left forces in which the Greek Communist Party was the dominant element; in Iran in 1953, where a mildly reforming regime was overthrown and replaced by the dictatorship of the Shah; in Guatemala in 1954, where an equally mildly reforming government was overthrown and the country delivered to a long succession of military dictatorships, with death squads, torture and massacre as a routine form of rule; in Brazil in 1964, where an 'unreliable' reforming nationalist regime was

[32] See e.g. his *American Power and the New Mandarins* (Penguin, London, 1969), *Towards a New Cold War* (Sinclair Browne, London, 1982), *Deterring Democracy* (Verso, London, 1991), etc.

overthrown; in the Dominican Republic in 1965, where American troops helped to overthrow an equally moderate regime; in Indonesia, also in 1965, where army commanders were encouraged to wipe out the Communist Party, and where up to half a million Communists and alleged Communists were exterminated; in Chile in 1973, where the radical government of Salvador Allende incurred the unrelenting hostility of the United States, and whose economic destabilization culminated in its overthrow in a military coup and the dictatorship of General Pinochet; in Nicaragua, where the United States gave support to the murderous activities of the Contras in the eighties. To this catalogue must be added the attempted destabilization of the Cuban regime; and the support which the United States, with the help of South Africa and Israel, extended to the armed struggle waged by the opponents of the revolutionary regimes in Angola and Mozambique. Millions upon millions of men, women and children paid with their lives for these policies.

All this, and a good deal else in the same vein that forms part of the history of the post-war years, was a gigantic endeavour, of global dimensions, to make the world safe for capitalism, whatever the cost this might involve for the people subjected to that endeavour. Of course, neither the government of the United States, nor any other, was propelled into interventionism by capitalist interests alone. Nor, clearly enough, was the invasion of Grenada under Reagan and of Panama under Bush a simple matter of defending capitalist interests. The motives were much more complex, and had to do with the wish in the case of Grenada, to get rid of a revolutionary regime, however tiny a speck the island was on the map; and in the case of Panama, to get rid of a dictator who, from being a paid client of the United States, had got out of control and had turned into an embarrassing nuisance. The unrelenting pressure on Cuba is another matter: for this was a revolutionary regime which could not be allowed to succeed, because of the danger that it would become a beacon for other countries in Central and Latin America. Much the same is true for Nicaragua. In all cases, however different the circumstances, the underlying purpose remains the defence of 'free enterprise' and the predominance of Western, particularly American, economic and strategic interests.

In Latin America, Asia and Africa, the main concern of governments acceptable to the West has generally been to defeat pressure from below for the remedying of crying grievances, and to block the possibility of reforms which are the essential condition for an amelioration of life for the mass of the people, but which might pose a threat to established interests and privileges. So long as these local power holders pursue the neo-liberal economic policies which the governments of advanced capitalist countries, the International Monetary Found and the World Bank favour, they may be assured of continued support. But this means a perpetuation of the grim conditions of life of the vast majority, with no likelihood whatever of real alleviation. The aid which the West dispenses to the countries of the 'third world' holds no such promise of alleviation, though much of it is certainly of great benefit to corrupt power holders themselves; and that aid is in any case more than compensated by the tribute which the poor countries pay to the rich ones by way of repayment of interest on debt, or by way of payment for the purchase from the West of enormous quantities of armaments by regimes which are not too poor to incur this kind of expenditure.

In recent years, a new emphasis has been placed in Washington and other Western capitals on the need for 'democracy' everywhere. Dictatorships are out of favour – though not where, as for instance in Saudi Arabia, they are useful allies. In former Communist countries, authoritarian regimes have been replaced by regimes which allow the functioning (or the malfunctioning) of democratic forms; and in Central and Latin America, viciously repressive dictatorships have for the most part given way to regimes which also allow opposition and political competition.

Democratic forms may encourage open pressure against existing structures of power, which is all to the good, but that pressure can usually be contained, and repressed where necessary within the framework of the constitutional order. In other words, a dictatorship in a capitalist context may be replaced by a 'democratic' regime in the same context. This is what has happened in Latin America and elsewhere; and it is what the United States and its allies want.

On the other hand, what they want in former Communist regimes is precisely the opposite. The change from dictatorship to 'democracy' is welcome, but only if it leads to a fundamental change in the social order, meaning the replacement of an economy in which the means of production are under public ownership with one where they are privatized, with the coming into being of a brand-new capitalist social order. In the one case, the Western concern is for the maintenance and defence of capitalism; in the second, it is for its establishment.

The struggle to make the world safe for capitalism will long continue, and will assume economic, political, cultural and, where necessary, military forms. So too will the struggle against governments which, whatever their ideological dispositions, might seek to disturb a status quo which the United States and other capitalist powers are concerned to maintain. The Gulf War with Iraq is the latest instance of this struggle. The murderous dictatorship over which Saddam Hussein presided was perfectly acceptable to Western governments, so long as it served their purposes, as was the case in Iraq's war with Iran. The invasion of Kuwait was a different matter; and any means other than war to bring the invasion to an end were quickly brushed aside by the United States. The point had to be made that leaders of countries in the 'third world' which gravely offended against what the United States and its allies considered to be their legitimate interests in a particularly important part of the world would expose themselves to fearsome retribution. The Gulf War is very unlikely to be the last such episode.

Even though it is too simple to say that capitalism makes for war, the defence of capitalist interests, and of 'free enterprise' in general, by the United States and its allies does nevertheless engender a powerful bias towards interventionism against deviant movements and regimes; and while this interventionism assumes many forms, it ultimately includes the threat and the use of force. A genuinely new world order will not come into being until this global defence of capitalism ceases to be the dominant concern of Western governments; and this will not come about until capitalist interests are sufficiently subdued to cease shaping the policies of Western governments. This will not mean that all conflict in the realm of international relations will come to an end. But it will at least dry up one of its main sources.

This then is the kind of indictment that may be drawn up against capitalism today. In this perspective, the notion that capitalism has been thoroughly transformed and represents the best that humankind can ever hope to achieve is a dreadful slur on the human race. All the same, the indictment does not indicate how precisely a socialist alternative would bring about a major change for the better in the way life is lived by the vast majority of people. This question and others related to it are taken up in the following chapters.

2

Socialist Aspirations

1

The disintegration of the Soviet Union and the collapse of Communist regimes in Eastern Europe obviously mark the end of the particular alternative to capitalism which was inaugurated by the Bolshevik Revolution of 1917. No one doubts the immense significance of this event; but how far is it relevant to the discussion of socialism?

The coming into being of the Communist alternative to capitalism had nurtured and sustained successive generations of people on the Left, and had seemed to them to provide a concrete, tangible proof that an altogether different (and immeasurably better) society than capitalism could ever achieve was not only possible in a remote future but was actually being built. Here at long last was the fulfilment of the promise of the French Revolution that had been aborted by Thermidor; here was the vindication of all the struggles and sacrifices which had marked history ever since then, the victory that redeemed the sufferings of the oppressed everywhere; and here too was the promise that what had been achieved in the Soviet Union could and would be repeated everywhere else.[1] From Paris to

[1] 'The Bolshevik revolutionary model has been decisive for all twentieth-century revolutions because it made them imaginable in societies still more backward than All the Russias. It opened the possibility of, so to speak, cutting history off at the pass.' B. Anderson, *Imagined Communities* (Verso, London and New York, 1991, rev. edn), p. 156.

Calcutta, from New York to Johannesburg, men and women who were among the most dedicated, militant and selfless activists on the Left drew strength from this conviction; and they unreservedly subscribed to Stalin's pronouncement, made as early as 1927, that 'a revolutionary is one who is ready to protect, to defend the USSR without reservation, without qualification, openly and honestly . . . for the USSR is the base of the world revolutionary movement and this revolutionary movement cannot be defended and promoted unless the USSR is defended.'[2]

There had been people on the Left, from social democrats at one end to anarchists at the other, who had always viewed the Soviet Union and later Communist regimes as a monstrous deformation of socialism. So too, from within the Marxist fold, did Trotsky and his disciples conduct from the twenties onwards an unremitting campaign against what they viewed as the betrayal of the Revolution; and there were over the years many Communists disillusioned with the Soviet Union who came to share that view. But all such people were summarily dismissed and denounced by a formidable Communist propaganda apparatus as by definition counter-revolutionary and as having, by their criticisms of the Soviet Union, 'objectively' sided with the forces of capitalism, imperialism and fascism. Communists and other unquestioning supporters of the Soviet Union were strengthened in their convictions by the Soviet Union's achievements, of which more in a moment, by capitalist hostility towards it, by the belief that the Soviet Union was the only true bulwark against fascism, by its decisive contribution to the defeat of Nazi Germany in World War II, and by Soviet hostility to the efforts of the United States and its allies to defeat by all means, including military intervention, all attempts at radical reform anywhere in the world.

Even ardent supporters of Communist regimes had to acknowledge, after 1956 and Khrushchev's 'secret speech' at the Twentieth

[2] J. V. Stalin, *Works* (Foreign Languages Publishing House, Moscow, 1953), vol. X, pp. 53–4. In a book published in 1968, Kim Philby, who may be taken to have had an extreme commitment to this view, was writing that his various appointments in the British Secret Intelligence Service must be regarded 'purely in the light of cover-jobs, to be carried out sufficiently well to ensure my attaining positions in which my service to the Soviet Union would be most effective. My connection with SIS must be seen against my prior total commitment to the Soviet Union which I regarded then, as I do now, the inner fortress of the world movement': K. Philby, *My Silent War* (Grove Press, New York, 1968), p. 21.

Congress of the Soviet Communist Party, that there was much, to say the least, that had been and remained unacceptable about the Communist experience; and this dissociation became more pronounced with every passing year. But the notion remained very widespread on the Left that whatever was wrong with Communist regimes was remediable in the long term and did not bring into question their very capacity to endure and develop further. This optimism was reinforced by the various attempts that were made by Communist regimes to implement reforms; and the early years of Gorbachev's endeavours after 1985 seemed to give further ground for the belief that, however haltingly and inadequately, the Soviet Union did seem to be moving in the direction of socialist democracy. This was the notion that was dealt a mortal blow by the events of 1989 and after. Socialists had no reason to mourn the passing of the old regime; but they had good reason to mourn the catastrophic failure of Mikhail Gorbachev to achieve a transition from the authoritarian collectivism of the Brezhnev era to something resembling socialist democracy. Whether this was ever a real possibility will of course never be known.

Anti-socialists gleefully point to the fact that no other alternative to capitalism than Communist regimes has ever come into being; and they easily move from that fact to the assertion that no other alternative can ever be realized. In other words, the death of Communism is synonymous with the end of socialism, save for the purely abstract, illusory and utopian constructions woven by ideologues remote from the real world. On this view, the only choice is between Communism as it was practised in Communist regimes on the one hand, and capitalism on the other. However, this is no choice at all, since Communism has so obviously failed. The *real* choice, so it is often claimed, is between different versions of capitalism – between, say, a more interventionist and socially minded capitalism of the Swedish type and a less interventionist, less welfare-oriented one. Nor is this belief confined to the Right: it has nowadays great currency within the Left, a phenomenon to which I will return presently.

As was noted earlier, there is no way to prove that a socialist alternative to Communism can be realized, except by actually constructing it. But, it will be argued here, to say that the only alternative to capitalism is Communism is to take far too restrictive, narrow and blinkered a view of what is possible by way of social construction.

2

We must begin with what socialism is not, and to do so first of all by reference to Communist regimes. There were many differences between them, but there was a 'model' which was common to them all, and which had a number of distinct features. One of these was their highly centralized command economy, with an all-embracing system of detailed and imperative planning, with all the strategic means of economic activity, and most other means as well, under state ownership and control, and with markets and prices allowed, at best, no more than a marginal role in the economy. Many attempts were made in the decades following Stalin's death in 1953 to reduce the rigidities of the 'model', but the main features of the system stubbornly endured.

Secondly, the Communist Party (under a variety of names) exercised what amounted to a monopoly of power in political life and beyond it throughout society. In some countries, other parties were allowed, but were only submissive adjuncts of the Communist Party. The Party itself, however, was only an instrument, alongside all other instruments of rule, notably the state apparatus, in the hands of the Party leaders. The monopoly of power of the Party was really that of its leaders, under the system of 'democratic centralism' in which centralism easily swallowed up democracy.

Relatedly, Communist regimes sought to stifle and suppress all manifestations of life that could not be closely controlled by the Party and the state. The degree to which this was achieved varied from country to country; and it was, at least in some of them, less strictly enforced in recent decades than in the heyday of Stalinism. Nor did control from the top preclude a certain 'pluralism' in the upper reaches of the system, in so far as diverse interests and lobbies competed with each other for resources and advantages.[3] Even so, the system everywhere remained essentially monolithic and repressive in intention and practice, with vast and arbitrary powers allocated to a gigantic police apparatus.

The suppression of dissent was carried out in the name of an official Party and state ideology, namely Marxism-Leninism, promulgated after Lenin's death in 1924, and supplemented in some cases

[3]   See e.g. S. G. Solomon (ed.), *Pluralism in the Soviet Union* (Macmillan, London, 1983).

by local additions, such as Mao Tse-tung Thought, or the thoughts of Kim Il Sung, or other variants. This was a catechism which did not admit any departure from it that was not officially sanctioned. It was impossible to get everyone to subscribe to the official ideology; but it was possible to punish overt dissent from it, in any sphere, and this was done, again with varying degrees of severity in different countries.

Finally, some Communist regimes, notably the Soviet Union, China, North Korea and Romania, fostered a cult of personality which reached quite extraordinary and grotesque dimensions, with the attribution of superhuman and quasi-divine qualities to the leader of the Party and state; and it was a cult which again admitted no overt dissent.

This is the 'model', which assumed its most extreme form in the Stalin years in the Soviet Union, and which has collapsed there and in Eastern Europe. In China, a Communist Party which remains in strict control presides over what appears to be a gradual transition from Communism to capitalism, even though the Chinese leaders deny that this is their intention and proclaim that their aim is the creation of a 'socialist market economy'. Only North Korea, Vietnam and, in very different ways, Cuba now remain Communist regimes; but for how long is uncertain. In any case, none of them is now believed to provide the 'model' of socialism which the Soviet Union, at an earlier time, was thought by many people on the Left to represent.

3

Of the many questions that may be asked about this Communist experience, two may be singled out here: how far was it the product of Marxism; and what relation, if any, does it bear to socialism?

Marxism has often been seen as the main source of the negative features of the Communist experience. How far is this justified?[4]

On any sober assessment, the answer, so far as classical Marxism is concerned, is 'not at all'. It is possible, in the vast corpus of the writings of Marx, and particularly of Engels, to find isolated

---

[4] For a useful survey of diverse views on the issue, see D. Lovell, *From Marx to Lenin* (Cambridge University Press, Cambridge, 1984), introduction.

formulations which have distinctly centralizing and even authoritarian overtones; but the whole thrust of their writings firmly and unequivocally points the other way. Nor is there to be found in any of their writings the slightest hint of some of the most distinctive features of Communist regimes – the one-party system, the domination of society by a dictatorial and repressive state, the cult of personality, of which both Marx and Engels would have been bitterly contemptuous. In relation to the state, there is, at the core of Marx's thought, a deep abhorrence – perhaps an exaggerated abhorrence – of its power, and an insistence on the need, in socialist terms, for its strict subordination to society; and it was Engels who looked forward to the 'withering away' of the state in the wake of a socialist revolution.

As for the public ownership of the means of production, it is indeed true that Marx and Engels did believe that common ownership was the essential basis of a socialist society. But they did not propose that the organization, control and management of the economy should be vested in an all-powerful state imposing its will on the producers and everyone else. For Marx, on the contrary, the basis of the socialist economy was to be constituted by the 'free association of the producers'. The point here is not whether the economic perspectives of classical Marxism are of relevance today; it is rather that these perspectives have very little to do with the organization of economic life that was typical of Communist regimes.

Against this, it is often argued that, whatever Marx and Engels may have said or intended, the implications of their mode of thought, with their faith in revolutionary and comprehensive social engineering, were inevitably 'totalitarian', and certain, once the attempt was made to put their aspirations into practice, to produce the regime that was established in the Soviet Union and elsewhere.[5]

This is a view of comprehensive social renewal which is inherently implausible. For it fails to take into account the specific conditions in which social renewal is undertaken, the degree of support it enjoys, the nature of the resistance it elicits from vested interests, the flexibility and cohesion of those in charge of it, in short all the historical conditions in which it occurs. This is in no way to say that comprehensive social change, even in the best of conditions, is an

---

[5] For an argument to this effect, see e.g. L. Kolakowski, 'Marxist roots of Stalinism', in *Stalinism*, ed. R. C. Tucker (W. W. Norton, New York, 1977).

easy matter, or that warnings of the dangers it entails can be brushed aside. The whole experience of the twentieth century shows well enough how real the dangers are; and I may say here that my own approach in this book to the question of socialist advance has been greatly influenced by my awareness of the delicacy of the enterprise and of the need to guard against authoritarian pseudo-solutions to the problems it must encounter. What this means in practical terms is discussed throughout the book; but when all due importance has been attached to the difficulties and dangers of radical social change, socialists are bound to reject the notion that the large-scale renewal of the social order which socialism implies is doomed by definition to turn into a self-defeating and catastrophic enterprise. To say that it must is to succumb to an extreme and debilitating form of determinism.

The leaders of Communist regimes claimed that they were faithfully following in the traces of Marx and Engels; and they may well have believed it. But neither claim nor conviction can be taken as proof of anything. The rhetoric and propaganda which were produced by these regimes were couched in carefully selected Marxist terms; but the practice amounted to a thorough repudiation of classical Marxism.

What shaped that practice was determined above all by the conditions in which the Bolshevik regime in Russia and later Communist regimes elsewhere came into being. For they were born in conditions of extreme crisis, dislocation, war and civil war, foreign intervention, huge losses of life and immense material destruction. Moreover, revolutionary change, whether internally produced or externally imposed, occurred in countries which, with the partial exception of Czechoslovakia and what became the German Democratic Republic, were at a low level of economic development, in some cases at an exceedingly low level. This meant, among other things, that far from proceeding from a mature industrial base, the new regimes had to foster an arduous process of economic development. Nor were their political circumstances any more propitious: again with the exception of Czechoslovakia, the countries concerned had all previously been ruled by authoritarian regimes of one sort or another, colonial or indigenous. To add to all this, many of the new regimes lacked legitimacy in the eyes of much of their population; and this was particularly true in countries where the new order had been imposed by the Soviet Union.

In the Soviet Union itself, adverse conditions greatly favoured the imposition of the Stalinist 'model'; and that 'model' was readily adopted elsewhere by leaders schooled in Stalinist thought and practice. Given these adverse conditions, one-party rule and the suppression of dissent appeared to them to be legitimate ways of running their countries. For were they not moved by the best intentions; and were not their opponents criminally perverse in obstructing the realization of their intentions?

So much was this system of rule attractive to leaders seeking revolutionary change in deeply unfavourable circumstances that revolutions born under wholly non-Communist auspices also soon gravitated towards the Soviet 'model': the Cuban revolution is the most notable example of such evolution, and other instances can be found in African regimes that formally adopted 'Marxism-Leninism'.

Communist leaders did not find self-legitimation only in their own good intentions, or in the reactionary opposition they encountered; they also found it in the very real social revolutions over which they presided. Whether imposed or indigenously generated, these revolutions did effect a radical change in property relations, in the class structure of their countries, in the political system, and in the vocabulary of politics. Nor were their actual achievements at all negligible, particularly in the early years, and in comparison with the record of the regimes they had replaced. In terms of economic growth, health and educational provision, security of employment, and opportunities for the mass of people who had hitherto been grossly disadvantaged, much was done. None of it affects the reality of the authoritarianism and repressiveness of these regimes; but neither do these features obliterate the advances that were made. As noted earlier, these advances greatly helped anyone so minded to overlook the negative aspects of Communist regimes and to foster the hope that whatever might be wrong would eventually be remedied.

4

The second and more important question which Communist experience invites is that of its relation to socialism.

The question is often dismissed as a mere exercise in arbitrary definitions. Thus, a distinguished socialist economist, Wlodimierz Brus, writes that 'to deny Communist countries the "title" of socialism would be tantamount to an a priori investment of socialism with fundamentally immaculate features, to an elimination of the negative by definition.'[6] For his part, Professor Brus accepts Joseph Schumpeter's 'institutional definition of socialism'. 'By socialist society', Schumpeter wrote in *Capitalism, Socialism and Democracy*, 'we shall designate an institutional pattern in which the control over means of production is vested with a central authority – or, as we may say, in which, as a matter of principle, the economic affairs of society belong to the public and not the private sphere.'[7] This 'Centralist Socialism', as he called it, is a purely arbitrary designation, sufficiently narrow to enable Schumpeter to advance the quite spurious claim that 'a society may be fully and truly socialist and yet be led by an absolute ruler or be organised in the most democratic of all possible ways; it may be aristocratic or proletarian.'[8]

This runs altogether counter to what socialism has meant to most shades of socialist thought; and such a consensus can hardly be dismissed as irrelevant. The world of socialism has always been one of extreme diversity, bitter divisions, enduring feuds. But there are certain core propositions which have attracted sufficient acceptance from most socialists to be legitimately taken to define the meaning of socialism; and it is, on this basis, perfectly possible to question the socialist credentials of Communist regimes without in the least investing socialism with 'fundamentally immaculate features'. Such questioning is in fact essential if we are to avoid a quite unwarranted degree of arbitrariness in defining socialism, or a degree of vagueness which robs the notion of any particular meaning. It is often said nowadays that this is precisely the case, and that socialism is indeed now so vague a term as to be virtually meaningless. This is a mistaken view.

There are in effect three core propositions or themes which define socialism, all three equally important, and each related to, and dependent upon, the others. These are democracy, egalitarianism, and socialization of a predominant part of the economy.

First, socialism incorporates the vision of a society immeasurably more democratic than any capitalist society could ever be. Socialism

---

[6] W. Brus, 'Socialism – feasible or viable?', *New Left Review*, 153 (Sept.–Oct. 1985), p. 45.
[7] J. A. Schumpeter, *Capitalism, Socialism and Democracy* (George Allen and Unwin, London, 1943), p. 167.
[8] Ibid., p. 170.

seeks to give real meaning to the notion of citizenship and popular sovereignty, well beyond universal suffrage, regular elections, political rights and other features of capitalist democracy. As noted earlier, capitalist democracy, in a socialist perspective, appears as a contradiction in terms, with its democratic forms fatally vitiated by the capitalist context in which they function; and socialism postulates that democracy has to encompass and pervade all aspects of the social order, which is certainly not the case in capitalist society.

It was the belief that socialism without democracy can, at best, only be a gross perversion which caused so many of the leading figures in the international labour and socialist movement at the time of the Bolshevik Revolution to take, from the start, a very critical view of the Bolshevik dictatorship. Thus in 1918, Karl Kautsky was writing that 'for us . . . Socialism without democracy is unthinkable. We understand by Modern Socialism not merely social organisation of production, but democratic organisation of society as well. Accordingly, socialism is for us inseparably connected with democracy. No Socialism without democracy.'[9] At the other end of the socialist spectrum, Rosa Luxemburg, while praising the Bolsheviks for having dared to seize power, was also sharply critical of their suppression of civic freedoms. 'Freedom only for the supporters of the government,' she wrote,

> only for the members of one party – however numerous they may be – is no freedom at all. Freedom is always and exclusively freedom for the one who thinks differently . . . Lenin and Trotsky have laid down the soviets as the only true representation of the laboring masses. But with the repression of political life in the land as a whole, life in the soviets must also become more and more crippled. Without general elections, without unrestricted freedom of press and assembly, without a free struggle of opinion, life dies out in every public institution, becomes a mere semblance of life, in which only the bureaucracy remains as the active element.[10]

[9] K. Kautsky, *The Dictatorship of the Proletariat* (Manchester, The National Labour Press, n.d.), p. 6. This was the pamphlet which provoked Lenin's furious response, *The Proletarian Revolution and the Renegade Kautsky*, published at the end of 1918, which insisted that 'proletarian democracy is *a million times* more democratic than any bourgeois democracy' and that 'the Soviet government is a million times more democratic than the most democratic bourgeois republic': in *Against Revisionism* (Foreign Languages Publishing House, Moscow, 1959), p. 404.

[10] R. Luxemburg, 'The Russian Revolution', in *Rosa Luxemburg Speaks*, ed. M.-A. Waters (Pathfinder Press, New York, 1970), p. 391.

However, the relationship of democracy to dissent is rather more ambiguous than these formulations allow. For democracy, whether understood as the rule of the majority, or in a much larger sense as the effective exercise of popular power, is quite compatible with the suppression of forms of dissent which come at some particular point to be unacceptable to power holders, who may well be supported by a majority, even the great majority, of the population. An obvious example is the harassment and persecution of Communists and others on the Left in which the government of the United States engaged after 1945 (and for that matter before), culminating in the McCarthy witch-hunt of the early fifties. To speak of this as a good example of John Stuart Mill's 'tyranny of the majority' is very misleading: the majority did acquiesce in the witch-hunt and even supported it, but it was not the majority which initiated it or engaged in it. That was done by power holders in government at central, regional and local levels, and by power holders in society at large (for instance, university presidents, trustees and administrators, Hollywood moguls, newspaper proprietors), and the population at large was subjected to a massive barrage of propaganda, conducted by the state and all means of communication, designed to convince it that the United States was in urgent danger from the Communist conspiracy. It was of course not only in the United States that harassment and persecution occurred, with the approbation of a majority: it was a part of the politics of all capitalist democracies in the epoch of the Cold War.[11]

Even so, it would also be misleading to suggest that these countries therefore ceased to be 'democratic' in the conventional sense of the term. The fact is that regimes can be democratic in that sense *and* repressive of dissent. The crucial difference between them and authoritarian regimes is that democratic regimes are much more constrained in their prosecution and suppression of dissent, and much more limited in what they do with dissenters. The American witch-hunt was a vicious business, which ruined many lives; and it dealt a terrible blow to the American Left in general, as it was intended to do. But it can hardly be compared to the treatment of dissent and dissenters by authoritarian regimes. Dissent in any society, however democratic, is always vulnerable to circumstances where

[11] On which, see e.g. R. Whitaker, 'Fighting the Cold War on the home front: America, Britain, Australia and Canada', in *The Socialist Register 1984: the uses of anti-Communism* (Merlin Press, London, 1984, and Monthly Review Press, New York, 1984).

its expression is easily taken as a menace to the social order. Nor would this have ceased to be a danger where a left government was seeking to advance radical measures of social renewal. On the contrary, it is in such a situation, where political polarization occurs, that the danger would be greatest; and it is also where a left government would have to tread very carefully in its attitude to dissent.

All democratic regimes impose certain limits on dissent, and on the means whereby dissent is articulated – on the right of expression, of assembly, of political activity. The crucial questions are how wide the limits are, and how effective the constraints upon power holders, in the state and in society, in their treatment of dissent and dissenters. The point of course applies to socialist democracy as well as to capitalist democracy; and it will be further discussed presently.

Intimately related to democracy is equality as the second core proposition of socialism. This entails a rough egalitarianism, which differs from perfect equality, an untenable notion, but an egalitarianism which does all the same seek the elimination of the major inequalities in every sphere of life which characterize societies deeply divided on the grounds of income, wealth, power and opportunities. In other words, socialism is about the coming into being of societies in which deep economic, social, political and cultural divisions will in time have ceased to exist; and in which the power now vested in a relatively small minority will be shared out throughout society. This is very different from a 'meritocratic' social order, which only means that access to 'the top' is made easier. Even this is fraught with major obstacles in class-divided societies where 'equality of opportunity' remains a slogan rather than a fact. In any case, however desirable it obviously is that people hitherto disadvantaged on the ground of class, gender, race etc. should no longer suffer discrimination and should be able to use their capacities to the full, their ascent to 'the top' would not do away with existing structures of domination. The assumption by women and black people of positions of power cannot by itself transform a system which is profoundly undemocratic.

The third, and most controverted, proposition is that socialism entails the coming into being of a socialized economy, in which at least the *preponderant* part of the means of economic activity, notably the 'commanding heights' of the economy, would come under various forms of public or social ownership, control and management.

In the introduction, I described socialization as an essential means to the realization of a democratic and egalitarian social order. As such, it is also a core proposition of socialism. This has long been strongly contested by social democratic writers and leaders, never more so than in recent years; and it has, in practical political terms, now been relegated to the margins of political life, and been the constant object of denunciation, dismissal and derision. However, the fact that the socialization of a predominant part of the economy is now discounted and rejected by the main political agencies of the Left cannot by itself be taken to invalidate the idea that it is an essential (though by no means a sufficient) condition for the achievement of a democratic and egalitarian society. The real question, in socialist terms, is not whether the socialization of a predominant part of economic life is an intrinsic part of the meaning of socialism, but how it is to be achieved in the context of an ever more multinational capitalism. This and other problems associated with socialization will be considered in chapter 4.

These propositions, it should be stressed, are inextricably intertwined and equally important. This is because there can be no true citizenship without a rough equality of condition, and no such equality is possible without the socialization of a predominant part of the economy. So too, as long and painful experience has shown, public ownership without democracy can only provide the basis for authoritarian statism.

Of the three propositions, it is only the third one, as noted, which has since the years following World War II been explicitly and fiercely rejected by people who have nevertheless called themselves socialists; and it is of course open to anyone who rejects socialization to appropriate the socialist label. But this rests on a failure to understand how much socialization is involved in the other goals of socialism, to which the same people theoretically subscribe. Whatever they choose to call themselves, they are in reality social reformers, concerned with the improvement of the existing social order rather than its replacement by an altogether different one. 'Social reformer' is not a term of abuse: it simply denotes a different position from that occupied by socialists. So long as the means of economic activity are under private ownership and control, so long must the social order be dominated by the drive for private profit, with the people who own and control these means exercising vastly disproportionate power and influence over government and society. Life for socialists would undoubtedly be a lot easier if socialization was not one of the core propositions of socialism. For not only is socialization a complex enterprise; also, many more people on the Left would then find it much more acceptable to subscribe to the idea of socialism as democracy and egalitarianism, at least in theory. An important reason for their recoil is the association of nationalization with centralism, bureaucracy and other ills. Conservative propaganda has greatly contributed to this image, but there is enough in it to make nationalization an unattractive notion, quite apart from the difficulties which implementation must encounter. This makes it all the more important for socialists to explain that old-style nationalization greatly differs in form, content and purpose from socialization, conceived as an intrinsic part of the democratic process.

Socialism itself must be viewed as part of a democratic movement which long antedates it, but to which socialism alone can give its full meaning. The idea of democracy has been drastically narrowed in scope and substance in capitalist societies so as to reduce the threat it posed to established power and privilege: socialism on the contrary is committed to a great widening of its compass. The unenthusiastic prophet of democracy in the nineteenth century was Alexis de Tocqueville. In his introduction to *Democracy in America*, published in 1835, de Tocqueville said that democracy, which he equated with the 'equality of condition' he thought he had found in the United States, was also making its way in Europe. 'A great democratic revolution', he wrote, 'is taking place in our midst; everybody sees it, but by no means everybody judges it in the same way. Some think it a new thing and, supposing it an accident, hope that they can still check it; others think it irresistible, because it seems to them the most continuous, ancient, and permanent tendency known to history';[12] and in a preface to the twelfth edition of the book, written in 1848, he also asked: 'Does anyone imagine that Democracy, which has destroyed the feudal system and vanquished kings, will fall back before the middle classes and the rich?'.[13] Dominant classes in all capitalist countries have ever since the nineteenth century fought hard and with a considerable measure of success to falsify de Tocqueville's prediction: socialism is the name of the struggle to make it come true.

[12]   A. de Tocqueville, *Democracy in America* (Doubleday, New York, 1969), p. 9.
[13]   Ibid., p. xiii.

Thus conceived, socialism is part of the struggle for the deepening and extension of democracy in all areas of life. Its advance is not inscribed in some pre-ordained historical process, but is the result of a constant pressure from below for the enlargement of democratic rights; and this pressure is itself based on the fact that the vast majority located at the lower ends of the social pyramid *needs* these rights if those who compose it are to resist and limit the power to which they are subjected.

This, however, is not enough. Socialism seeks, not only the limitation of power, but *its eventual abolition as the organizing principle of social life*. This, incidentally, or not so incidentally, is ultimately what Marx was about. It is of course a notion which constitutes an immense wager on the capacity of the human race to achieve unforced cooperation, and may be dismissed as absurdly 'utopian'. For socialists, it forms an essential part, in however long-term a perspective, of the promise of socialism.

There is a profound sense in which democracy, equality and socialization must be taken to be means to an end which ultimately defines socialism, namely the achievement of a greater degree of social harmony than can ever be achieved in societies based on domination and exploitation. Such harmony would be based on what might be called civic virtue, according to which men and women would freely accept the obligations of citizenship as well as claiming its rights; and they would find no great difficulty in the cultivation of a *socialized individualism* in which the expression of their individuality would be combined with a due regard for the constraints imposed upon it by life in society.

In the light of the meaning that is properly attached to socialism, it is obvious that the practice of Communist regimes was for the most part a denial rather than an affirmation of that meaning. They did bring the main means of economic activity (in most cases all of them) under public ownership; but they also demonstrated the point that this, without democracy, amounts to no more than authoritarian collectivism. Nor were these regimes egalitarian, for they created structures of power and privilege which made a mockery of any notion of equality of condition. Communist regimes have been described on the Left as being socialist, or degenerate workers' states, or state capitalist, or bureaucratic collectivist, and so on. But it is at any rate clear that they constituted at best a terrible deformation of socialism, and at worst its total repudiation.

5

It is hardly necessary to insist, at this moment in history, that the realization of the core propositions of socialism, or even the advancement towards their realization, is certain to be an exceedingly arduous project, full of pitfalls and tensions; and much of the Left has now accepted an 'epistemic conservatism', previously cultivated by the Right, about the limits of what is possible by way of social renewal.

The appropriate response to this is not to deny the problems posed by socialist construction, but to see how they could be solved, or, in the first instance at least, how they could be attenuated, on the assumption, which lies at the root of socialism, that their resolution or attenuation is not only desirable but possible.

Of all the problems which arise, there are three which are of quite exceptional importance, in so far as they question the socialist enterprise at its very roots; a legion of other problems seems by comparison to be less challenging.

First, there is the challenge posed by history itself, not least recent history, to the fundamental optimism about human capabilities which pervades the socialist enterprise – a belief, inherited from the Enlightenment, in the infinite perfectibility of human beings; or, to put it in more contemporary terms, the belief that human beings are perfectly capable of organizing themselves into cooperative, democratic, egalitarian and self-governing communities, in which all conflict would certainly not have been eliminated, but where it would become less and less frequent and acute. It will take a long time for this to be fully realized; but socialism's essential point of departure is – has to be – that there is no implacable curse which dooms humankind to perpetual division and strife.

All history, and certainly the history of the twentieth century, has seemed to provide a bitter rebuttal of any such optimism. Hegel once said that 'history is a slaughterhouse'; and he was echoing Joseph de Maistre's remark that 'the stench of blood rises from the pages of history.' Never has this been more true than in this century. The violent ending of millions upon millions of lives in World War I and World War II, the Nazi extermination camps, the murderous record of Stalinism, the human cost of Maoist adventurism; the mass killing associated with the war waged by France in Algeria and by the United States in Korea and Vietnam, the slaughter associated with 'ethnic cleansing' in former Yugoslavia, and countless other man-made disasters and wars since 1945, with the atrocities accompanying them, all appear to testify against socialist optimism and to justify the pessimism of the Right. So too, to all appearances, do the cruelties which human beings inflict upon each other in the course of their daily lives.

The question which this endless catalogue of horrors insistently presses upon anyone committed to the kind of enterprise represented by socialism is obvious: is this the human material out of which societies based on cooperation, sociality and altruism are to be constructed? Does it not on the contrary invite the deepest scepticism about the possibility of constructing the sort of social order to which socialism aspires? Is not the notion of human perfectibility an illusion daily denied by stark and irrefutable reality?[14] And is it not therefore a thousand times more reasonable to settle for improvements in the kind of social order which has been established in capitalist democratic societies, rather than to strive for a certain-to-fail wholesale recasting of society?

One retort to such questions is that socialism does not claim to provide a 'perfect solution' to humanity's problems; nor does it promise a social order – indeed a world – where all is forever sweetness and light. This, however, is too facile. For even a much less ambitious project needs to confront the question of whether the progressive attenuation of conflict and the notion of social harmony are not dangerously 'utopian'.

On this, there are some points to be made which suggest that the case is not quite as starkly hopeless as is often made out.

One such point is that the great collective blood-lettings which form so large a part of the historical record have never been the

---

[14] These are questions which Isaiah Berlin has repeatedly asked in his work, invoking Immanuel Kant's image of 'the crooked timber' from which human beings are made to argue that 'no perfect solution is, not merely in practice, but in principle, possible in human affairs, and any determined attempt to produce it is likely to lead to suffering, disillusionment and failure': I. Berlin, *The Crooked Timber of Humanity* (John Murray, London, 1990), p. 48. In a review of the book, Perry Anderson has argued that Kant was not in fact referring to humanity as a whole but to the fallibility of any individual as sovereign: P. Anderson, 'The pluralism of Isaiah Berlin', in *Zones of Engagement* (Verso, London and New York, 1992), p. 233. This does not of course invalidate the question which Berlin is asking.

product of purely spontaneous action from below. The easy notion that 'we are all guilty' and the attribution of guilt to human nature mask the crucially significant fact that it was from above that have almost always come the initiation and the organization of mass killings. It was not 'the masses' who decided to build the gas chambers, who organized the Gulag, who initiated the disastrous policies associated with Maoism, who planned the bombing of Korea 'back to the Stone Age', who decided on the saturation bombing of Vietnam and Cambodia, and who prepared the ground for and organized 'ethnic cleansing'. Most such collective actions have been initiated and organized by people of power in pursuit of whatever purposes and fantasies moved them. 'The masses' cannot at least be held responsible for the decisions which produced wholesale slaughter. In fact, the mass of 'ordinary people' have seldom if ever had any direct involvement in such slaughter: even in periods of the greatest horrors, most people have tended to be the spectators of what was being done, often in their name.

This said, it is true that 'ordinary people' have generally at least acquiesced in the horrors that were being perpetrated, and often cheered the perpetrators. Active disapproval in the face of power has for the most part been confined to a minority, and the more ruthless the power, the smaller the minority. Moreover, people of power, having made their decisions, have never found it difficult to enlist people for the execution of murderous deeds. At their behest, enough have always been found to inflict violence, torture and death on other human beings. Execution squads have never lacked recruits, including volunteers; and such squads have never suffered much from desertion. In the rather different case of armies in the field, participants in mass slaughter have found justification in the slogan 'kill or be killed', and additional justification in whatever sacred cause they believed they were serving.

The perpetration of atrocities on a huge scale has never been confined to any particular part of the human race. In appropriate circumstances, a lot of people – perhaps most people – may be induced or driven to participate in collective slaughter, even though only a minority is likely to be called upon to do so. But it is a very large and unwarranted step to move from this to the notion that humanity as such cannot escape from the slaughterhouse, and is doomed to add, generation upon generation to the end of time, to the catalogue of collective cruelty. It is much more reasonable to believe that it should be possible, without any utopian illusions, to create a context in which collective cruelty would be seen for the abomination that it is, and made impossible by the resistance which it would evoke. Indeed, it may well be said that it is precisely the existence of so much evil which makes it essential to create a context in which evil may be conquered, or at least attenuated; and it is a counsel of despair to say that it cannot be done, that evil on a huge scale is part of the human condition, that its conquest is impossible.

The same point goes for the individual acts of cruelty perpetrated by men and women upon each other, or upon children, or for that matter upon animals. Here too, the notion that such acts are to be explained by traits ineradicably embedded in human nature is much less plausible than the view that they are mainly produced by the insecurities, frustrations, anxieties and alienations that form an intrinsic part of class societies based on domination and exploitation. The 'injuries of class', allied to injuries of race, gender, religion and many others, readily lend themselves to pathological and morbid deformations which deeply and adversely affect human relations. This can only be effectively tackled in societies where conditions are created which foster solidarity, cooperation, security and respect, and where these values are given substance by a variety of grassroots institutions in all areas of life. It is these conditions which socialism seeks to advance. Collective and individual cruelty is a terrible and pervasive reality. But it also meets with strong opposition. Indeed, there is now much greater abhorrence of cruelty than has ever been common in earlier epochs: much that was easily accepted in the past, even the recent past, like racist and sexual oppression and discrimination, and horrendous crimes by state agents, is now actively denounced and opposed. It is not in the least 'utopian' to think that conditions can be created where collective and individual misdeeds can be turned into increasingly marginal phenomena.

All the same, it cannot be expected that the demons which have been at work throughout history will not continue to cast their evil spell for a long time to come; and the struggle against them is bound to affect very substantially the ways in which a new social order is constructed. More precisely, that struggle has a direct bearing upon the mode of government that would be required in a society which was beginning to move in socialist directions. The power of the state in such a society would be variously constrained; but, as will also be argued later, the notion that state power, and therefore state coercion, would no longer have a substantial place in the conduct of affairs belongs to the realm of fantasy, at least for the relevant future. The day may come when state coercion will no longer be required, and when the state will indeed 'wither away'; but it will long remain an essential element in the construction of a new social order.

A second issue which challenges socialist optimism is what Robert Michels long ago called the 'iron law of oligarchy'. Socialism is based on the view that it is possible for power to be distributed and decentralized in genuinely democratic ways, to the point where much of government is self-government. This, a variety of elite theories proclaims, is an absurd expectation. For, so it is argued, it ignores the fact that minority rule, with power firmly concentrated in the hands of a relatively small number of people, is an inescapable feature of the human condition; and that, whatever may be intended by revolutionaries and reformers, and however resolute may be their attempt to achieve a democratic distribution of power, minority rule will inevitably defeat their intentions and their endeavours.

This assertion of the inevitability of minority rule rests on one of two propositions. One of them is that there is a 'natural' division in any society between a minority destined by virtue of its attributes to appropriate power, and the majority destined by reason of its lack of the required attributes to constitute the subordinate population. The required attributes may vary over time, and particular merit may be assigned to physical strength, or courage, or mental ability, or specialized knowledge, or wealth, or cunning, or a combination of them; but however this may be, the unequal distribution of attributes will ensure the perpetuation of minority rule. The minority may be challenged; but the result of the challenge, if successful, will always be the substitution of one ruling minority by another. 'History', as Pareto once put it, 'is the graveyard of aristocracies.'

The other proposition proceeds from a view of the nature of organization. The claim is that in any organization, power will inevitably come to be concentrated in relatively few hands; and that those who enjoy this power will want to keep and enlarge it, and use all the resources at their disposal to fend off any challenge to their predominance. Michels formulated his 'iron law of oligarchy' in relation to the German Social Democratic Party before World War I, and was concerned to argue that what was intended as an instrument of working-class liberation was in fact an instrument for the mastery of the Party by its leaders; but the idea, as Michels argued, can easily be adapted to any kind of organization. Elite rule is inevitable.

How far do such notions undermine the democratic purposes of socialism? And does not Communist experience, and the experience of rule elsewhere, even in the name of democracy, serve to validate theories of ineluctable minority rule?

There is no doubt that any kind of organization must involve the attribution of a degree of power to some people; and that power is most likely to accrue to people who have more energy, drive, purpose, ambition or whatever than others. The propensity to activism is not equally distributed; and it is quite likely that people to whom power has accrued will find its exercise agreeable, and will therefore seek to cling to it, and will find excellent reasons for doing so.

The real question is whether people to whom power has been attributed can be so controlled and constrained as not to allow them to constitute an oligarchy. This is not simply a matter of rules and regulations governing the exercise of power, for rules and regulations can always be circumvented. Much more important is the economic, social, political and moral context in which power is exercised. In societies where vast inequalities of every kind are an intrinsic part of daily life, it is indeed inevitable that power should assume concentrated and oligarchic forms, however loud the democratic rhetoric or elaborate the formal procedures which mask the fact. But the propensity to activism is not fixed; and, given favourable conditions, it could well spread. In societies where an egalitarianism of condition is in the process of being created, and where citizens are deeply conscious of their democratic rights, including their right to voluntary and effective participation, it is realistic to think that leadership need not be turned into oligarchic rule. Nevertheless, the *tendency* to oligarchy will long endure;[15] but a tendency can be countered and defeated. An iron law of oligarchy is a different matter; and there is no good reason to think that, given the right context, such a law must implacably govern the exercise of power.

[15] Michels himself generally speaks of a 'tendency' to oligarchy, as when he writes, for instance, that 'organisation implies the tendency to oligarchy. In every organisation, whether it be a political party, a professional union, or any other association of the kind, the aristocratic tendency manifests itself very early': *Political Parties* (Dover Publications, New York, and Constable, London, 1959), p. 32. The subtitle of the book is 'a sociological study of the oligarchical tendencies of modern democracies'.

A different challenge to socialist optimism has made its way to the top of the political agenda in recent decades, namely a 'neo-Malthusian' reading of the ecological dangers which threaten humankind. On this reading, population growth and the erosion and exhaustion of resources turn the development which so many parts of the world so badly need into an ever greater threat to life on the planet; and the obsessive productivism and consumerism of the developed world itself make a disastrous contribution to the aggravation of the threat.

The dangers to which ecologists point are real enough. What is at issue, however, is the 'neo-Malthusian' insistence that humanity is in the grip of forces which it cannot control. It is this which socialists, without indulging in a silly under-estimation of the dimensions of the threat, are bound to contest. As Ted Benton has observed, 'neo-Malthusianism' plays down 'qualitative differences in the organisation of societies as of only secondary causal significance in the face of large-scale natural or quasi-natural quantitative tendencies and limits'.[16] In fact, these 'qualitative differences in the organisation of societies' are of primary importance in relation to ecological and other dangers. Nor is this argument in the least weakened by the experience of Communist regimes. Their own record in relation to the environment was truly appalling; but this only points to the fact that, in this as in all other areas, authoritarian rule and the suppression of dissent are certain to produce dire consequences. Communist rulers were moved by strong productivist impulses, with industrial growth as their highest priority; and they were able to give free rein to these impulses, and to do great environmental damage with complete impunity.

In capitalist societies, on the other hand, it is the drive for profit which has been a main source of ecological vandalism. In this area as in others, the very nature of the system compels those who run it to treat any consideration other than profit as, at best, secondary.

Corporations and governments do nowadays proclaim their concern for the environment, and so do many international agencies. Conferences are held and pious resolutions passed. But to tackle

---

[16]   T. Benton, 'The Malthusian challenge: ecology, natural limits and human emancipation', in *Socialism and the Limits of Liberalism*, ed. P. Osborne (Verso, London and New York, 1991), p. 252.

ecological dangers, the depletion of resources, the over-population of the planet, is a task which requires very different priorities from those which move the capitalist state, not to speak of corporations. It requires an organization of society whose dominant principle is not the drive for the maximization of private profit; and it also requires a degree of public intervention in economic life which is anathema both to corporate and state power holders, and to international agencies inspired by neo-liberal principles.

This is not to under-estimate the reality of the dangers and the immensity of the task involved in seeking to tackle them effectively. Yet the real problem is not the fact of pollution, the scarcity of resources or over-population, but the extent to which a world dominated by capitalist imperatives is able to tackle them. On this count, there is justified pessimism. It would be idle to claim that socialism offers an instant solution to the problems which confront the planet. But it is at least legitimate to claim that socialism, in so far as it does stand for intervention and the frustration of capitalist drives, offers a chance that the problems would be tackled with all the determination that is required. This, however, is for the long term. Meanwhile, there is the struggle in which socialists, with many others, must engage against all the forces which threaten the planet.

6

A crucial consideration, in assessing the plausibility of socialism, is what it is taken to promise. In the history of socialist thought, there has always existed a quasi-religious, salvationist view of socialism, a belief that it would cure all ills, solve all problems, end all conflicts, finally lift all the burdens which have always plagued humankind. Socialism meant redemption, making the world anew, creating a new man and woman. This, it was acknowledged, might not happen all at once; but it would not be very long before it did happen after the old order had been swept away.

This vision of a total rupture with the present, of a complete cleansing of all that was evil in the world, has always had a powerful appeal through the ages. Added to this, and logically following from it, there is the notion that, in the formulation which Marx and Engels used in *The German Ideology* in 1846, revolution was necessary 'not only because the *ruling* class cannot be overthrown in

any other way, but also because the class *overthrowing* it can only
in a revolution succeed in ridding itself of all the muck of ages and
become fitted to found society anew.'[17] The issue here is not whether
revolution *is* the only way to achieve a new social order, but rather
that it does not rid the revolutionaries or society of the muck of
ages. In dictatorial regimes, revolution is very likely to be an imperative necessity, and it may open the way as nothing else could to
great progress. As Lenin also once said, 'revolution is the festival of
the oppressed.' But festivals do not last very long, and revolution is
often accompanied by bitter resistance. The dislocation and suffering
this causes greatly affects revolution's redemptive quality, and has a
profoundly adverse effect on it. In any case, it clearly takes a great
deal more than revolution to dispose of the muck of ages; and it was
Marx himself who also said in his *Critique of the Gotha Programme*
of 1875 that many 'defects' were 'inevitable in the first phase of
communist society as it is when it has just emerged after prolonged
birth pangs from capitalist society'.[18] This situates revolution in a
realistic perspective. A crucial distinction has to be made between
what can be hoped for in the short and middle term, and what may
be achieved in the long term by generations which have been nurtured in a world in which values such as cooperation, egalitarianism,
democracy and sociality have come to constitute the dominant common sense.

Such a long-term perspective is bound to be exceedingly unattractive to people who do view the achievement of socialism in much
more immediate and dramatic terms, and who view anything else
as smacking of a dangerous and discredited reformism. For them,
socialism is unthinkable without revolutionary upheaval, in the
aftermath of which an entirely new social order must be created
without any delay.

These are, however, two different propositions. For even if a revolutionary upheaval is necessary, the fact remains that to make a
reality of its promise is certain to be a difficult enterprise, which is
most likely to succeed if it is undertaken with great care and
deliberation.

This view is in any case dictated by the nature of capitalism as a

[17]   K. Marx and F. Engels, *The German Ideology*, in *Collected Works* (Lawrence and Wishart, London, 1976), vol. 5, p. 53.
[18]   K. Marx, *Critique of the Gotha Programme* (1875), in Marx and Engels,
Collected Works, vol. 24, p. 87.

mode of production. Earlier modes of production could, in given historical circumstances, be declared by fiat to be at an end. Lincoln's 1863 proclamation of emancipation in the United States – one of the greatest acts of expropriation in history – provides a dramatic illustration of the point. The same may be said of serfdom, brought to an end in Russia in 1861 by Czarist decree. Socialism, for its part, has as a cardinal aim the abolition of wage-labour, as defined in chapter 1; but it is clear that this abolition presents very different problems. Its transformation into labour performed under entirely different, non-capitalist conditions is more likely to be a lengthy process: the notion that it can be done at a stroke, and achieve desirable results, is belied by the dismal experience we have of such voluntarism. Relations of production, based on exploitation, as defined earlier, in a minority but far from negligible private sector, in a society moving towards socialism, will for a long time continue to exist alongside a public sector which will have been freed from it. The private sector will of course be subject to stringent regulation, and exploitation will thereby be tempered, but it will not have been abolished.

Marxists and socialists in general have always tended to underestimate the problems that must arise in the organization and administration of a post-capitalist society. A notable example of such under-estimation is to be found in Lenin's *The State and Revolution*, with its view of how easy the task would be – a view that was very soon changed once the Bolsheviks had come to power.[19] A rather different kind of 'utopianism' was also a marked trait of Stalinism, with its conviction that society was instantly and infinitely malleable, and that all that was required to shape it in any desired direction

---

[19] 'We, the workers, shall organise large-scale production on the basis of what capitalism has already created, relying on our own experience as workers, establishing strict, iron discipline backed up by the state power of the armed workers. We shall reduce the role of state officials to that of simply carrying out our instructions as responsible, revocable, modestly paid "foremen and accountants" (of course with the aid of technicians of all sorts, types and degrees) . . . Such a beginning, on the basis of large-scale production, will of itself lead to the gradual "withering away" of all bureaucracy, to the creation of an order . . . under which the functions of control and accounting, becoming more and more simple, will be performed by each in turn, will then become a habit and will finally die out as the *special* functions of a special section of the population.' V. I. Lenin, *The State and Revolution*, in *Selected Works* (Lawrence and Wishart, London, 1969), p. 298, emphasis in text.

was an iron will and ruthless leadership. Precisely the same was true
of Maoism, under whose auspices and at the command of Mao Tse-
tung was launched the 'great leap forward' which resulted in a
famine that cost the lives of millions of people. This voluntarism was
a prominent – and disastrous – feature of Communist thinking and
practice and led Communist leaders to embark on vast schemes of
social engineering which took little or no account of the real human
and material costs they must involve. A favourite slogan at the start
of the 'revolution from above' which Stalin initiated was 'there is no
citadel which Bolsheviks cannot storm': the trouble with this is that
the storming of citadels inevitably left many of them in ruins.

To repeat a point made earlier, any serious view of socialism
today has to accept the fact that the creation of a new social order,
even in the best of circumstances, which are most unlikely to obtain,
is bound to be a very difficult enterprise, full of hard choices and
great tensions. Socialists have always dwelt on the contradictions of
capitalism, and have been right to do so; but experience shows that
much attention has also to be paid to the contradictions which are
an inevitable part of the socialist enterprise.

Particularly important in this perspective is the fact that habit and
tradition, deeply encrusted beliefs and ancient prejudices, inherited
patterns of thought and behaviour, form a stubborn part of reality,
with a remarkable capacity to endure, even under the most adverse
circumstances. The experience of post-Communist regimes shows
this well enough, with the resurgence of long-suppressed national,
ethnic and religious sentiments. There is a very difficult path to be
explored between a reckless – and catastrophic – voluntarism on one
side, which starts from the premise that everything is immediately
possible, and an exaggerated caution on the other, which can easily
turn into retreat and paralysis. Socialism has to be perceived as a
process whose development occurs in societies each of which forms
an exceedingly tangled whole, whose history has to be taken into
careful account and whose complexities have to be reckoned with.
Socialism cannot reject out of hand everything that has been woven
over the years into the texture of the social order, much of it the
result of bitter struggles from below; but neither can it afford to be
mired in the 'muck of ages'. It is about a new social order, but a new
social order which will be marked by continuities as well as
discontinuities. It both is rooted in the reality of the present and
continually strives to transcend it. A central theme of this book is

precisely that socialist democracy represents both an *extension* of capitalist democracy and a *transcendence* of it.

Socialism represents a liberation of society from the constraints placed upon it by the imperative requirements of capitalism. Much scorn has been cast on Marx's notion that capitalism at a certain stage of its development becomes a 'fetter' upon the productive process. This, as noted earlier, has not happened, even though capitalism imposes upon that process priorities dictated by the striving for private profit rather than humane and rational ends. But in any case, it will be argued here that capitalism *has* come to be a fetter upon the most beneficent use of the immense resources it has itself brought into being. Great improvements have undoubtedly been achieved in the conditions of life of the vast majority of the population in the societies of advanced capitalism. But these improvements have been undermined and limited by the very nature of the system in which they have occurred. The point is to change the system and to remove the constraints which impede the proper use of resources. Nor is it only a matter of material resources: the notion of liberation goes very far beyond this and encompasses every aspect of the social order, not least its moral quality. By their very nature, capitalist societies are profoundly immoral societies, in so far as they are inherently based on domination and exploitation – features which decisively affect human relations. This view formed an essential part of an earlier socialism: it badly needs reaffirmation nowadays.

In recent years, it is the very notion of socialism as a comprehensive reorganization of the social order which has come under fire, often from people who have remained more or less committed to the progressive side of politics. Each in its own way, post-Marxism, post-modernism, post-structuralism and related currents of thought, has served, whatever the intentions of its protagonists, to strengthen the recoil from general notions of human emancipation, particularly Marxism. Any such 'meta-saga', in the contemptuous formulation of one of the prophets of post-modernism, Jean-François Lyotard, is viewed as a dangerous illusion. All large schemes of social renewal, however cautious and qualified, attract suspicion, hostility and denunciation. This was always an intrinsic part of conservative thought: it has also now become part of the thinking of a substantial part of the intellectual Left. The accent is now on partial, localized, fragmented, specific goals, and against universal, 'totalizing' perspectives.

Much of this stems from the many defeats and disappointments which the Left has suffered in recent decades – the catastrophic failures of Communist regimes; the ever more pronounced integration of social democratic parties and governments into the fabric of capitalist society; the dissipation of the hopes generated by the spasm of 1968; the resilience and vitality of post-war capitalism; and, relatedly, the confidence of the Right in recent decades, its electoral victories, its affirmation of the virtues of the market, of the superiority of 'free enterprise' and competition, its glorification of socially indifferent individualism as against the socialized individualism to which socialism is committed.

This has greatly encouraged the many currents of thought which have helped to subvert any belief that a comprehensive alternative to capitalist society was possible or even desirable. The erosion of that belief is a matter of immense importance. For, in suggesting that there is no real alternative to the capitalist society of today, it plays its own part in creating a climate of thought which contributes to the flowering of poisonous weeds in the capitalist jungle – weeds whose names have already been noted – racism, sexism, xenophobia, antisemitism, ethnic hatreds, fundamentalism, intolerance. The absence from the political culture of the rational alternative which socialism represents helps the growth of reactionary movements which encompass and live off these pathologies and which manipulate them for their own purposes.

Such movements are in any case quite likely to prosper as a result of the multiple crises which capitalist societies cannot resolve, however loud the cries of triumph of their apologists may be. This makes all the more necessary the advancement of the case for a radically different social order.

3

Mechanisms of Democracy

1

There would of course be wide variations in the specific forms which socialist democracy would assume in different countries. Capitalist democracies have enough fundamental features in common to warrant the common label, even though there are countless constitutional and political differences among them. The same would be true of socialist democracies.

The present chapter is primarily concerned with the institutional and social changes which movement towards socialist democracy would entail. The next chapter deals with the changes that would be needed in the economic organization of society. The division is in some ways artificial, in that changes in one realm are intertwined with changes in the other. For the sake of clarity of exposition, however, it is best to take each in turn.

Both chapters are essentially concerned with the radical extension of democracy in all areas of life, and with the measures this requires. This striving derives from a commitment to democratic forms throughout society which has already been referred to as being fundamental to socialism. Capitalist societies are unable to achieve this democratization, and their rulers are much concerned to limit it. It is also worth recalling that the striving for a radical extension of democracy builds upon age-long struggles designed to achieve a similar purpose. In the same vein, a point made in chapter 1 needs to be reiterated here, namely that socialist democracy will, in many instances, take up and greatly strengthen the democratic forms which are already to be found in capitalist democracy. Norman Geras makes the point well:

> The insistence, under the rubric of 'smashing' the state, on a total discontinuity between bourgeois democracy and projected socialist politics has tended to obscure for too many revolutionary socialists the value of certain norms and institutions which any real socialist democracy would need to incorporate: amongst them, a national representative assembly elected by direct universal suffrage, some separation of powers, the independence of judicial from political processes, the protection of individual rights, a constitutionally guaranteed political pluralism.[1]

There is more to socialist democracy than this, but the insistence on the incorporation of these 'bourgeois freedoms' into any serious notion of socialist democracy serves to highlight the point that what is involved in the enterprise is not a utopian construction, plucked out from the blue yonder, but giving a new substance to what already exists, as well as seeking more ways of enriching the meaning of democracy. As has also been noted earlier, the gains which have been achieved under capitalist conditions are constrained and corrupted by the context in which democratic forms function, and by the determination of conservative forces in the state and in society that these forms should not endanger the existing structures of power and privilege.

The state, in this context, is a highly conservative mechanism when it comes to promulgate and implement measures which challenge established power and privilege. Its institutions are well geared to the weakening and deflection of pressure for radical change and for limiting the impact which such pressure might have on policy and action. At every turn, existing structures of power in the state and in society deeply affect the functioning of constitutional forms, so much so that their workings cannot be understood without reference to their social context. For instance, the American Congress is a legislative institution far more independent from the executive than any other legislature. But simply to note this and to make it a matter of executive–legislative relations, as is commonly done in the political science literature, is to ignore a crucial fact,

---

[1] N. Geras, 'Our ethics', in *The Socialist Register 1989*, eds R. Miliband, L. Panitch and J. Saville (Merlin Press, London, 1989, and Monthly Review Press, New York, 1989), p. 208.

namely how much senators and representatives, independent as they are from the executive, and free from party discipline, are dependent for election purposes on the support of corporate business and the lobbies associated with it. Institutional independence masks the very real dependence of legislators on the 'special interest' represented by business. Corporate power is not the only such interest, but it is by far the most important one: the labour interest is by comparison of marginal account. In other systems, the legislature is less subject to the influence of business; but the class context nevertheless crucially affects its mode of being. Socialist governments would have it as their purpose to change this context, to reduce the ability of corporate power to weigh upon the making of policy, and in due course to eliminate it as a major point of reference.

In immediate terms, the question is whether the state can be so reorganized as to turn its mechanisms into a help for radical reform rather than its adversary. This is a difficult task, not only because of the opposition which it is bound to encounter, but also because the attempt to achieve a radical extension of democracy is beset with contradictory pulls which are bound to complicate the socialist enterprise. A good example of what is involved is provided at the outset by the very notion of constitutionalism. A socialist democracy would obviously be ruled by well-defined constitutional provisions and by a framework of law. But constitutional and legal provisions are a constraint, not only on the power of the executive, which is why they were promulgated in the first place, long before there was any question of democracy: they are also a constraint on the democratic process, which involves the exercise of popular power in regard to the orientations and policies of the government and other public bodies.[2] Constitutionalism has often been a bulwark against democratic intrusion upon entrenched class interests. But it is also crucial for the protection of basic rights. It may well be said that constitutionalism cannot by itself guarantee any such protection; and that, however 'basic' these rights may be declared to be, they can always be circumvented and abrogated where circumstances are deemed by the powers that be to demand it. Nevertheless, constitutionalism is bound to remain crucial in the working of a socialist

---

[2] For some interesting essays on this issue, see J. Elster and R. Slagstad (eds), *Constitutionalism and Democracy* (Cambridge University Press, Cambridge, 1988).

democratic regime. The dictatorship of the proletariat was taken by
Lenin to mean 'rule won and maintained by the use of violence
by the proletariat against the bourgeoisie, rule that is unrestricted by
any laws'.[3] What this means in practice is not popular rule, but
dictatorial rule by those who purport to represent the people. But
even if it did mean popular rule, it would be wholly incompatible
with any notion of socialist democracy, simply because socialist
democracy involves constraints on all forms of power, including
popular power.

2

Let us begin with the organization of the state itself, with the clear
understanding that this is only part of the problem, and that the
democratization of the state is closely related to the democratization
of society.

To begin with, it has to be said that a socialist government newly
come to office would need to be strong if it was to deal effectively
with the immense problems that it would immediately confront; and
the need, regrettably, would remain for a long period of time. This
is the first and most obvious point of tension in the construction
of a socialist regime; for socialists rightly recoil from the notion of
a strong government, given all this has meant by way of arbitrary
and repressive rule in the twentieth century. The problem is to find
ways in which the executive power can be strong *and* limited. That
this is not impossible is amply demonstrated by the experience of
capitalist democracy. For bourgeois governments in capitalist
democracies have generally had the power they needed to implement
their policies, but have nevertheless been circumscribed in various
ways in the exercise of that power. There is a great difference between
a strong executive working within constitutional rules and subject to
other constraints as well and an executive power free from constraints.
Socialist democracy would seek to achieve the combination in its
own ways, but it is unrealistic to think that this would not constitute
a constant terrain of struggle. Nor is this a bad thing. There is bound,
in the advance towards socialist democracy, to be a permanent

[3]   V. I. Lenin, *The Proletarian Revolution and the Renegade Kautsky*, in *Against
Revisionism* (Foreign Languages Publishing House, Moscow, 1959), p. 392.

see-saw between the power of the state and constraints upon it, as there is in capitalist democratic regimes.

Similarly, there is also, in the process of radical reform, bound to be a constant clash between contradictory rights, most notably but not only between the rights of private property and the requirements of the public good, as interpreted by democratically elected public authorities. The age-long struggle for the extension of democratic rights has largely been a struggle against the right of property owners, in the eighteenth-century formulation, to do 'what we will with our own'. Working-class movements have been at the heart of this struggle; and a socialist government would press it a lot further – against the rights of property owners where these rights conflict with the requirements of public policy. The obvious danger in this as in all other realms is that the requirements of public policy would be arbitrarily invoked; and a socialist government would be constrained to proceed with a scrupulous regard for set legal procedures. Socialist democracy would be a regime in which regard for legal procedures would be taken to be of the greatest importance, with the recognition that such a regime would need to encompass independent adjudication between competing claims. The notion that in a socialist society, law would become superfluous because class antagonisms would have disappeared belongs to 'utopian' thinking.[4] But however scrupulous and fair adjudication would seek to be, it would inevitably be bound to deny certain rights in the advancement of others, with the use of state power to ensure the progress of the reforms to which the government was committed.

What follows is an enumeration of some of the institutional changes which the advance towards socialist democracy would entail in the state and the political system.

(i) In liberal theory, the first bulwark against state power has traditionally been seen as a separation of powers between the executive, legislative and judicial branches of government. In practice, such separation, whatever else it achieved, was also a useful device for the protection of property and privilege from encroachments, with opposition to such encroachments solidly entrenched in legislatures and the judicial process. Also, what made the separation of

---

[4] For a cogent defence of the need for a system of law under socialism, see C. Sypnowich, *The Concept of Socialist Law* (Clarendon, Oxford, 1990).

powers viable as a feature of government was the high degree of *ideological congruence* that existed between the three branches. For all their differences, ministers, legislators and judges were for the most part agreed on the fundamental features of the social order. Where agreement broke down, the functioning of government was impaired, and was followed in extreme cases by a reordering of the relations between the branches, usually by way of a strengthening of executive power, often in the form of outright dictatorship.

A socialist regime would certainly include a separation of powers. It may be assumed that, in time, a sufficiently high degree of ideological congruence would have been created in the state to attenuate if not to remove the sources of severe conflict between executive, legislature and judiciary, and the separation of powers would then mean no more – but no less – than a built-in tension in the relations between them. Such tension means that the power of government is being constrained, but not subverted, which is precisely what is wanted.

In this process, a particularly important place has always been allotted to the judiciary; and judges have traditionally used their power to impede legislation which offended their conservative prejudices. This is not, however, inherent in the judicial function; and it is quite possible to conceive of a judiciary that would not have a settled prejudice against progressive legislation. After all, there have been a fair number of such judges in capitalist democracies, who have done honour to the judicial function by the liberal attitudes which they brought to the discharge of their duties. Socialist democracy would no doubt seek to limit the scope of judicial review, for the simple reason that important issues of policy ought as far as possible to be determined by democratic process. But a change in the character of the judiciary does all the same create new perspectives about the meaning of judicial review. Objections have often been raised in Britain to the promulgation of a declaration of rights, on the ground that any such declaration enhances the power of judges who could on the whole be relied on to apply conservative criteria in the interpretation of cases brought before them.[5] But this would no longer necessarily be the case if the selection of judges was

[5] See e.g. J. A. G. Griffith, 'The rights stuff', in *The Socialist Register 1993*, eds R. Miliband and L. Panitch (Merlin Press, London, 1993, and Monthly Review Press, New York, 1993); also his *The Politics of the Judiciary* (Fontana Press, London, 1977, 4th edition).

based on criteria which favoured rather than worked against the appointment of progressive judges. In any case, in a political system subject to legal constraints, an element of judicial review is inevitable, and should indeed be welcomed, in so far as it provides an important source of redress for abuses of power by state authorities.

On the assumption that the judiciary would in due course be generally composed of men and women of liberal disposition, judges would be able to cooperate in a task to which they have mostly failed to make a significant contribution, namely the humanization of the system of justice. The administration of justice in most capitalist democracies, in terms of its cost, delays, sentences, conditions of incarceration and its class and racial bias, is disgraceful, and its shameful character will seem scarcely credible to future generations nurtured in a very different social climate. Judges have for the most part stoutly upheld the system of which they were a part. Theirs has not been a voice for the reform of the system they were expected to administer; and it is not unfair to say that, had it been left to them, capital punishment would still prevail in the capitalist democracies where it has been abolished. In the one such regime where it continues to be widely applied, namely the United States, opposition to it by judges has been conspicuous by its absence. A socialist government would make it its business to reform the administration of justice root and branch; and it would be helped in this task by reforming judges. Among other things, socialist democracy would have as one of its urgent tasks the achievement of cheap as well as prompt justice and would regard this as an intrinsic part of the democratic process.

(ii) However the state was organized, it would include a vast army of officials that would remain in being for a long time to come. A main aim of 'participatory democracy', to be discussed presently, is to enable 'ordinary people' and grassroots organizations to take over many of the functions performed by officials, and thus to give effective meaning to the notion of self-government. This too comes very high on the socialist agenda; but it is all the same unrealistic, for the relevant future, to think that officialdom can be done away with, and that the state and its bureaucracy can be made to 'wither away'.

'Bureaucracy' is now a term of abuse both on the Right and on the Left, though for different reasons. On the Right, the insistence that state bureaucracy is inherently inefficient and unnecessarily intrusive in people's lives is a useful part of the battle against state 'interference' with the rights of property and business; and the implication that it is the state alone which is subject to the real or alleged vices of bureaucracy also serves to hide the fact that all large organizations, as Max Weber noted long ago, are run on 'bureaucratic' lines. The notion that corporate business is not run on these lines and is not subject to bureaucratic vices is a travesty of reality.

On the Left, bureaucracy has been taken to be contrary to democratic rule; and antagonism towards bureaucracy has been greatly reinforced by the experience of Communist regimes and the belief that the promise of the October Revolution had been fatally thwarted by an all-encompassing and self-perpetuating officialdom.

There is much to justify the hostility of the Left towards bureaucracy. Even if Communist regimes are treated as extreme examples, much milder forms of bureaucracy are not free from familiar vices – inflexibility, arrogance, inefficiency, contempt for 'ordinary' citizens.

However, what the wholly negative view of bureaucracy ignores is the degree to which the rules which govern it may, in a democratic context, serve to limit rather than enhance the exercise of arbitrary power. This is no argument for its extension; it is merely to say that, in so far as officialdom is an inevitable part of the contemporary state, the real issue is how its own power may be made democratically accountable.

A distinction needs here to be made between the higher and the lower levels of the bureaucracy. At the higher levels, where policy is determined and action taken, it may be assumed that officials in all branches of the state, including the military and police apparatus, should be subordinate to ministers. This is much more easily said than done. For ministers come and go, while officials may stay where they are for a long time, develop a personal or departmental view and can, if so minded, exercise so much influence over policy as to turn the notion of subordination into something of a sham. The danger this would present to a socialist government would be reduced by the ideological congruence which would have been established between ministers and top officials.[6] But this would not prevent disagreements from arising on important issues; and it is all

---

[6] For a discussion of the renewal of the top ranks of the state personnel which a socialist government would need to undertake, see ch. 6.

the more important that the organization of the state at this level should be strictly guided by the principle that officials are subject to ministerial direction. Even so, much here, as elsewhere, must depend on the quality and resilience of ministers themselves.

It is at the lower levels of the state that the citizen usually encounters officialdom, and where vices such as incompetence, indifference, sloth and, in the case of the police, brutality as well have their most immediate effects. At these levels, it is essential that the checking function should be exercised by a variety of agencies, from the national legislature to local bodies representing individual and aggrieved citizens, on the basis of information made freely available.

In the end, none of this, however elaborate, is adequate if the political culture in which state officials operate does not compel them to have a strong sense of the respect which is due to 'ordinary' citizens. Such a sense is not easy to foster in societies where deep inequalities of every kind prevail. For great inequalities of condition produce great inequalities of treatment, not least by state officials, many of whom, engaged in the supervisory, controlling and repressive activities of the state at the grass roots, tend to deal with people in need or in trouble, and are often working under very difficult circumstances. It is only where inequality has been drastically reduced, and where citizenship and community become more than mere words, that the vices of officialdom can themselves be effectively subdued.

The accountability of officials, in the upper echelons of the state, and in some lower ones as well, would be enhanced if they were subject to election. In a socialist democracy, it would be a matter of course that, where people are in positions of substantial power, in the state and in society, they should wherever possible be so subject. This might not be practical in the case of officials in the upper layers of administration, whose selection should be the responsibility of ministers, with the consent of the legislature. But it is desirable that judges and police chiefs, and others in government agencies with important responsibilities, should be elected, after having met stipulated criteria of eligibility, promulgated by the relevant professional bodies. There is no good reason why electors should not be able to choose judges on the basis of their stated attitude to the administration of justice, the treatment of offenders, the issue of abortion, and other questions with a bearing on their function. The same goes for police chiefs in relation to issues which come within their field of concerns. The objection, in the case of judges, that this would fatally prejudice their work as judges is unwarranted: a statement of attitudes leaves plenty of room for the independent judgement of particular cases.

(iii)   A socialist regime in unitary states would certainly favour a considerable devolution of power to elected regional and local authorities, on the ground that these authorities would, in regard to a whole range of issues, be better able to represent the interests and wishes of their constituencies than the central state. Such devolution, however, is by no means synonymous with democratic self-government. For the attribution of power to sub-central government, however desirable, may not mean much more than a proliferation of bodies and the reinforcement of the rule of local and regional 'notables', with a vast increase in the state personnel, and with no significant strengthening of 'participatory democracy' – what a former French prime minister, Pierre Mauroy, once called 'Jacobin decentralization'.[7] The same point applies to the devolution of power to states or provinces in federal systems. Such devolution is inherent in such systems but does not in itself amount to an extension of democracy.

The principle of decentralization also poses another problem to a government embarked on radical reform. For such a government, duly legitimated by majority support, would clearly be concerned to ensure that legislation in regard to many important issues should be applied *nationally*. It would be intolerable for legislation regarding health care, educational facilities, safety at work, environmental protection, abortion rights and much else as well to be disregarded or circumvented in the name of local or regional autonomy and freedom from central 'interference'. Once this is out of the way, there is everything to be said for giving local and regional authorities the possibility of adapting nationally agreed policies to specific local and regional needs and wishes – on the understanding that adaptation is not used to stultify reform. Here too, contradictory pulls are at work, and a balance would need to be struck between the power of the centre and that of the periphery.

[7]   Quoted in V. A. Schmidt, 'Decentralization: a revolutionary reform', in *The French Socialists in Power 1981–1986*, ed. P. McCarthy (Greenwood Press, New York and London, 1987), p. 95.

(iv)   Something needs to be said about the organization of executive power. The movements which had made electoral success possible would inevitably have placed a number of people in leading positions, with one individual as the standard-bearer of collective aspirations. In a world of politics dominated by television and tabloids, such a personalization is bound to be greater and more strident than at any previous time. A presidential system greatly accentuates the trend, but it is also at work in parliamentary systems.

Socialist democracy would have an inherent bias against great executive power being vested in the hands of any one individual, whether president, chancellor or prime minister. Such a concentration of power means that major decisions are made without much or any reference to anyone outside a small coterie of advisers. Prime ministers in capitalist democracies are generally rather more constrained in the exercise of personal power than presidents elected by universal suffrage, but experience here too shows that a prime minister determined to exercise great power has a good deal of room to do so.

It would be naive to think that this can easily be avoided, whatever the system. But it is nevertheless worth saying that a socialist democratic regime ought to enshrine the principle of 'collective leadership', and ensure that no single person should be given a preponderance of power. Socialist democracy would establish a political climate in which great personal power would be viewed as an undue and dangerous privilege, and any 'cult of personality' taken for an unacceptable deviation from democratic values.

(v)   Of course, it is not only the power of the head of the government which needs to be circumscribed: so does the power of government as a whole. This brings into focus the role of the legislature, and its relationship to the executive.

The assumption was made in an earlier chapter that a socialist government would need to be backed by a solid parliamentary majority if it was to be successful in its reforming endeavours; and it would for the purpose also need to have control of the legislative programme and agenda. This, however, cannot be taken to mean that the legislative branch would be an obedient and subordinate adjunct of the government. The majority would be made up of men and women who, though broadly united, would nevertheless have different views and positions on many issues; and this diversity would be enhanced if the majority consisted of different parties and groupings within a coalition. The general support which the majority would be expected to give to the government, and which it would want to give to it, is not at all synonymous with the surrender of an essential critical and checking role. The legislature in a socialist democracy, and its specialist committees, would need to be armed with enough power in relation to the executive to constitute a reference point which the government could not ignore.

The opposition parties in the legislature could be counted on to do what they could to act as a check upon the government. Their effectiveness would no doubt be limited by their minority status, but much of the responsibility for the critical examination of the government's policies and actions would fall upon them. For the party or parties supporting the government would obviously suffer from certain inhibitions in exercising a critical role. A government engaged in the arduous task of radical reform, and faced with much opposition, would not greatly welcome criticism from its own side; and parliamentarians of the majority would themselves find it very awkward, to put it no higher, to appear to be siding with the opposition at a time of great conflict. Yet the legislature does need to exercise a critical function, and should be empowered to do so by formal constitutional provision, with a particularly important investigative role allotted to its committees. This is another instance of the inevitable tension which is bound to arise between what the democratic process requires on the one hand, and the requirements of government on the other.

In *The Civil War in France*, Marx, in praise of the Paris Commune, said that it was to be 'a working, not a parliamentary, body, executive and legislative at the same time';[8] and the same notion was later taken up by Lenin.[9] This rejection of the separation between legislature and executive is not realistic. Government by assembly, at least for a whole country, is not possible: sooner rather than later, an assembly would need to delegate power to an executive able to make policy. What is needed is both a strong government and a legislative assembly capable of playing an effective role vis-à-vis the

---

[8]   K. Marx, *The Civil War in France*, in K. Marx and F. Engels, *Collected Works* (Lawrence and Wishart, London, 1986), vol. 22, p. 331.
[9]   Lenin, *The Proletarian Revolution and the Renegade Kautsky*, p. 400.

government. This too is much more easily said than achieved; but there is at least no question that it is what is needed.

(vi)   The legislature to which I have referred so far is the first chamber in a bicameral system, and a word needs to be said about second chambers. In the past they were armed with vast powers, and were intended to make as difficult as possible the passage of any legislation which might pose a threat to property or which might, more generally, disturb the status quo in progressive and democratic directions.[10] These powers have been steadily reduced, at least in unitary states, in the course of this century. The bias of socialist democracy, again in unitary states, would be towards unicameralism. Alternatively, second chambers might be used to give representation to economic, social, regional, cultural and other interests. This would raise no issue of principle, so long as the bodies in question had a purely consultative and advisory role, and posed no challenge to the first chamber.

The question would present itself differently in a federal system, where states or provinces would want representation in a second chamber, specifically constituted to defend their prerogatives and interests. In such cases, the second chamber would obviously need to have a degree of power adequate to the purpose.

(vii)   Whether a national assembly is strong or weak, its composition should reflect with a fair degree of accuracy the votes cast in a general election. On this score, the first-past-the-post electoral system is clearly unsatisfactory. For it makes a mockery of the notion of accurate representation; and it commonly creates situations where governments elected with the support of a minority of voters, and with an even smaller minority of the electorate, are given full power to rule. It is on this basis that Margaret Thatcher, with a minority of votes in 1979, 1983 and 1987, was able to proceed with her counter-revolution; and the same goes for John Major's election in 1992. Labour supporters of the first-past-the-post system argue that it also gives the Labour Party a chance to win an election and form a government of its own. This may be true, but it ignores some important facts, quite apart from the point of principle that the

---

[10]   See e.g. A. J. Mayer, *The Persistence of the Old Regime: Europe to the Great War* (Pantheon Books, New York, 1981).

electoral system should not greatly distort representation. One fact the argument ignores is that a government engaged in fundamental reform needs a much greater measure of support *in the country* than does a conservative government. It is only thus that a radical government could hope to achieve its purposes; and that support ought to be reflected in voting figures. Fifty-one per cent is no magic figure; but achieving that figure, alone or if need be in coalition, is none the less very helpful.

A socialist democratic regime would have an electoral system which ensured a high degree of congruence between votes cast and parliamentary seats. Perfect congruence, in the form of a strict system of proportional representation, tends to allow minor parties to exercise a wholly disproportionate amount of power in fragile coalition governments. But between the first-past-the-post system on the one hand and strict proportional representation on the other, there is a wide range of options which obviate, at least in some measure, the undemocratic defects of both.

(viii)   Whatever electoral system is in operation, elections – or at least elections which are not a complete sham – mean that the party or parties in government may lose. Where parties are not fundamentally divided, and where democratic forms are solidly implanted, this possibility is taken for granted: it is assumed that the 'rules of the game' will prevail and that a government defeated at the polls will resign and make way for a successor. So, in a presidential system, does the defeated incumbent give way to the successful challenger.

One of the distinctive features of the evolution of Communist parties in the sixties and seventies – the period of Eurocommunism – was their unqualified acceptance of what in France was called 'alternance', their acceptance of the 'rules of the game' in this as in other respects. This stood in sharp opposition to the politics of Stalinism, as practised in Eastern Europe after 1945, not to speak of the Soviet Union, where, given the monopoly of the Communist Party, the question did not arise. Given the Stalinist experience, anti-Communists in France and elsewhere were able to claim that an election won by a Communist Party and its allies would be the last one held, or at least the last one held in fair competition with other parties. This was probably true, not only because Communist leaders would have so willed it, but because their success at the polls – which was in any case never likely – would most probably have been followed by conditions approximating to civil war, in which the holding of elections would have been next to impossible.

How does the matter present itself in relation to a socialist government, elected by due process and facing a general election?

The stakes in such an election would clearly be a good deal higher than is normally the case, with an opposition seeking to regain power so as to reverse many of the government's most important reforms. For its part, the government and the parties supporting it would be acutely conscious of the fact that the process of reform had only begun and could only be advanced and strengthened over a long stretch of time. In these terms, the possible loss of an election would be a great setback, fraught with dire consequences. On an optimistic view, it is possible that the government's record and the zeal of its supporters in the country would have created a solid body of support sufficient to ensure continued electoral success. This is what the Swedish Social Democrats achieved again and again, until growing economic problems, and the adoption of neo-liberal measures in the eighties to solve them, brought their conservative opponents back to office. Where defeat, for whatever reason, seemed possible, a socialist government would have no option but to go to the polls and accept its results. The alternative, namely the refusal to hold an election, would amount to a pre-emptive coup which could only be sustained on the basis of rule lacking all legitimacy and with the prospect of bitter resistance.

This, however, is not quite the end of the matter. The assumption I have made here is that, however keen the opposition would be to undo the government's work, it would itself remain wedded to constitutional forms. It may be said that this is a very large assumption, and that conservative parties hitherto wedded to constitutional forms might change and turn fascist. This under-estimates the distance that normally separates such parties from outright fascist ones. Given that distance, it would be difficult for conservative parties to turn themselves into such parties.

Perry Anderson writes that 'the Italian and German experience between the wars is a reminder that there is a parliamentary road to fascism.'[11] Actually, that experience does not show that there is a parliamentary road to fascism. At the time of the so-called March on

Rome in 1922, Mussolini's Fascist Party had 35 deputies in the Chamber of Deputies. There was never any question of his winning power in a free election. His strength lay in the militancy of the Fascists in the country, the weakness of the government, the sympathies which he evoked in the Italian ruling class, and the support he had in the state apparatus at local and regional level. His assumption of the premiership at the invitation of the king had nothing to do with a parliamentary road to fascism. Hitler did very much better electorally and his Nazi party was by 1932 the largest party in the Reichstag. But he had not won a majority and there was no constitutional requirement that he should be appointed chancellor, not least because everything the Nazis had said and done previously showed conclusively that they were not running a 'normal' party, and that they quite clearly intended to destroy the democratic forms of the Weimar Republic. Hitler's appointment was the result of the divisions and consequent weakness of the Left, and, in this case too, of the lack of serious opposition which he and his policies encountered on the Right – indeed, the belief of many powerful and influential people in the state and in the country that he was the answer to Germany's problems. In France in 1940, in the wake of defeat, a majority of parliamentarians voted to make Pétain head of state with full powers, and thus gave legitimation to what amounted to an authoritarian regime. But this, in the particular conditions of the time, can hardly be taken to mean accession to power by the 'parliamentary road'.

That road has also been closed to neo-fascist parties since World War II. Such parties led a mostly marginal existence until the eighties. They have achieved a greater measure of electoral success since then, but nowhere have they become major parties with any chance of coming to power as a result of electoral success. They might well gain greater support if a socialist government came to power; but the real danger they would present is that they would increasingly resort to violence and thus create conditions approximating to civil war; and the further danger is that they would find allies in the state apparatus and among conservative politicians hitherto committed to constitutionalism.

In such conditions, it would be right for a socialist government to invoke emergency powers and suspend the normal workings of institutions until civil peace had been restored. Also, the government would come down at a fairly early stage on fascist leaders and their parties, and make them liable to prosecution on a variety of grounds.

The invocation of emergency powers and the suspension of the normal workings of institutions are hardly to be welcomed, but this is a price that would have to be paid to meet the threat of a neo-fascist bid for power.

This is very different from the achievement of power by anti-socialist parties committed to constitutional rule. Even an anti-socialist government thus committed would presumably want to undo much that had been done by the previous government. The hope for the Left would be that a socialist government would have used its term of office to make the roll back of reform a very difficult business; and that, despite their defeat at the polls, the forces which had brought a socialist government to power would remain sufficiently strong and entrenched to make a successor government hesitate to push too far its counter-reforming zeal. The Thatcher governments in the eighties had no such strong and entrenched opposition to deal with, which is why they were able to carry through so wide a range of regressive policies. When they did encounter real resistance, as over the poll tax, they retreated.

It is always the weakness of the Left which gives strength to the Right: a socialist government would have as one of its major tasks the reinforcement of the forces of the Left throughout the country. Also, it may be presumed that it would have striven to begin the process described by Francis Castles in relation to Sweden: 'Social Democrats and their sympathizers', he wrote in 1978, 'are integrated into the institutional machinery at all levels. They constitute a sizeable proportion of the higher state bureaucracy, the provincial administrations, the judiciary and, indeed, every major political instrumentality in Scandinavia.'[12] This would do no more than replicate the situation to be found in the bourgeois state, and it is in the creation of sufficiently strong 'earthworks' and 'fortresses' committed to the Left in society and the state that would lie the best hope that a successor government would be thwarted in its endeavours, and that it would represent no more than an interlude in the process of radical reform. The resistance that it would encounter on the Left would be part of the democratic process, and would only replicate the resistance that a socialist government would encounter from conservative forces. Victory at the polls, by either the Left or the Right, can hardly be taken to mean that opposition comes to an end.

[12] F. Castles, *The Social Democratic Image of Society* (Routledge and Kegan Paul, London, Henley and Boston, 1978), p. 96.

3

All the reforms discussed so far, and others of the same kind, would amount to a significant democratization of the state system. But it would all the same remain a system of *representative* democracy, in which the people's participation in public affairs and the decision-making process would be fairly limited. For its participation would largely consist of voting for representatives at various levels of government and seeking to influence them through various channels of pressure – parties, civic associations etc. As I noted in chapter 2, this more or less defined the meaning of participation for democratic theorists in the decades following World War II, and many of them found even this to be rather dangerous. In *Capitalism, Socialism and Democracy*, Joseph Schumpeter had declared that what he called classical democratic theory had 'demanded too high a level of rationality' from ordinary citizens.[13] In a similar vein, a Report of the Trilateral Commission, a prestigious body initiated by David Rockefeller in 1973 and bringing together academics and politicians from around the world, warned that 'a pervasive spirit of democracy may pose an intrinsic threat and undermine all forms of association' as well as causing 'an "overload" on government and the expansion of the role of government in the economy and society'.[14]

Classical democratic theory, for its part, had, in Lane Davis's formulation, sought in participation 'the education of an entire people to the point where their intellectual, emotional, and moral capacities have reached their full potential and they are joined, freely and actively in a genuine community'.[15]

In actual fact, participation, in classical democratic theory, mainly meant participation in a process designed to select representatives. Thus, John Stuart Mill in *Representative Government* (1865) declared that 'the only government which can fully satisfy all the exigencies of the social state is one in which the whole people participate.' But he then went on to say that 'since all cannot, in a community

[13] J. A. Schumpeter, *Capitalism, Socialism and Democracy* (George Allen and Unwin, London, 1943), pp. 253–4.
[14] M. J. Crozier, S. P. Huntington and J. Watanuki, *The Crisis of Democracy*, Report on the Governability of Democracies to the Trilateral Commission (New York University Press, New York, 1975), pp. 162, 164.
[15] L. Davis, 'The cost of realism: contemporary restatements of democracy', *The Western Political Quarterly*, XVII, 1 (March 1964).

exceeding a single small town, participate personally in any but some very minor portions of the public business, it follows that the ideal type of a perfect government must be representative.'[16]

This view that 'participatory democracy' really meant 'representative democracy' under conditions of universal suffrage was far too restrictive for many people influenced by the 'spirit of 1968'. This, as I noted in an earlier chapter, had always been true for classical Marxism, not to speak of anarchism.

Representative democracy and the parliamentarism associated with it had always had a bad name with these currents of thought. For it was, in practice, taken to mean the continued exclusion of the mass of the people from the decision-making process, the maintenance of a great distance between representatives and those they were meant to represent, politics as an activity mainly to be engaged in by professionals skilled in the business of bargaining and compromise, and prone to corruption.

From the sixties onwards, the notion of participation as an activity far transcending voting and 'traditional' political activity gained much ground, and increasingly came to mean the radical enlargement of the sphere in which people could assume 'control of their own lives'. As Benjamin Barber put it, in a rather exaggerated but not untypical formulation, 'without participation in the common life that defines them and in the decision-making that shapes their social habitat, women and men *cannot become individuals*.'[17]

The issue here is not participatory democracy, in the strong sense, *or* representative democracy. In its strongest sense, participatory democracy means something like direct democracy, virtually without mediation, or with representatives totally controlled by their constituents. This is not a realistic view of what is possible. Representation is inherent in organizations at all but the most immediate and local level, and even there it will be found to be needed; and representation does involve *some* distance between representatives and represented.

Given this, two questions arise: first, how to reduce this distance; and secondly, how to *combine* representative with participatory democracy.

---

[16] J. S. Mill, *Representative Government* (Blackwell, Oxford, 1946), p. 151.
[17] B. Barber, *Strong Democracy* (University of California Press, Berkeley and London, 1984), p. xv, my emphasis.

To begin with, a distinction needs to be made between official bodies, state agencies, parliamentary, regional and local assemblies on the one hand; and parties, trade unions, associations, clubs and voluntary agencies of many different kinds on the other. The first might be called the official sector, the second the citizen one.

In relation to the official sector, effective participation means resort to the various devices and procedures which have been outlined earlier, and which are designed to make representation as faithful, responsive and accountable as is possible; and this also involves that attribution to agencies of the citizen sector of a definite consultative and advisory role in the decision-making process. This is of particular relevance to local and regional government, but is obviously of wider application. Indeed, socialist democracy would encourage the devolution of as much responsibility as possible to citizen associations at the grass roots, with effective participation in the running of educational institutions, health facilities, housing associations and other bodies which have a direct bearing on the lives of the people concerned.

The citizen sector, as understood here, extends right across society and represents all the innumerable interests and concerns which are part of civil society. It is in society itself as much as in the organization of the state that the life of most people is affected by the exercise of power by those who control its main resources. This is most obviously the case in factories and offices, and in all places of work, but it also applies to all other institutions where structures of power are in place. In a socialist democracy, all such structures would be subject to the greatest possible measure of control by the people located in them. This is simply to say that democracy would pervade all of society and be part of the to-be-taken-for-granted organization of the social order, with participation as a 'natural' right of citizenship.

This would at least attenuate a danger to which reference was made in chapter 2, namely that of oligarchy. This danger is present wherever power is exercised, in the private as well as the public sector, in trade unions, parties and associations as well as in the state and economic enterprises. The only answer to it is the practice and the habit of democracy. There is a distinction to be made between hierarchy and oligarchy. Democratically run organizations may well have structures of power, and most probably do need structures where some people have more power than others. What this requires not to turn into oligarchy is that those who have a greater measure of power should have been given it freely by their constituents, that they should be accountable, and that the decision-making process should involve effective participation.

Effective participation is clearly a defining feature of socialist democracy. But it is worth saying that with this goes the right *not* to participate. There are people who, for whatever reason, will choose to remain uninvolved in the life around them, and who will instead cultivate privacy. It is rather unlikely that anyone would really choose to remain uninvolved in *any* sphere of common activity at all. But if people did choose uninvolvement, this would have to be accepted. Participation should be seen as a right, not an obligation.

More important, however, is that the principle of effective participation should be recognized as a crucial feature of the social order and as giving meaning to citizenship. It is thus that what I have called civic virtue can be cultivated, and that socialized individualism can truly find expression.

4

Unfortunately, all this belongs only to the realm of good intentions. For the intentions to be turned into real advances, certain conditions imperatively need to be met. If these conditions do not obtain, as they do not in capitalist democracies, the democratic process, as described here, is fatally undermined.

The most important by far of these conditions is the drastic attenuation of the multiple inequalities which mark capitalist societies. I noted earlier that these inequalities related to all aspects of life – income, wealth, education, life chances etc. But with these goes another one, an inequality in citizen power. It bears repeating that, despite all proclamations of the people as sovereign, the crucial means of power – economic power, administrative and coercive power, and power over the means of communication and persuasion – remain in the hands of a relatively small minority of people who enjoy a high degree of independence, particularly in the economic realm, in the wielding of that power. It is this which justifies the description of capitalist democracies as oligarchies tempered by democratic forms. So long as this endures, notions of citizenship and community must remain thin of meaning.

Another way of saying the same thing is that the vast majority of people are separated from these means of power. Political democracy, in any but a narrow sense of the concept, is not compatible with the oligarchic control of the means of power. This is precisely why so much effort has been deployed in the last hundred years to obfuscate the reality of oligarchic power, and to turn into an unarguable truth the notion that capitalist regimes really are regimes of popular sovereignty. The reality of oligarchy is most readily obfuscated in the political realm by the existence of democratic forms; there is no need to repeat here what has already been said about the limitations of these forms in the context of class rule.

The attempt is also made to mask the reality of oligarchic power in the economic realm, by reference to the constraints to which corporate power is subject – government intervention, competition, the market, employees, trade unions, public opinion and so forth. But it is nevertheless the case, as was argued earlier, that corporate power, in charge of immense resources, remains remarkably free in the making of decisions of crucial importance for society at large. Indeed, this freedom of capitalist enterprise is commonly declared by its apologists to be a matter for rejoicing, and 'interference' by the state or anybody else to be deplored and opposed. For their part, socialists start from the premise that the construction of socialist democracy is impossible so long as the main means of economic activity remain under the control of corporate power. The private ownership and control of these means is also a primary source of the other inequalities which are part of a capitalist-dominated social order, and which make impossible that rough equality in citizen power which socialist democracy requires. How this is to be tackled is discussed in the next chapter.

5

There is also the question of the control of the realm of communications and persuasion. It is clear, in the light of what was said about this in chapter 1, that a commitment to socialist democracy demands that this too be subjected to radical change. The trouble, however, is that an alternative model to the one which prevails in capitalist democracies, and which would be congruent with the aims and values of socialist democracy, is not readily available. Here too, the Communist experience is of no use, save as an anti-model. The very first decree of the Council of People's Commissars, issued two days after the Bolshevik seizure of power, was a decree on the press which authorized the government to close down all newspapers that printed false information or promoted resistance to Soviet power. This was followed ten days later by a resolution of the central executive of the all-Russian Congress of Soviets, drafted by Trotsky, which confirmed the decree.[18] Subsequent Soviet history saw party-state control of all means of communication strengthened and extended to the point where nothing could be legally transmitted which was not under the strict control of the party and the state. It was not until Gorbachev came to power in 1985 and introduced *glasnost* that freedom of communications acquired real meaning in the Soviet Union.

Freedom of the press, and of communications in general, in a socialist democracy would mean neither the kind of capitalist predominance which is now the rule, nor the state-party monopoly that existed in Communist regimes. The alternative organization of the media would encompass three different types of regime. First, there would exist a public sector, in which public corporations with a high degree of autonomy would control and manage the world of radio and television; and this would include a large network of regional and local stations. Public corporations in charge of radio and television already exist in all capitalist democracies; what would be different about socialist democracy is that it would greatly extend the share of the public sector.

Secondly, there would exist a large cooperative sector, constituted on the basis of the ownership and control of newspapers, magazines, local radio and television stations, cinemas and theatres by journalists and other media people themselves, by political parties, trade unions, schools, universities and other bodies, some with a local reach, others with a larger one, up to national or international dimensions. In many cases, these cooperative enterprises would be self-financing; in others, they would rely, at least for part of their revenue, on public subsidies, administered by agencies working according to well-defined criteria of fairness.

[18]   J. Bunyan and H. H. Fisher (eds), *The Bolshevik Revolution, 1917–1918* (1934), and Y. Akhapin (ed.), *First Decrees of Soviet Power* (1970), quoted from W. M. Evers, 'Liberty of the press under socialism', in *Socialism*, eds E. F. Frankel, F. D. Miller, Jr, and J. Paul (Blackwell, Oxford, 1989), p. 215.

Thirdly, there would exist an area of private ownership, with strict limits on what could be owned by one individual or company. Capitalist democracies already impose certain restrictions on such ownership. But these do not prevent giant corporations from owning and controlling an extraordinary range of means of communication. No socialist democracy could ever tolerate the kind of ownership enjoyed by Berlusconi's Fininvest empire in Italy, which

> comprises the ownership of the three main national private television channels (which strongly influence other networks by providing them with programmes, advertising and personnel), a lucrative film production company, two national newspapers, magazine publications, a radio network, the biggest Italian publishing company (Mondadori), and television channels in France, Germany and Spain. Fininvest also has interests in the insurance sector, the financial market and the real estate and construction sectors. It owns a national supermarket chain (Standa), about three hundred cinemas and a football team.[19]

Rupert Murdoch's own communications empire, though less ramified, is scarcely less impressive. For it comprises a substantial part of the British press, including ownership of *The Times*, *Today*, the *Sun*, the *Sunday Times* and the *News of the World*, as well as newspapers in the United States, Australia and Hungary; and the television stations it also owns give it a reach stretching to more than two-thirds of the planet.

Such ownership and control would have no place in a socialist democracy. In such a regime, private individuals would not be prevented from owning a newspaper or magazine, or a radio or television station, or a publishing house, or a cinema or theatre. But no individual or company would be allowed to own or control more than *one* such means of communication. This would no doubt be attacked as an intolerable infringement of freedom. It would in fact be no more than the protection of society from a degree of private ownership and control which gives to wealthy individuals a power which no truly democratic society should countenance. The combination of public corporations, cooperative enterprises at local, regional and national (and international) level, and limited private ownership, would ensure a far greater degree of pluralism than is now provided, and it would also give far more ample and richer meaning to the

[19] J. Keane, *The Media and Democracy* (Polity Press, Cambridge, 1991), p. 71.

notion of freedom of expression. So too would it remove the weight of capitalist imperatives from the media, without substituting for it the heavy hand of the state. It would also strengthen the media's role as an educational and enlightening influence, and encourage a 'politics of truth' in the dissemination and discussion of public affairs. In short, socialist democracy would free the media from their capitalist fetters, and thus help them become valuable allies in the enhancement of democratic citizenship.

6

The achievement of what I have called a rough equality of conditions, without which democratic citizenship remains little more than an aspiration, has many different facets. One of the most important of them is education.

Education in capitalist society has always been characterized by a deep division between elite education on the one hand and mass education on the other. Nor has that division been much lessened by the fact that children from the working class have in increasing numbers gained access to elite education. For this leaves the vast majority of the population receiving an education greatly inferior in terms of resources and facilities to that of the minority.

A fundamental issue is at stake here, namely whether the division between elite and mass education simply reflects a division between the more able and the less able parts of the population; or whether the division is to a large extent based not on 'innate' ability but on extraneous factors, in which class plays a critical role. It is of course true that some children nurtured in very adverse circumstances do overcome them and gain access to elite education, or reach 'the top' without it. But this does not negate the fact that class location, for the majority, plays a decisive role in the determination of their 'life chances', including the chance for people to develop their full potential. At the core of socialism, there is the belief that there is potential in most people, and that a prime objective of socialist democracy is to create the conditions in which this potential can be given its full scope. Lip service is nowadays paid to this objective by most governments by reference to equality of opportunity. But equality of opportunity is a mere slogan in societies marked by deep inequalities of condition: it could only acquire real meaning where all children started off under circumstances which were not thus marked.

The negation or stifling of individual potential is an abomination, first because of what it does to people, and also because it represents a terrible waste for society at large: an immense pool of ability and talent remains only very partially tapped. Progress towards socialist democracy would require the will to obliterate the great gap which now exists between the private and the public sector at primary and secondary level, and to devote all the resources needed to turn the public system from the dead end which it now so often is into a preparation for various forms of further education.

Under-education is also a blight upon the effective citizenship of the majority which is affected by it. Education for citizenship means above all the nurturing of a capacity and a willingness to question, to probe, to ask awkward questions, to see through obfuscation and lies. It means the nurturing of a climate of thought in which racism, sexism, xenophobia, antisemitism are seen for the pathologies they are. It further means the nurturing of that socialized individualism to which I have referred earlier and which is synonymous with civic virtue. To say this is to tread on dangerous ground, since it might suggest that schools should be turned into instruments for the propagation of a set of not-to-be-questioned ideas. This would be anathema to the spirit of socialist democracy. What is involved is something very different, namely the cultivation of an awareness that the quest for individual fulfilment needs to be combined with the larger demands of solidarity and concern for the public good. Effective citizenship does not mean the automatic acceptance of the definition of the public good from on high. On matters large and small, different individuals will in fact give it a different meaning, based on their own experience and reflection. This is as it should be, with a resolution of the differences based upon agreed procedures between alert and informed citizens.

All that has been said in this chapter leaves open the question of the economic 'base' on which socialist democracy is to rest. The point has already been made that socialist democracy absolutely depends upon a growing socialization of the economy. Unless this is achieved, all that is being proposed by way of reform really means the attempt to humanize the workings of a capitalist-dominated social order. This attempt has gone on for many years, and I have noted that what has been achieved is far from negligible. But it still leaves in being capitalist societies, with the failings and shortcomings that have been discussed here. There is no way in which this can be fundamentally remedied without the socialization of the larger part of the means of economic activity. What this involves is the subject of the next chapter.

4

The Mixed Economy,
Socialist Style

1

In the economic realm as elsewhere, socialist democracy represents both an extension of capitalist democracy, and a transcendence of it.

State intervention in the economy is the best example of what this means. The fashion in recent years has been to denigrate state intervention and to exalt the virtues of the market. Yet one of the most notable features of the history of capitalism from its beginnings right up to the present day has been its reliance on the state and its dependence upon it.

For the state is, by its very nature, inevitably involved in 'economic life' by virtue of the budgetary and taxation policies which it alone can promulgate and implement. But state intervention goes far beyond this. For it is the state, even in the regimes most dedicated to 'free enterprise', which provides capitalism with protection and help, not only in political, legal, police and military terms, but also in strictly economic terms as well, by way of subsidies, allowances, tariffs, concessions, contracts, rescue of failing banks and other enterprises, protection from foreign competition, and a host of other measures designed to help capitalist enterprise. So too has the state had to intervene in economic life in order to protect society from the depredations wrought by a capitalism which cannot afford to be unduly concerned with the individual and social costs generated by the logic of the system. Governments have had to save capitalism from itself, and to deploy on its behalf a consciousness which, left alone, it has been unable to develop in relation to what is required for its preservation and strengthening. In short, the survival of the system has always depended on government intervention in the economy; and it is worth stressing how much, as a system of domination and exploitation, it has depended on the coercive power of the state.

In recent years, strenuous attempts have been made by market ideologists in government, spurred on by ideologists outside it, to reduce intervention to a minimum by deregulation and privatization, and to shrink the public sector in favour of the private one. But even they have been unable to do more than make a dent in the responsibilities which the deficiencies of 'free enterprise' impose upon governments. Again and again, conservative governments have been compelled, against their own dogmatic convictions, to attenuate and correct the failings of unregulated capitalism. They have done so reluctantly and unwillingly; and they, or rather their populations, have paid a heavy price for that reluctance and unwillingness, by way of economic decline, social neglect and individual suffering. Britain and the United States in the eighties are prime examples of the nefarious effects of the market dogmatism which guided the Reagan and Thatcher governments.

For its part, a socialist government would have a powerful interventionist vocation, and would consider intervention in economic life as a major responsibility. However, its interventionism would have purposes fundamentally different from those of anti-socialist governments and would take very different forms. For unlike such governments, a socialist government would be seeking not only to improve the performance of the economy or to attenuate its most manifest inadequacies, but to transform it altogether. In no way is this to suggest that state intervention would always and necessarily be of the right kind and achieve beneficial purposes. But the errors committed by a socialist government subject to democratic constraints would at least be due to a mistaken application of socially defensible purposes, rather than to the socially deleterious purposes so often pursued by conservative governments.

2

The most far-reaching form of interventionism is clearly the transfer of enterprises from the private to the public domain. Conservative and liberal governments, and authoritarian governments of the Right, have often in the past resorted to measures of public ownership, notably but not only in basic utilities; and there have been many instances in the twentieth century when mild social democratic governments have also embarked on programmes of public ownership. Indeed, there was a time when the extension of public ownership, to the point where it would encompass most of economic activity, was, at least in theory, part of a programmatic consensus on the Left.[1] For it was agreed that great economic power should not be wielded by private capitalists, that governments needed to control the levers of economic power, that private profit was not an acceptable criterion for economic activity, that economic democracy in the firm could only be achieved under public ownership – in short, that social ownership was an intrinsic part of the definition of socialism.

The debate in the ranks of social democracy therefore then centred not on whether the extension of public ownership was desirable, but on how much of it should be undertaken and what forms it should assume. Nor, in the case of the Labour Party in Britain, was there any vocal opposition until the late fifties to Clause Four of its constitution, with its commitment to the eventual public ownership of the means of production, distribution and exchange.[2] That clause, drafted by Sidney Webb in 1918 and incorporated in the revised constitution of the Labour Party, was intended to pacify rank-and-file activists at a time of great radicalism at the grass roots, and it never seriously affected actual policy. But there were few people until the late fifties who were willing to say that the commitment to public ownership was obsolete and altogether

[1] In the 1930s, quite moderate social democrats in Britain, such as Evan Durbin and Hugh Gaitskell, advocated (at least for a time) the nationalization not only of the Bank of England but of the joint stock banks as well; and more radical Fabians called then for the nationalization of insurance and building societies as well. See Elizabeth Durbin, New Jerusalems: the Labour Party and the economics of democratic socialism (Routledge and Kegan Paul, London, 1985), p. 168. For its part, the Socialist League, founded in 1932 as a pressure group for socialism in the Labour Party, and originally including a wide diversity of people, ranging from Clement Attlee to Aneurin Bevan and from R. H. Tawney to Harold Laski, had in its programme a demand for the immediate nationalization of the banks, land, the mines, power, transport, iron and steel, cotton, and the control of foreign trade.

[2] In New Fabian Essays, first published in 1952, Roy Jenkins, then as later on the right wing of the party, was pleading for 'a substantial extension of public ownership': 'Equality', in New Fabian Essays, ed. R. H. S. Crossman (J. M. Dent, London, 1970 edition), p. 83.

irrelevant to the achievement of socialist purposes. Even in the seventies, there were social democratic parties, for instance in Sweden with the Meidner Plan,[3] and much more emphatically in France with the Common Programme of the Socialist and Communist Parties, which gave to the extension of public ownership a prominent place in their plans; and the French socialist government elected in 1981 did carry through a substantial programme of nationalization.

Since then, with the aggressive propagation of neo-liberal ideology in the eighties, and the Left in retreat before it, public ownership has all but disappeared from the social democratic agenda. It is now resolutely shunned, save for a very cautious and reluctant acknowledgement that there might be occasions when one or other measure of public ownership would be necessary. Nor even is there any great willingness to consider seriously the return to public ownership of the utilities, services and other enterprises which have been privatized by conservative governments. Public ownership is declared to be more than ever irrelevant to socialist purposes, and also electorally damaging; and there is also the argument that ownership has in any case undergone rapid changes, with a variety of institutions, like insurance companies and pension funds owning a growing proportion of shares, thus making obsolete many of the earlier arguments in favour of public ownership. Moreover, even though the percentage of shares in private ownership has greatly declined, a far greater number of people now own these shares than was the case in the past: 'people's capitalism', which was much touted in the United States a great many years ago, is now claimed to have arrived everywhere else in the advanced capitalist world, and to have been greatly enhanced by privatization.

This ignores the fact that by far the largest part of individual share ownership is highly concentrated.[4] But in any case, the

---

[3] The Meidner Plan envisaged the gradual transfer of shares from private firms into a 'wage-earner fund', which was intended to ensure, in the long term, a fundamental shift in the distribution of control in the Swedish economy. The plan, for all practical purposes, was stillborn.

[4] 'There are many more shareholders [in Britain] than there were before privatization. In 1981, only 7 per cent of Britons held shares, says the Treasury. By 1992, 22 per cent did. But the newcomers' stakes are tiny. Even before the sale of the last slab of BT's equity in July [1993], 54 per cent of its shares were held in blocks of less than 400 ... More than half of those who snapped up privatization issues own shares in no more than one company.' The *Economist* (6–12 November 1983). The same source notes that individual owners still account for half the value of the New York exchange and a third of Paris's, whereas in Britain they hold just 20 per cent by value of British shares.

argument also fails to take into account the fact that, however own-ership is distributed, the *control* of enterprises remains vested in a small group of people, whose primary concern is, and is indeed required to be, the interests of shareholders. Nor is the point af-fected by the fact that the same people are in control of vast pension funds. Privatization further reduces the capacity of governments to 'interfere' with business activity. The regulation of what have become private monopolies is generally weak and limited, intentionally so. A significant recent example of the abdication of responsibility by government which privatization involves is provided by the decision of Michael Heseltine, the Secretary of State for Trade and Industry, in October 1992, to close 31 pits and thus throw 30,000 miners out of work at a time of mass unemployment. The uproar this produced caused the government temporarily to reprieve a few of the threat-ened pits, but the point which Heseltine made again and again was that, in a 'free society', he could not compel the (recently privatized) electricity industry to enter into contracts with the coal industry which were 'uneconomic'. In fact, the point Heseltine was unwit-tingly underlining was that a democratic government which did not have ultimate control over the major decisions of enterprises must find it very difficult to impose upon them policies congruent with social purposes which their controllers do not share and to which they are opposed.

The point applies with great force to the banking system and financial institutions. No society can be deemed to be democratic in which crucial financial decisions are taken by small groups of peo-ple, with no democratic credentials whatever, whose first concern is the profitability of the institutions which they command, and who enjoy a remarkable degree of freedom from government 'interfer-ence'.[5] Banking and finance are too serious a business to be left to the mercies of bankers and financiers: no socialist government could tolerate a situation where its purposes, legitimated by the democratic process, would be stymied by such people. They are not, and cannot be, the custodians of the common good; and the mistakes in policy

[5] It was this freedom which made it possible for United Kingdom firms to engage in direct foreign investment in the eighties to an amount representing 65.6 per cent of net direct business investment. The next largest such investment was made by German firms, with 16.1 per cent: A. Glyn and B. Sutcliffe, 'Global but leaderless? The new capitalist order', in *The Socialist Register 1992*, eds R. Miliband and L. Panitch (Merlin Press, London, 1992, and Monthly Review Press, New York, 1992), p. 85.

they are driven to make in their search for greater profits (as in their accumulation of bad debts), not to speak of the endless scandals and misdemeanours which attend the management of banking and finance, constantly reinforce the point, or should do so.

The propagation of the view that public enterprise is inherently beset by crippling vices has traditionally been one of the main ideological and political endeavours of anti-socialist ideologues, politicians and commentators, united on this as on nothing else; and their endeavours have been greatly helped by the experience of Communist regimes, where public enterprise, imprisoned in an authoritarian system and in a comprehensive command economy, did have many of the negative features attributed to public enterprise as such. Closer to home, the experience of public ownership under social democratic auspices did not help either. For it was not intended by social democratic leaders in government that public enterprise should be more than an adjunct to capitalist enterprise, with as little departure as possible from business lines in the direction of socialization under democratic control.[6] Proposals by the Labour Party for getting the private sector to help finance infrastructure investment are well in line with this approach.

The ideological shift which has occurred on the Left in regard to the socialization of the economy, even as a long-term prospect, is very remarkable; and that shift, it should be noted, occurred well before the growth of multinational companies was taken to mean that nationalization was no longer feasible. What was proposed instead was the greater regulation of business. This, however, fails to take account of the fact that regulation, in areas where business is strongly opposed to it, is fraught with great difficulties, which can only be overcome by a large bureaucratic apparatus and draconian penalties for failure to comply. Regulation of private business, in a democratic context, has a limited and uncertain reach. Public ownership avoids most of the problems which regulation encounters: the latter is no substitute for the former.

The virtual rejection of nationalization by most social democratic

[6]   For an instructive account of the various and stultifying constraints to which nationalized enterprises in Britain were subjected from 1945 onwards, see R. Saville, 'Nationalization', in *The Labour Government 1945–51*, ed. J. Fyrth (Lawrence and Wishart, London, 1993). It is also relevant, as Saville notes, that the boards of nationalized utilities and industries were mainly composed of businessmen and military men who had no interest in the larger hopes which socialists (but not Labour ministers) invested in nationalization.

parties has in effect meant the abandonment of any attempt to bring about a fundamental transformation of the economy and therefore of the social order itself. What makes the shift all the more remarkable is that there was nothing in the nature of capitalism which warranted it. For, as will be argued below, the negative features of that experience were not *inherent* in public ownership, but the result of a context deeply hostile to its serving any purposes other than those dictated by the logic of capitalism.[7]

3

A major criticism raised against public enterprise is that it fatally discourages entrepreneurship and innovation, and therefore makes for stagnation, obsolescence and inefficiency. Thus, Brus and Laski, writing from within the left spectrum, ask whether entrepreneurship is 'at all imaginable for economic actors who are not principals operating on their own risk and responsibility, but only agents employed by a public body which itself is rather unfit for entrepreneurial behaviour'.[8]

There are a number of possible answers to the question. One of them is that the authors seem unduly influenced by Communist experience. They themselves note the negative economic consequences of a political system which paralysed individual initiative and boldness at all levels of the productive process, most of all for managers for whom a minimal condition of survival was acceptance of directives from on high.[9]

Public enterprise in a socialist democracy would not be run on any such basis. Also, a different answer to the question which Brus and Laski pose is that most economic actors in capitalist corporate enterprise are not 'principals' operating at their own risk, but agents of the corporation who own at most a small fraction of its stocks and shares. These people may run some risk in the exercise of

---

[7] As Robin Murray notes in relation to the pattern of nationalization in Britain, 'the Morrisonian corporation is designed ... to strengthen management, and weaken workers, users and politicians': 'Ownership, control and the market', *New Left Review*, 164 (July–Aug. 1987), p. 103.

[8] W. Brus and K. Laski, *From Marx to Market: socialism in search of an economic system* (Oxford University Press, Oxford, 1989), p. 59.

[9] Ibid., p. 47.

entrepreneurship, namely that of being dismissed or demoted for inadequate performance, though this risk, at the uppermost levels of corporate managerialism, is small. In any case, the same risk applies, or could well be made to apply, to the managers of public enterprises. Indeed, it could well be made to apply a lot more strongly in public enterprises than is the case in the private sector, where top managers form part of a protected environment and easily move from one top job to another. It is only gross fraudulence which is seriously punished.

Another answer to the question of whether public ownership can foster efficient and innovative economies is provided, paradoxically enough, by the experience of countries which are extolled as shining examples of unfettered capitalism, namely those of the Asian Pacific Rim. As Jeffrey Henderson and Richard Appelbaum, among other writers on the subject, have noted, 'state policy and influence should now be accepted as the single most important determinant of the East Asian economic miracle.'[10] State intervention in these countries took many forms, which varied in scope and character; but they included, notably in South Korea and Taiwan, a large and powerful state sector.[11] In addition, there were the creation of new private industries by way of subsidies and direction, protection from foreign imports, the setting up of government-sponsored research facilities, the expansion of education. In South Korea, the state also initiated a major land reform which 'destroyed the land-owning class and created a large population of small farmers that, with state support, dramatically improved agricultural productivity'.[12]

[10]   R. P. Appelbaum and J. Henderson (eds), *States and Development in the Asian Pacific Rim* (Sage, Newbury Park, Calif., London and New Delhi, 1992), p. 23.
[11]   In Taiwan, 'in 1952, as much as 57 per cent of total industrial production . . . and 56.7 per cent of manufacturing output were accounted for by public corporations.' 'By the early 1980s, the share of the public sector had been reduced to less than 20 per cent, but the government remains dominant in such fields as heavy machinery, steel, aluminium, shipbuilding, petroleum, synthetics, fertilizers, engineering, and, recently, semi-conductors'. A. H. Amsden, 'The state and Taiwan's economic development', in *Bringing the State Back In*, eds P. B. Evans, D. Rueschmeyer and T. Skocpol (Cambridge University Press, Cambridge, 1985), p. 91. Also, 'almost every bank in Taiwan is . . . wholly or partially owned by the state (foreign banks were not allowed to establish operations until 1969). The lending activities of all financial institutions have been under strict state supervision' (ibid., p. 91).
[12]   M. Castells, 'Four Asian tigers with a dragon head: a comparative analysis of the state, economy and society in the Asian Pacific Rim', in Appelbaum and Henderson, *States and Development in the Asian Pacific Rim*, p. 42.

The most remarkable example of successful state intervention in a capitalist economy is Japan, whose 'economic miracle' is largely due to it. As Chalmers Johnson notes, Japan is the best example of a state-guided market system currently available, the guidance being provided by the bureaucrats of the Ministry of International Trade and Industry (MITI), who have a direct and intimate involvement in the fortunes of what are taken to be 'strategic industries'.[13] As Chalmers Johnson also notes, Japan provides a good example of the interaction of two sub-systems, one public and geared to developmental goals, the other private and geared to profit maximization; and this has involved the penetration of government at microeconomic as well as macro-economic level, and the wielding of much influence over whole economic sectors, whole industries or individual enterprises.[14]

However, these countries are hardly to be taken as exemplars of socialist democracy. State intervention in Japan occurred under a regime which Chalmers Johnson calls 'soft authoritarianism', marked by the uninterrupted rule of one party and a remarkable degree of freedom and power for the bureaucracy. Also, economic growth in the 'four tigers' – South Korea, Taiwan, Singapore and Hong Kong – occurred under the auspices of authoritarian regimes which were not 'soft' at all; and this of course made effective intervention a great deal easier. This raises a crucial question: how far would a socialist government, operating in a context where democratic forms make opposition possible, be able to enforce its will on private business? The chances are that it would be nothing like as successful as was the case in authoritarian regimes. This is why public ownership is an inescapable condition for the effective control and regulation of the more important parts of economic activity. Even so, it is quite clear from the experience of the countries of the Asian Pacific Rim that the notion, so assiduously peddled by ideologues of the Right, that state intervention and public enterprise are inherently inefficient and destructive of entrepreneurial initiative is not well founded.

The same conclusion must be drawn from the experience of public ownership in capitalist democratic countries. For publicly owned firms in these countries have shown again and again that they were perfectly capable of doing at least as well, in strict efficiency terms,

[13]   C. Johnson, *MITI and the Japanese Miracle* (Stanford University Press, Stanford, Calif., 1982).
[14]   Ibid.

as firms in the private sector. The evidence strongly supports the quite modest claim of Bob Rowthorn and Ha-Joon Chang that 'as far as large-scale enterprises are concerned, there is no activity which the public sector cannot in theory perform as efficiently as the private sector.'[15] Similarly, the authors of a study of public enterprise in Western Europe conclude a chapter on the performance of the public sector with the observation that 'the wave of nationalisation in France after 1981, and the present day trend towards privatisation in a number of European countries, may owe as much, if not more, to political considerations as to economic rationality.'[16]

The drive to privatization should be seen for what it is – a *political* enterprise based upon the wish to widen the scope of the private sector, to weaken government's capacity to direct economic life according to criteria determined by democratic deliberation and decision, to foster 'popular capitalism' and thereby strengthen conservative propensities among new shareholders, to make more difficult the extension of the public sector by a government of the Left, and to raise revenue from the sale of what Harold Macmillan (by then Lord Stockton) called the 'family silver'. Privatization is an up-to-date and extreme application of the demand that business should be left free from government 'interference' – except of course where government help to business is required, at which point interference turns into sound economic policy.

What the private sector can achieve can be done at least as well by the public one, given a favourable context; and public enterprise also makes possible, even though it does not make certain, the avoidance of the failings which the micro-rationality of private enterprise imposes upon it. There is another aspect to this: public enterprise makes possible a democratization of economic activity far beyond anything that capitalism can achieve. More will be said about this presently.

[15] R. Rowthorn and Ha-Joon Chang, 'The political economy of privatization', in *The International Theory and Practice of Privatization*, eds T. Clarke and C. Pitelis (Routledge, London and New York, 1993), p. 59. For a positive assessment of the French experience of public ownership, see P. Dreyfus, 'The efficiency of public enterprise: lessons of the French experience', in *Public and Private Enterprise in a Mixed Economy*, ed. W. J. Baumol (Macmillan, London and Basingstoke, 1980). For a negative assessment of a number of public enterprises in Britain in the seventies, see R. Pryke, 'Public enterprise in practice: the British experience of nationalization during the past decade', in the same volume.
[16] H. Parris, P. Pestieau and P. Saynor, *Public Enterprise in Western Europe* (Croom Helm, Beckenham, 1987), p. 150.

4

What then of the problem which the internationalization of capital would pose to a socialist government determined to extend public ownership?

Much here depends on what firms, industries, utilities or services are in question. There is a great difference to be made between firms which are owned by foreign multinational companies, and the rest. Thus, Robin Murray notes that 'today, the nationalization of Ford UK would give public control over factory buildings, an assembly line which would be starved of key inputs from Ford Europe, and components which would be largely useless outside Ford Europe's production and marketing operations.'[17]

'The answer', he suggests, 'may be to support the expansion of a British-based firm or – where indigenous production no longer exists – to adopt a strategy for rebuilding it.'[18] This would certainly be on the government's agenda; but it may well be that, meanwhile, a socialist government would not make the public ownership of foreign-owned subsidiaries one of its priorities.

A lot, however, turns on how large a part of a country's economic resources is owned by foreign firms. Murray also suggests that 'an important part of British industry' is made up of foreign-owned branch plants.[19] In fact, the great majority of British corporations, not to speak of smaller units, remain wholly or largely British owned; and the same predominantly national ownership is true for other advanced capitalist countries, even though foreign companies, notably American and Japanese, have made inroads in their industrial, commercial and financial sectors.[20] One of the main features of dependency in countries of the 'third world' is that foreign companies do actually *dominate* these sectors, which does make outright nationalization an exceedingly difficult enterprise in economic terms, and also in political ones. The best that can be hoped for in such circumstances is for a socialist government to negotiate new terms

[17] Murray, 'Ownership, control and the market', p. 91.
[18] Ibid.
[19] Ibid.
[20] Thus, Glyn and Sutcliffe note that typically in advanced capitalist countries, 5–10 per cent of capital stock is owned overseas, and that this 'presents a picture of important but hardly overwhelming internationalization of production': 'Global but leaderless?', p. 84.

on which the activities of foreign firms are conducted, including partial and gradually extended state ownership.

Where foreign ownership is confined to a part interest in a given enterprise, the remaining ownership in the hands of local owners could be transferred to the public sector, thus creating joint ownership with foreign owners, with the public controllers clearly predominant.

On this view, the internationalization of capital does not, for advanced capitalist countries, present any major technical obstacle to the socialization of an important part of economic life, though it may well present other problems. Foreign firms might well decide to close the operations of their local subsidiaries, not because they were under threat of public ownership, but because they did not like the whole thrust of government policy and feared its consequences. It would be for the government to decide whether it was possible to replace them with nationally owned firms. Nationally owned firms might also think of emigration: a socialist government would have to decide whether to prevent them from doing so.

The point also needs to be made that though socialization is technically possible, its pace is not thereby determined. The aim is to achieve the socialization of a predominant part of the means of economic activity; but how rapidly this should be done is an open question, subject to many different considerations. A socialist government, having been brought to power by a great wave of popular support, would no doubt want to make a beginning with the programme of socialization to which it was committed. On the other hand, a substantial programme of socialization (or de-privatization) presents many problems; a socialist government would have to take the long view and see socialization as a process extending over many years, on the basis of well-laid and flexible plans.

Among other problems it would need to cope with, the government would have to decide how to deal with the issue of compensation to shareholders for firms taken into public ownership. It is not possible for a democratically elected government to adopt a policy of simple confiscation, not least because this would be unjust to many small investors, among whom must be counted many wage-earners. On the other hand, immediate compensation in full would saddle the government with crippling burdens at a time when money was badly needed elsewhere. The solution would probably lie in compensation by way of the issue of government bonds, redeemable over an extended period of time; and a considerable degree of differentiation would also have to be made between small and large investors, with facilities for more rapid redemption available to small investors.

However carefully the government sought to proceed, its measures would be certain to produce strong internal opposition, and also opposition of an even more formidable character from governments committed to neo-liberal policies, and from international institutions like the IMF, the World Bank, the European Commission and other international institutions, for all of which economic interventionism and socialization constitute mortal sins. How a socialist government would deal with this opposition is discussed at length in chapter 6.

5

A socialized economy would consist of three distinct sectors. First, there would be a predominant and varied public sector. Secondly, there would exist a substantial and expanding cooperative sector. Thirdly, there would endure a sizeable privately owned sector, mainly made up of small and medium firms, with an important part to play in the provision of goods, services and amenities.

The public sector in a socialist context would assume a number of different forms, with economic units owned and managed by the central state, regional and municipal authorities, and with various forms of democratic control, depending on the nature of their activities. They would be subject to competition from alternative sources of provision of goods and services, either from other public sector firms or from private ones.

Public sector enterprises would enjoy a high degree of autonomy in the running of their own affairs. This cannot, however, amount to complete autonomy – a situation which does not even apply to capitalist firms in non-interventionist capitalist regimes. A socialist government would want to retain a decisive say in a number of realms to ensure compliance with its macro-economic policies and objectives, and with its concerns about health and safety, employment and the rights of workers. The government would have an ultimate power, sparingly applied, to intervene in matters of investment, pricing, location and other issues of concern beyond those of the firm. Even with publicly owned firms, there would be a tug of war between them and the government, based on differences that are likely to arise between the interests of the firm, as perceived by managers and employees, and the government's policies. André Gorz notes that

> there exists, up till now, no other science of management except the capitalist one. The question is solely to what extent the criteria of economic rationality should be subordinated to other types of rationality within and between companies ... Socialism must be conceived as the binding of capitalist rationality within a democratically planned framework, which should serve the achievement of democratically determined goals, and also, of course, be reflected in the limitation of economic rationality within companies.[21]

The point is obviously germane to public enterprises but is clearly a source of potential conflict.

Also, the controllers and managers of public enterprises would be subject to scrutiny from various sources – trade unions and workers' councils, committees of the legislature, consumer councils, the press. These are qualifications to the notion of autonomy which a democratic order clearly requires. 'Management' in a socialist context cannot be taken to mean decision making by a small number of people at the head of the enterprise, free from a considerable measure of democratic control. Public enterprise in such a context must be taken to include as a matter of course the greatest possible degree of participation in the determination of policy by everyone employed in the enterprise who wishes to be involved, and the attribution of real power to employees in regard to all issues which most directly affect them – for instance, health and safety, the process of production, conditions of work etc. One of the main purposes in moving from private to public enterprise is to affect decisively 'relations of production' and to create conditions which approximate as closely as possible to what Marx called the 'free association of the producers.'

It is as well to recognize, however, that here is another point of tension because of contradictory pulls. So long as a distinction between management and employees endures, there is bound to be an area of dispute in regard to the prerogatives of management on the one hand and the right to participation by employees on the

---

[21] A. Gorz, 'The new agenda', in *After the Fall: the failure of Communism,* ed. R. Blackburn (Verso, London and New York, 1992), p. 296.

other. The point about public enterprise in the context of socialist democracy is that its spirit would be such as to make the conflicts that do arise capable of being resolved without bitter confrontation, though the possibility of such confrontation cannot be discounted. Managerial prerogatives have always been a subject of fierce contention, with managers determined to surrender as little as possible of their power over employees – not surprisingly, since they represent interests fundamentally opposed to those of employees. There would be no such fundamental opposition of interests between the 'two sides of industry' in the socialized sector of the economy. For the first time, there would come into being a genuine community of interests between all those engaged in the work of the firm, irrespective of their location in the process of production; and this could be expected to produce a spirit in the enterprise altogether different from that which prevails in capitalist enterprise. This is not to say that a socialized enterprise would bask in perpetual sweetness and light, but it is nevertheless the only form of enterprise in which community of purpose could be made to acquire real meaning.

As noted earlier, state enterprises are only one part of the public sector. Another is constituted by the large range of activities undertaken by regional and municipal authorities, notably in the provision of services and amenities. There is of course nothing new in this: regional and local authorities in many countries are responsible for theatres, opera houses, restaurants, daycare centres, summer camps, swimming pools, leisure facilities of every sort – quite apart from the services which they render as part of their statutory duties. Socialist democracy would widen the scope of their activities, and require that what they do should involve as much citizen participation as possible.

Local and regional authorities would also be involved in the activities of a host of small and medium firms located in their region, and based on 'flexible specialization'. Such involvement was one of the notable features of economic development in the 1980s, with local and regional government providing a variety of services to these firms. 'Local governments, banks, employers associations and trade unions', one writer noted, 'work together to regulate the local economy and provide collective access for small firms to key services from factory premises, loan finance and marketing to research and development training and technical education.'[22] Here too, a socialist regime would encourage this kind of decentralized cooperation between local and regional authorities and enterprises.[23]

In this connection, and more generally, an important concern of a socialist regime would be to strengthen another sector of the economy, namely the cooperative sector, in the field of production as well as distribution, and in the provision of services. Cooperatives now play a very subsidiary role in capitalist economies.[24] A socialist regime would make it its business to help cooperative enterprises play a much more important role in the economy than has ever been sought by bourgeois regimes.[25]

As noted earlier, an economy that had been largely socialized would nevertheless comprise a large scatter of small and medium-sized firms, individually owned and controlled. To accept the existence of such firms for an indefinite period of time – indeed as a permanent and desirable feature – must no doubt offend purists. But it should be recognized that a private sector of this kind has a number of advantages. It introduces an additional element of competition in the provision of goods, services and amenities. It gives an opportunity to individuals who are so inclined to try their hand at independent ventures, and to experiment with new products and services. A socialist regime would not only find this acceptable, but would actively encourage such individual initiatives. But it would at the same time see to it that the private sector remained a subsidiary part of the economy as a whole.

---

[22] J. Zeitlin, 'Local industrial strategies: introduction', in *Economy and Society*, Special Issue: Local Industrial Strategies, 18, 4 (November 1989), p. 369.

[23] For an account of what was done in this area by the Labour-controlled Greater London Council in the eighties, see M. Mackintosh and H. Wainwright, *A Taste of Power: the politics of local economics* (Verso, London and New York, 1987).

[24] Even the legendary Mondragon cooperative venture in the Basque country has been a marginal adjunct to the Spanish economy: 'By the end of the 1970s,' H. Thomas and C. Logan note, 'there existed in the province a modern co-operative system of technical education, 70 cooperative factories with a workforce of more than 15,000 cooperators and a credit coop bank with 93 branches and 300,000 deposits.' H. Thomas and C. Logan, *Mondragon: an economic analysis* (Allen and Unwin, London, 1982), p. 1.

[25] For a discussion of the problems which affect cooperative enterprises, see e.g. J. Elster, 'From here to there; or if cooperative ownership is so desirable, why are there so few cooperatives?', in E. F. Paul et al., *Socialism*.

6

What is the place of planning and markets in a socialist economy?

The first thing to be said about planning in a socialist democracy is that it would bear no resemblance to the Stalinist model of total, comprehensive, detailed planning in which all enterprises were required to conform to the plan, with no reference to the market. This was not how planning had been conceived after the Bolshevik Revolution. Alec Nove notes that Trotsky, speaking in 1922 of a 'transitional period', had said that 'it is necessary for each state-owned factory with its technical director to be subject not only to control from the top – by state organs – but also from below, through the market, which will remain the regulator of the state economy for a long time to come.'[26] R. W. Davies also notes that 'until 1928 every one assumed that plans must be made compatible with market equilibrium, and with a non-coercive economic relationship with the peasantry.'[27]

Stalinist planning brushed all qualifications aside. It is now fashionable to view it as a total disaster; and so it was in terms of the horrendous human and material costs which it exacted. But it was a great deal more effective in setting the Soviet Union – and later other Communist countries – on the path of rapid industrialization than is generally acknowledged. Indeed, its achievements, in strictly quantitative terms, were, as Paul Kennedy notes, nothing short of staggering, 'first in the production of steel, pig iron, coke, oil,

---

[26]   A. Nove, *Socialism, Economics and Development* (Unwin Hyman, London, 1986), p. 33. In 1923, Trotsky was also saying that 'for the next period . . . we shall have a planned state economy, allying itself more and more with the peasant market and, as a result, adapting itself to the latter in the course of its growth.' But, he added, 'although this market develops spontaneously, it does not follow at all that state industry should adapt itself to it spontaneously. On the contrary our success in economic organization will depend in large part upon the degree to which we succeed, by means of an exact knowledge of market conditions and correct economic forecasts, in harmonizing state industry with agriculture according to a definite plan': L. Trotsky, 'The new course', in *The Challenge of the Left Opposition (1923–5)* (Pathfinder Press, New York, 1975), p. 119.

[27]   R. W. Davies, 'Gorbachev's socialism in historical perspective', *New Left Review* 179 (Jan.–Feb. 1990), p. 9. Davies adds, however, that 'all Communist economists assumed that this was a transitional stage; eventually planning would replace the market, and product exchange would replace trade' (ibid.).

machine tools, diesel and electric trains, cement, mineral fertilizers, tractors, shoes, prefabricated concrete structures' as well as 'one of the most comprehensive educational systems in the world' and the provision of 'more active physicians . . . than any other country in the world.'[28] This success of Soviet planning obscured its cost and the waste that went with it; and it greatly helped to spread the popularity of the idea of planning in the thirties. So did the element of planning which governments undertook in World War II and in the years of reconstruction after it. In a book published in 1978, Stuart Holland noted that even 'in the 1960s virtually every leading Western European country – with the exception of West Germany – was committed to some kind of economic planning', which he defined as 'the combination of indicative targets and aid and incentives'.[29] Fashions quickly changed thereafter. As Holland also notes, 'in the 1970s the flight from planning has been dramatic';[30] and it became even more so in the eighties.

Yet this is in some ways misleading. For despite all rhetoric, the fact is that some measure of planning is engaged in by all governments in advanced capitalist countries, however dedicated such governments may proclaim themselves to be to 'free enterprise', the market economy and non-interference in economic life. Governments, of whatever complexion, are compelled to set targets for a range of projects which they cannot avoid undertaking, and must allocate resources for the purpose. Defence is an obvious case in point, where the development and production of weapons, tanks, aircraft, warships etc. have to be planned in detail for years and even decades ahead. The same goes for programmes of road construction, airports, the building of schools, hospitals, prisons etc. Whether governments use private firms or publicly owned ones for the purpose is in this respect largely irrelevant, save for the fact that publicly owned firms are much more readily accountable than private ones, and therefore much less likely to engage in the kind of profiteering which has been a familiar part of the practice of firms engaged in government work. Capitalist governments are deeply involved in issues of cost, performance and delivery, even though their system of control is

[28]   P. Kennedy, *Preparing for the Twenty-First Century* (HarperCollins, London, 1993), p. 229.
[29]   S. Holland (ed.), *Beyond Capitalist Planning* (Blackwell, Oxford, 1978), p. 1.
[30]   Ibid.

generally weak. It is government which has to decide on priorities, and plan for their realization. Where governments neglect this obligation, the results are grievous. Thus, Robert Heilbroner, writing in 1991, noted in relation to the United States that 'for something like twenty years the condition of our infrastructure – our streets, highways, bridges, tunnels, airports, navigation facilities, and water and sewage systems – has been steadily deteriorating for lack of adequate investment.'[31] Nor can 'the market' be expected to compensate for government neglect. It is no part of business, nor can it be, to initiate projects which are inherently the responsibility of government. It is precisely market forces which induce firms *not* to invest in projects which are essential to society's well-being, but which hold no promise of profit to them.

The planning favoured by socialist governments would involve the setting of targets for key sectors of the economy, encompassing the infrastructure, public utilities, other major elements in the productive process, and also provision for training, education and a variety of services. The targets would be subject to regular reappraisal and modification as circumstances required; and they would be achieved by a combination of 'indicative' and 'imperative' planning, with the government using various inducements and pressures as well as instructions to achieve purposes which had been subject to democratic determination.

Both Japan and France provide much experience of the weapons which are at the government's command if it is determined to play a positive role in the steering of economic activity. Martin Cave and Paul Hare note that 'in a mixed economy like France . . . the ability of authorities to implement the plan is restricted.'[32] Nevertheless, the 'indicative' planning current under the relatively weak regime of the Fourth Republic was highly successful in what it sought to achieve. By the mid-sixties, under the Fifth Republic, planning had ceased to be a serious instrument of economic policy. Nor did the Mitterand regime seek to give it new strength. But it did set out 'priority programmes', as in the Ninth Plan, for 1983–8, which included such goals as the modernization of industry, education and training, the development of communication industries, employment policies and

[31]   R. Heilbroner, 'Lifting the silent depression', *New York Review of Books*, XXXVIII, 17 (24 October 1991), p. 6.
[32]   M. Cave and P. Hare, *Alternative Approaches to Economic Planning* (Macmillan, London, 1981).

so on. The plan had little influence on the policies of a government bent on policies of 'austerity' and retrenchment. A different kind of socialist government would also have its 'priority programmes', but it would pursue them in a very different spirit.

Markets would have a definite place in a predominantly socialized economy. But market forces, in such an economy, would not be the ultimate determinant of economic life. The submission of the economy to unregulated market forces means the abdication by government and the society which sustains it of responsibility for deciding what needs to be done for the common good and the achievement of social justice. Indeed, it means the return of the 'invisible hand' and the destructive assumption, contradicted by ample evidence, that what the market dictates necessarily results in the common good. A socialist economy would not be ruled by such market fetishism.

One of the major objectives of a socialist government, operating in the context of a mainly socialized economy, would be to extend the area of 'decommodification', from which market forces are excluded. Such 'decommodified' areas already exist in capitalist economies, and are largely the product of pressure from below in the decades following World War II to ensure that access to health, education and other services should be viewed as rights inherent in citizenship, without any regard to ability to pay. As G. Esping Andersen puts it, 'the outstanding criterion for social rights must be the degree to which they permit people to make their living standards independent of pure market forces.'[33] This notion of citizenship constitutes an essential difference between socialism and conservatism, with the latter concerned to reduce the area of 'decommodification' and to establish the principle that provision of services and benefits free from ability to pay should be confined, on strict criteria of eligibility, to the most deprived and destitute members of society. The privatization of services is part of this endeavour.

Alec Nove makes the point that 'health, education; (public) housing, posts, urban public transport, environmental protection, water supply, street lighting and cleaning, parks, etc. are not (should not be) provided because of a desire to make money.'[34] How far and

[33]   G. Esping Andersen, *The Three Worlds of Welfare Capitalism* (Polity Press, Cambridge, 1990), p. 3.
[34]   A. Nove, 'Markets and socialism', *New Left Review*, 161 (Jan.–Feb. 1987), p. 102.

how soon such a list (which is hardly revolutionary) should be extended is a question that cannot be settled in advance. For his part, Ernest Mandel adds to it 'cultural and information (communication) services and basic foods and clothing'; and this, he notes, would cover 'between 70 and 80 per cent of civilian expenditure in most of the industrialized countries of the world'.[35] This probably goes well beyond what is possible in the relevant future; but the principle that decommodification should cover an extended area of life is an essential part of socialism. This does not mean the imposition of a uniformity of consumption and the absence of choice. Decommodification is not in the least intended to create a 'dictatorship over needs'; and it is not at all incompatible with the provision of a wide range of goods and services which would remain subject to the market.

A social order in which basic needs are no longer subject to ability to pay would create conditions in which a sense of community, diffused through the whole of society, would be encouraged to flower and would enrich both individual and social life. The notion of 'basic needs' is often repudiated by anti-socialist writers in the name of a wholly spurious relativism. Thus, one such writer, John Gray, speaks of 'the incommensurability of preferences and values in modern societies, which sustain a diversity of traditions and ways of life', which are allegedly 'evaded by theories of basic needs or primary goods which suppose that these can be made the objects of public provision by institutions whose mode of operation is subject to democratic control'; this is rejected on the ground that the 'ranking among basic needs [is] a matter of intractable dispute unsettleable by reason', and that 'their content and definition of the needs itself will vary across different traditions and ways of life.'[36] In fact, there is no real problem in identifying basic needs, as the same author acknowledges in a different publication.[37] There may be argument as to how far the list of such needs should be extended, but it is perfectly possible to settle this by reason.[38]

---

[35]   E. Mandel, 'The myth of market socialism', *New Left Review*, 169 (May–June 1988), p. 112.
[36]   J. Gray, 'Marxian freedom, individual liberty, and the end of alienation', in *Marxism and Liberalism*, eds E. F. Paul, F. Miller and J. Paul (Blackwell, Oxford, 1986), p. 181.
[37]   J. Gray, *Beyond the New Right* (Routledge, London, 1993), *passim*.
[38]   For an interesting discussion of the issue, see L. Doyal and I. Gough, *A Theory of Human Needs* (Macmillan, London, 1991).

Clearly, goods, services, benefits, amenities that had been wholly or largely decommodified would still have to be paid for; and the payment would mainly take the form of various types of direct and indirect taxation. Neo-liberal dogma has turned direct taxation into one of the great hate-phrases in its repertoire. But as Mr Justice Frankfurter once put it, 'taxation buys civilization.' Even so, it is never likely to be very popular, but it can be made acceptable if the burden is spread fairly. A socialist government would have this as a major aim. It would, in a transition period in which exorbitant incomes and great wealth had not been wholly eliminated, clearly place the heaviest burden of taxation upon them; and it would also seek to close off the many loopholes whereby corporations greatly reduce the taxes they pay, or avoid paying them altogether. The point is to move towards a situation where the vast inequalities of income and wealth typical of a capitalist society would have been steadily diminished; and this could be expected to foster a greater willingness on the part of most people to view both direct and indirect taxation as a necessary price to pay for the amenities which benefit them and society at large.

In the sixties and seventies, at a time when unions were relatively strong and influenced by the militancy of their members, great efforts were deployed in many capitalist countries (not least by social democratic governments) to implement incomes policies that would contain and subdue wage demands: in this realm at least, market forces were then thought to be detrimental to the 'national interest'. These endeavours achieved varying degrees of success;[39] but success largely meant that the main burden of the policies fell on wage-earners. As always in a capitalist context, such policies meant in practice that it was they, rather than employers and others in higher income groups, who were detrimentally affected. By the eighties and the early nineties, different forms of pressure on wages had come into operation: mass unemployment, the attack, in Britain and else-where, on trade union rights, with the consequent retreat from militancy by wage-earners.

A socialist government, clearly pursuing egalitarian aims, and subject to strong inflationary pressures which it would imperatively

[39] See e.g. R. J. Flanagan, D. W. Soskice and L. Ulman, *Unionism, Economic Stabilisation, and Incomes Policies: European experience* (Brookings Institute, Washington, D.C., 1983).

need to subdue, might not resort to an incomes policy of the old style. But as part of the demand management in which it would be engaged, it would need some understanding with trade unions, and wage-earners in general, particularly those in strong bargaining positions, that they would agree to some restraint in their wage and other demands. To say this may well seem ridiculously unrealistic; but this is to ignore the fact that a socialist government would be seen to be striving for a just society; and it would also ensure that restraint applied with full force to the inflated salaries and other financial advantages which high executives and others in positions of power enjoyed. It would certainly seek to affirm the principle that, while men and women in the service of the state should be adequately paid, their salaries and other advantages should not be grossly out of line with the income of their fellow citizens. The immediate cry this would provoke is that it would drive away the best people from the service of the state and also produce a 'brain drain' of such people to countries where they would receive much higher salaries. In fact, the chances are that a large number of highly qualified people would wish to stay and help in the social construction that was under way; and in any case, people who could only be induced by inflated salaries to work in the service of the state or in public enterprise would not be the kind of people that were wanted. In reality, it is reasonable to expect that most people would, reluctantly or not, accept the new conditions, not least because these new conditions would hardly condemn them to penury.

7

In the perspective of what has been said in this chapter, what are the fundamental changes that would result from the achievement of a socialized economy? Before answering that question, a point that has repeatedly been made in other contexts needs to be reiterated, namely that in no way is the claim made here that the change would automatically usher in a new world, altogether free from the evils of the old one. Such 'triumphalism' would by now be entirely out of place. For a long time to come, old problems would endure, and new ones would arise. The point, however, is that there are two different ways of accepting that this would be so. One of them is to say that the problems are intractable, inherent in the human condition, and therefore beyond real and effective solution. This is the traditional conservative view, and it treats as dangerously 'utopian' hopes of a radical improvement in the way life is experienced. Indeed, a corollary of this view is that attempts at radical reform, of the kind proposed here, are bound to make a bad situation infinitely worse.

The other position is that no problem is intractable and that the potential for radical change for the better is enormous; that the human race has hardly begun to tap this potential; and that, while the determination to tap it will not create a paradise on earth, it will create an immeasurably more favourable environment for the majority to fulfil the best that is in them.

The differences between a capitalist economy and a socialized one are clearly not purely 'economic': they are economic, social, political and moral, and affect the whole texture and mode of being of the social order.

The first difference is of course that the private ownership and control of the main economic resources of society would have ceased to be the dominant form of economic organization. As a result, a determinant source of unequal power and position in society would progressively dry up. This would mean a fundamental change in the social structure, with the eventual disappearance of the most important part of the capitalist class, namely the owners and controllers of the major and privately owned means of economic activity. This would bear some similarities to what happened in the twentieth century to the land-owning aristocracy in Western Europe: it did not actually disappear, but it lost most of the power which land-ownership had previously given it. The power it continued to enjoy derived from other sources, not least the entrenched position of aristocrats in the state service. The controllers of corporate power would also lose that power, even though many of them would no doubt find their way into strategic parts of socialized enterprise; but the power they would wield would not be based on their control of major private resources.

This invites the retort that this could well mean no more than the consolidation of a 'new class', a 'state bourgeoisie', made up of the people in high positions in the state and public enterprise; and, in the same vein of thought, it could be said that such people would be the beneficiaries of an all-encompassing 'statism', which would give them a degree of power and privilege not much different from that enjoyed by people in power in capitalist democracies, or indeed even greater.

I have noted in an earlier chapter that this is a possibility which is not to be treated lightly. On the contrary, it would have to be taken with the utmost seriousness as a crucial point of tension between democratic aspirations on the one hand, and the tendency of people in power to seek its extension and to abuse it on the other. As was also said in previous chapters, the way to resolve that tension, and to attenuate the risks of overweening and arbitrary power, is first to build institutional barriers to it, and secondly to rely on the critical vigilance of a multitude of organs of opinion, and on the spirit of an alert citizenry imbued with a sense of what civic virtue demands of people in power.

The disappearance of corporate power over the main means of economic activity also means that the dynamic of that activity would have been radically changed. Its main purpose would no longer be the maximization of profit for the benefit of the owners and controllers of corporate power. The organizing principle of a socialized economy would be the satisfaction of individual and collective needs, with the priorities for the satisfaction of these needs having been democratically determined. Exploitation would have no place either in public enterprise or in the cooperative sector. It would endure in the remaining private sector, but would be strictly controlled. This relegation of exploitation to a subsidiary part of economic life would represent a fundamental transformation of the social order, and could be expected to have a tremendous impact on the ways in which people viewed the social order and how they responded to the demands which it made upon them.

Both the level of productive activity and its goals would be subject to democratic decision making, with the producers having a major (but not an exclusive) voice in the process. There would be plenty of room for informed debate on the issues involved; for instance, the length of the working day, the length of the working week, the requirements of rapidly changing patterns of work, the allocation of resources etc. For some general purposes, the debate would be conducted at national level – eventually for some purposes at international level. For other purposes, it would be conducted on a regional or local basis. But the crucial point is that it would not be conducted in the shadow of the imperative requirements of capitalism.

I have already referred to democracy at the workplace. Suffice it to repeat here that a socialized economy would make possible an entirely new set of 'relations of production', in which genuine, unforced cooperation would become the norm, with opportunities for the full development of individual capacities which are now thwarted.

The right to work was a right to which bourgeois governments were forced to subscribe during World War II because of the radical expectations that were then aroused, and because of the need to assure the population that the sacrifices they endured would have their due reward. Lip service continued to be paid to the right to work for some time thereafter – it was included in the preamble of the Constitution of the French Fourth Republic in 1946 and also in that of the Fifth Republic in 1958; but it has long ceased, in practice, to be a major aim of capitalist governments and is indeed now widely taken to be an unrealistic and undesirable goal. Unemployment on a large scale may be ritually deplored by people in power but is a permanent feature of economic and political life, and not a particularly unwelcome one, since it greatly helps to curb the militancy of wage-earners. Government complacency would be punctured if the unemployed made a real nuisance of themselves, and could be organized as a militant pressure group, but unemployment, with all its other soul-destroying features, helps to isolate people and to discourage collective action. Even in the thirties, the Hunger Marches in Britain involved a relatively small minority of the unemployed and only occurred because they were organized at the behest of the Communist Party.

A socialist government would give a very high priority to the achievement of full employment and would seek to turn the right to work into reality. In an age of ever greater advances in technology, with more and more sophisticated machines taking the place of human labour, this would need many measures to adapt to these advances – a shortening of the working week, a lowering of the age of retirement, the proliferation of services, the strengthening of state, municipal and voluntary agencies involved in the provision of caring services. A fundamental aspect of policy would be the provision of ample facilities for retraining and the renewal of skills. In this realm also, what is now generally done very inadequately would be treated as an essential part of the process of production. Even though a socialist society would be committed to full employment, it would also wish to reduce the amount of time which men and women had to devote to 'earning a living', and thereby increase the amount of time they would be able to devote to 'living' and to engaging in whatever pursuits they found most fulfilling. This, in a socialist society, would not be subject to the kind of commercialization and exploitation of leisure which occurs in capitalist society. At local, regional and national level, a variety of public and cooperative agencies, supplemented by private ones, would compete in the provision of facilities and services; and this, save for private firms, would be done without the deforming distraction constituted by the striving for maximum profit.

An economy under effective socialist control would also be sharply alert to the social costs of the productive process, and would subject it to stringent ecological controls. Here too, what capitalism does grudgingly and inadequately would be done wholeheartedly in a context in which the requirements of capital would have ceased to weigh upon governments.

A further consequence of socialization is that the kind of frantic pushing of products which now goes under the name of advertising would cease. Under capitalism, vast armies of skilled, often talented, men and women devote their skills and talents to the production of a barrage of tendentious advertising on behalf of their clients, one of its features being the implicit or explicit praise for free enterprise and its blessings. Advertising would certainly not be abolished in a socialist society; but it would be greatly reduced and would lose its frantic and biased character. This would cut costs considerably and would also be of great benefit to cultures now saturated with low-grade commercial propaganda.

In short, a socialized economy, to reiterate a fundamental theme of this book, would free the whole of society from the 'fetters' imposed upon it by the rationality of capitalism, and substitute for it an altogether different rationality, attentive to human needs and seeking their satisfaction under the least onerous conditions possible. This liberation of society from the domination of capital is the essential condition for the creation of a social order in which a degree of cooperation and harmony unattainable under capitalism would become possible.

All the reforms which have been proposed in this chapter and the previous one clearly need detailed elaboration. But these proposals also raise a set of different and crucial questions: what are the constituencies available, or potentially available, for the kinds of reform which socialist democracy demands? What are the agencies available for the purpose? And what are the strategies most likely to advance the process? Scarcely less important, there is, as noted earlier, the question of the opposition which a socialist government determined to carry out these reforms would inevitably encounter, and how it would cope with that opposition. It is with these questions that I am concerned in the next two chapters.

5

Constituencies, Agencies, Strategies

1

However profound their disagreements on other counts, most social-ists have shared the view that the achievement of power, and its use for socialist purposes, imperatively required a very large measure of popular support. For those socialists eager to follow an electoral path, popular support was mainly to be expressed at the polls, in an electoral process that would in time give them a majority of votes and parliamentary preponderance. For socialists at least willing, in the conditions of capitalist democracy, to explore this path, popular support would find expression in vigorous extra-parliamentary forms as well as electoral ones. For revolutionary socialists, popular sup-port would, at a time of extreme crisis, be manifested in the streets and the countryside, and lead to the overthrow of the existing re-gime and its replacement by a mode of rule based on popular power. Even ardent Leninists and 'vanguardists' dismissed as mere 'putschism' any notion of power obtained by a small minority, on the basis of a coup engineered by a group of conspirators (the kind of people whom Marx once contemptuously called the 'alchemists of revo-lution'), without popular backing. In the months following the February Revolution in Russia in 1917, the Bolsheviks were able to claim a substantial measure of support; and they stilled what doubts they might have had about its extent, particularly after their seizure of power in October 1917 and the dissolution of the Constituent Assembly in January 1918, with the belief that in any case they represented the best interests of the masses.

In contemporary terms, three questions are raised by the notion of popular support, as outlined in the preceding chapter: what constituencies are actually or potentially available for change in socialist directions? What agencies may be expected to advance the enterprise? And what strategies are appropriate to the purpose? What follows by way of an answer to these questions mainly refers to advanced capitalist countries.

'Popular support' means mainly the support of a large part of the wage-earning population, now mostly urban, for the simple reason that wage-earners, as noted in chapter 1, constitute a large majority of the population. This focus on wage-earners is not, contrary to what is often claimed, in the least intended to ascribe a 'privileged' role to them, or to invest them with an 'historical mission', or to proclaim them to be members of a 'universal' class, whose emancipation entails the liberation of everybody else who is subject to oppression. None of these notions is required. The focus on wage-earners stems rather from the common-sense observation that, if popular support is indeed essential for the advancement and success of the socialist enterprise, then the support of wage-earners is obviously of the first importance. This is not, of course, to say that support from other classes – members of the lower middle class and even members of the dominant class – is not necessary, a point that will be taken up presently.

It was also noted in chapter 1 that, even though wage-earners did constitute a majority in objective terms, this was very different from a solid political majority, particularly one committed to radical change. The fashion in recent times has been to argue that achieving such a majority was nowadays out of the question. For one thing, it is said, any such notion of an objective majority tends to obscure the very disparate nature of its constituent elements. Also, the profound internal divisions of that majority are supposed to render a 'totalizing' label like 'working class' or 'wage-earning class' quite misleading, in so far as it suggests a degree of cohesion which is not there; and it also ignores the individuality and specificity of every single person. As if this were not enough, it is said as well that deep changes in the production process, with the erosion of the industrial working class, the waning of 'traditional' occupations, the break-up of settled communities and the pervasive spread of consumerism have created a 'working class' (very much in inverted commas) which finds its real identity in the supermarket and the shopping mall rather than in dingy party meeting halls and in political activity in general. The working class, so it is claimed, is now an ever more amorphous, atomized mass of people in societies which have turned reality into spectacle, and in which ideology and political commitment are an irrelevant distraction from the real concerns of wage-earners.

There is nothing new in the view of the working class as fatally contaminated by the values of 'possessive individualism'. In every generation, the point is made, gleefully or dolefully, that the working class has been 'bourgeoisified', that it has been finally reconciled to capitalism and integrated into the political system, that it has ceased to be a 'dangerous class', that its concerns have come to lie in privatized activity, not in public affairs, save as spectacle. Even as spectacle, public affairs could not begin to compete with sport and other forms of entertainment.

How true is this picture today? In order to answer that question, it may be useful to probe Marx's notion of 'social being'. In his preface to *A Contribution to the Critique of Political Economy* (1859), Marx wrote that 'the process of social, political and intellectual life in general is determined by the mode of production of material life', and that 'it is not the consciousness of men that determines their being, but their social being that determines their consciousness.'[1] For him, and for later Marxists, social being was taken to be pre-eminently shaped by class, and class itself to be determined by location in the process of production. The location of the working class in that process entailed its subjection to domination and exploitation, and this must in turn lead it to develop a 'class consciousness' infused with the will to achieve an altogether different social system. This conception of social being and of its consequences for consciousness has clearly been proved to be greatly flawed.

The essential mistake, however, lay not in the emphasis on the importance of class as an objective fact but rather in reading from it a revolutionary consciousness in the making. There is here an 'imputation' of a 'revolutionary consciousness' to the proletariat, which is in some ways akin to Rousseau's 'general will', which is the will that the people would will if they knew what they ought to will. In later developments of the notion of class consciousness, it was the Party which became its embodiment, as the agency which did will what the proletariat ought to will. This, it should be stressed, is not

---

[1]   K. Marx, preface to *A Contribution to the Critique of Political Economy* (1859), in K. Marx and F. Engels, *Collected Works* (Lawrence and Wishart, London, 1980), vol. 16, p. 469.

Marx, but the fact remains that the link between class and class consciousness is a great deal more complex than Marx's formulations allowed. For social being encompasses a number of identities other than class which may be of primary importance to individuals: gender, race, ethnicity, nationality, religion, youth, old age, disability, sexual preference, or a combination of them.

These other identities do not change an individual's class location; and the ways in which other identities are experienced are deeply affected by this class location. A woman who belongs to the dominant class and a woman worker may both find their primary identity in their gender, as *the* defining aspect – for them – of their being, but the ways in which that identity is experienced will be different in each case. Both suffer male domination and discrimination in what remain profoundly male-dominated societies; but they do not suffer in the same manner. The same point applies to a black middle-class person as against a black worker; and so on.

Also, identities which co-exist in a person's social being may assume different degrees of importance according to circumstances. Thus a black woman worker, in a conflict with her employer in which her fellow workers, black and white, male and female are engaged, may well perceive her class position to be pre-eminent, and to feel a strong bond of solidarity with her fellow workers, irrespective of colour; whereas in circumstances where she is the victim of discrimination, possibly by her white fellow workers, it is her identity as a black woman which is of the greater importance.

Identities other than class and location in the process of production may well obliterate class solidarity altogether: nationality, ethnicity, religion, for instance, often assume compelling, all-encompassing importance in the minds of men and women, and thus lead them to reject any kind of solidarity with other men and women who, though they have the same objective class identity, belong to a different nationality, ethnicity or religion. Recent literature has emphasized that neither ethnic nor national sentiments should be taken to be inborn, 'natural', and that both should rather be seen as engendered from many different sources, and often deliberately manipulated to achieve integrative purposes.[2] But true and important though this is,

---

[2] See e.g. E. Gellner, *Nations and Nationalism* (Blackwell, Oxford, and Cambridge, Mass., 1983); E. J. Hobsbawm, *Nations and Nationalism since 1870* (Cambridge University Press, Cambridge, 1990); B. Anderson, *Imagined Communities* (Verso, London and New York, 1991, rev. edn).

the fact remains that ethnic and national sentiments do create loyalties which have again and again involved workers of different ethnicities and nationalities in mutual slaughter. The former Yugoslavia provides a recent and catastrophic instance of the phenomenon. 'Proletarian internationalism' and the obstacle it was thought to present to wars between nations were one of the great illusions nurtured by the Second International; and it has played very little part in international relations ever since the great bloodletting of World War I.

Marx also believed that the process of production would result in a working class that was made more or less uniform and brought together by the common condition of its members. This greatly underestimated the enduring nature of the divisions which have marked the working class, and which have grown rather than diminished.

This under-estimation has vast implications. For Marx, proletarian class consciousness meant that the working class, united by the nature of capitalism, would in time overcome its various divisions (of which he was well aware), that it would obtain a clear perception of its position in society, of its class interests, of who its real enemies were, and of what should be done to achieve its emancipation. Given this view, it is easy to understand why Marx and Engels held throughout their life to the firm conviction that, as Marx put it in drafting the Rules of the First International in 1864, 'the emancipation of the working class must be conquered by the working class itself', since that working class, steeled by its many struggles, would in due course acquire the clear-sightedness and the will required to achieve emancipation. Lenin's departure from this view in *What is to be Done?* (1902) lay in his affirmation that 'the working class, exclusively by its own efforts, is able to develop only trade-union consciousness';[3] and by 'trade-union consciousness' he meant of course something very different from revolutionary class consciousness, namely the struggle for limited gains within the existing social order. That struggle was not to be despised. On the contrary, it should be helped in every way possible; but it was all the same essentially different from the struggle for revolutionary change.

There is a sense in which Lenin's departure from Marx, though considerable, was less dramatic than might appear at first sight. For Lenin did believe that, with the guidance and the leadership of the

---

[3]   V. I. Lenin, *What is to be Done?* (Lawrence and Wishart, London, 1937), p. 32.

party, the working class *would* acquire the necessary revolutionary class consciousness and *would* make the revolution.

It may be argued that what happened in Russia in the course of 1917 bears some distant relationship to this model of revolution, and that there have been other episodes in the twentieth century which also bear some similarly distant approximation to it. But the model has all the same failed to be justified by historical experience.

However, while the class location of the working class has not for the most part produced revolutionary class consciousness, this cannot be taken to mean that the link between class and political orientations in all classes is not quite strong. That link has always been very strong in dominant classes: the overwhelming majority of their members do not tend to support reformist, let alone revolutionary, parties. On the contrary, the class location of members of dominant classes leads them, quite naturally, to support parties which are committed to the maintenance and strengthening of the social order of which they are the beneficiaries. But this common 'world view' admits of endless variations within its compass – not least over the ways in which the social order may be preserved and strengthened. This is simply to say that the link between class and ideological orientations is complex and subject to great variations.

This is even more true for wage-earners, large numbers of whom, not least the most deprived among them, have often supported bourgeois parties. Also, some wage-earners, angry at their condition, have at times been lured into supporting far-right parties and movements which attacked immigrants, blacks, Jews and other minorities, but also promised social and political renewal. It is not for nothing that the Nazi Party called itself national-socialist, and that other such parties and groupings everywhere have usually proclaimed their will to achieve radical change and engaged in a 'populist', anti-Establishment rhetoric. This support which members of the wage-earning population have given to racist, xenophobic and antisemitic groupings shows well enough that the link between the class location of the wage-earning population and its political orientations can assume reactionary as well as progressive forms.

It should also be said, however, that the great majority of organized workers has always shown a remarkable resistance to parties and movements of the far right. It should not be forgotten, for instance, that in the election of November 1932 in Germany, the last election before the Nazis' accession to power in January 1933, in circumstances when Social Democrats (SPD) and Communists (KPD) were engaged in a fierce struggle with each other, the SPD obtained 20.4 per cent of the vote, as compared with 21.6 per cent in the election of July 1932 and 24.5 per cent in the election of September 1930; but the KPD, for its part, obtained 16.9 per cent of the vote, as compared with 14.3 per cent in July 1932 and 13.1 per cent in September 1930.[4] The bulk of the votes for the SPD and the KPD came from wage-earners; and the determined campaigns of the Nazis to attract working-class voters met with little success.[5] The real strength of the Nazis lay in their support from other sources – the petty bourgeoisie in town and country, and the bourgeoisie; and it is also relevant that it was not wage-earners who brought Hitler to power but the support which he received from the most highly respectable people in the land, culminating in President Hindenburg's invitation to him to assume the chancellorship.

More recent history also shows the reluctance of the great bulk of the working class to heed the appeal of neo-fascist groupings. A small fraction of the wage-earning population in advanced capitalist countries with well-implanted labour and socialist movements has on occasion given electoral support to far-right and neo-fascist movements, which, like their predecessors in Italy and Germany, have based their appeal on some kind of 'national populism' with nationalism, xenophobia, racism and a spurious denunciation of bourgeois power holders as its main ingredients. But the major support of these parties has not come from the working class: in general, wage-earners have shunned such movements, and have either remained faithful, electorally, to parties of the Left or to constitutional conservative parties, or have kept out of 'politics' altogether.

Also, long experience shows that the divisions which do exist in the working class are not insuperable: there are innumerable instances of working-class struggles in which workers, separated by gender, ethnicity, religion etc. have managed to make common cause against employers and the state in the struggle for common objectives;

[4]   T. Childers, *The Nazi Voter: the social foundations of Fascism in Germany, 1919–1933* (University of North Carolina Press, Chapel Hill and London, 1983), pp. 141, 209, 211. The Nazi Party obtained 37.3 per cent in July 1932 and 33.1 per cent in November 1932. In the election of September 1930, it had received 18.9 per cent (ibid.).
[5]   Ibid., pp. 243ff. See also T. Mason, 'National Socialism and the working class 1925–1933', *New German Critique*, 11 (Spring 1977).

and I will argue in a moment that much the same has occurred in the political realm.

The struggle, however, has mostly been of an emphatically non-revolutionary and strictly 'reformist' character. The reasons for this are a combination of economic, political, social and cultural factors: the resilience and expansiveness of capitalism, and the expectation and actual achievement of improvements within the system; social mobility, if not for oneself at least for one's children; the risks there may be in the involvement with 'extreme' politics; the fear that in any case alternatives to the present are not available, or would make things worse, linked to the repulsive features and the failures of Communist regimes; unrelenting conservative propaganda against the Left, and also attacks by social democratic leaders against anything to the left of them; above all, the existence of democratic forms and of the mechanisms which they provide for reform. Clearly, it is only under the most exceptional circumstances that 'revolutionary situations' occur in capitalist democratic regimes and that the risks they entail are accepted by a substantial part of the population.

This, however, is not the end of the story. For whereas it is perfectly true that the bulk of the working class has generally refused to play a 'revolutionary' role, at least a large part of it has frequently supported left parties which promised far-reaching changes in the social order, nothing less, in the words of the Labour Party's election manifesto of February 1974, than 'a fundamental and irreversible shift in the balance of power and wealth in favour of working people and their families'. The same kind of language has often been used by social democratic and other left parties in many countries, with very good electoral results.[6]

It is of course true that many wage-earners (and others) who voted for left parties did not do so because they were committed to programmes of radical renewal and reform; and some of the support which these parties attracted was fragile and conditional. But the fact remains that a considerable part of the wage-earning population

---

[6] A study of 'electoral socialism' by A. Przeworski and J. Sprague opens with the sentence 'No political party ever won an electoral majority on a program offering a socialist transformation of society': A. Przeworski and J. Sprague, *Paper Stones: a history of electoral socialism* (University of Chicago Press, Chicago and London, 1986), p. 1. This is manifestly false, unless 'a socialist transformation of society' is taken to mean an explicit commitment to revolution, in the strong sense of the word.

in many countries has come together at election time in support of radical programmes, and has, at least for electoral purposes, overcome its many divisions; and has done so again and again. It is this electoral availability for such programmes which worries conservative forces, and which leads them to conduct a daily assault, by way of their parties, the media which support them, and other agencies, on the consciousness of working-class voters and others, in the hope that they might be weaned from dangerous thoughts and inclinations. Unlike all the prophets of the transformation of the working class into an amorphous mass mesmerized by consumption, conservatives everywhere know that the working class, from their point of view, remains a potentially dangerous class, and that the battle for its mind and heart is a hard and never-ending necessity.

This is a much more realistic view than that embodied in J. K. Galbraith's notion of a now prevalent 'culture of contentment' according to which 'the controlling contentment and resulting belief is now that of the many, not just the few.'[7] Galbraith, whose book is focused on the United States, notes that 'the economically and socially fortunate ... are now a majority not of all citizens but of those who actually vote.'[8] But a majority of those who vote in the United States means a majority out of some 50 per cent of the electorate, which may be taken to mean something over 25 per cent of Americans; and it may well be that this is indeed a 'contented' minority, which hardly justifies any notion of a 'culture of contentment'. Galbraith also suggests that 'a contented majority ensured the rule of the government of Margaret Thatcher for eleven years.'[9] But Thatcher never had a majority of voters on her side in any election. Nor is there any reason to believe that a majority of those who did vote Conservative were in any way 'contented'.

Marx over-estimated the solidity of the link between class location and the political orientations it would produce among wage-earners; but his critics, for their part, greatly under-estimate its strength. A major reason for this is the devaluation of the importance of work in the life of wage-earners. André Gorz has long been one of the main proponents of this devaluation. In a recent formulation which is typical of this vein of thought, he writes that 'we are dealing with

---

[7]   J. K. Galbraith, *The Culture of Contentment* (Sinclair-Stevenson, London, 1992), p. 10.
[8]   Ibid., p. 15.
[9]   Ibid., p. 153.

a social transformation that is leading to a situation in which work occupies only a modest place in people's lives';[10] and he goes on to say that 'individuals transferred the search for self-realization to other terrains.'[11] It may be doubted whether more than a minority of wage-earners ever found much 'self-realization' in wage-labour. Be that as it may, the notion that 'work occupies only a modest place in people's lives' can only be taken to mean that the work they do is of no great interest to them, and is no more than a means to an end. True though this may be, work, as Robert Dahl notes,

> is central to the lives of most people. For most people, it occupies more time than any other activity. Work affects – often decisively – their income, consumption, savings, status, friendships, leisure, health, security, family life, old age, self-esteem, sense of fulfillment and well being, personal freedom, self-determination, self-development, and innumerable other crucial interests and values.[12]

This is very well said; but what also needs to be said is that the work people do is intimately related to their class location. Neither class location nor work automatically produces a left-inclined consciousness; but the need to seek reform is nevertheless 'organic' to the working class, given its location in the productive process and in society at large: wage-earners are driven, by the nature of that location, to demand better wages and conditions, shorter hours, the extension of rights and benefits, and other related reforms. The strength of the striving for reform depends on many different circumstances; but it is never far from the surface. This helps to explain the support which large parts of the wage-earning population have given to the major agencies of reform in capitalist societies. Also, Lenin's notion of 'trade-union consciousness' greatly under-states the substance and scope of this pressure, ranging as it has from mundane but crucial demands for better wages, shorter hours and better conditions to the enlargement of civic and political rights, and much else that has threatened and indeed affected the status quo. It is this pressure which has been mainly responsible for such 'social democratization' as capitalism has undergone. That the pressure has

[10] A. Gorz, 'The new agenda', in *After the Fall: the failure of Communism* (Verso, London and New York, 1992), p. 293.
[11] Ibid.
[12] R. A. Dahl, *Democracy and its Critics* (Yale University Press, New Haven and London, 1989), p. 327.

not achieved more cannot be laid at the door of the working class: again and again, it is left leaders in opposition or in government who have decided that retrenchment rather than an attempt to seek further advance was the course of wisdom.

Parties of the Left also have a vital role in the articulation of 'organic' demands and in their coherent formulation; and they are (or should be) a crucial source for the articulation of a value-system which directly challenges the prevailing one and which puts forward a radically different 'world view'. The failure of social democratic parties to perform this function, ever more marked in recent decades, is not the least important explanation of such de-radicalisation as has occurred in the wage-earning population of advanced capitalist countries. Przeworski and Sprague note in the work already cited that 'the ascendancy of motivations other than class is a consequence of strategies of political parties: when parties do not seek to organize workers as a class, class ideology is altogether absent from political life and other principles of organization and identification come to the fore.'[13] This is an exaggeration. In fact, the ascendancy of motivations other than class is often the consequence of many different factors; but the virtual occlusion of class from political discourse certainly owes much to a social democratic determination to avoid the dread accusation of being 'class parties' and thus the obscuring of their 'national', class-free vocation. It needs also to be said that an insistence on the importance of class does not involve a self-defeating narrowing of focus, if the working class is taken to encompass, as noted earlier, that large majority of the population which is made up of wage-earners and their families. Nor does this emphasis preclude concern for other layers of the population, notably the business and sub-professional petty bourgeoisie. Avoidance of the class dimension is merely an obfuscation of the most important aspect of the reality of capitalist societies.

Pressure for reform is not of course confined to wage-earners. It also comes from the ranks of the lower middle class; and movements of reform of one kind or another have also attracted a fair number of members of the bourgeoisie.

I noted in chapter 1 that the lower middle class encompasses two distinct elements: on the one hand, small business people, shopkeepers,

[13] Przeworski and Sprague, *Paper Stones*, p. 59.

small farmers, independent artisans – the small fry of the world of capitalism; on the other hand, teachers, journalists, technicians, social workers, supervisory personnel in the state and the private sector.

In political terms, the business part of the lower middle class has commonly been viewed as a conservative, often a reactionary force, prone to support self-proclaimed saviours who promise to protect small business from both big business and organized labour. But the conservative inclinations of small business are not irremediable; and parties of the Left, such as the former Communist Party of Italy, have had some success in attracting support from small entrepreneurs, shopkeepers and artisans.[14] Much the same has occurred elsewhere as well. To achieve such support is of great importance. Alec Nove notes that in Chile, there was 'a very large class of small shopkeepers, owners of workshops, artisans, owner-drivers of trucks, small peasantry, and other members of what must be called the petty bourgeoisie'.[15] Their alienation from the Allende regime, notably the (CIA-fomented) strike of truck drivers, played a part in its destabilization.

It is, however, the sub-professional side of the petty bourgeoisie which offers the most promising constituency for left parties and movements. For a large part of that constituency consists of men and women who are employed in the state sector and who therefore have personal experience of the inadequacy of the state's provision for welfare and collective services, and who themselves suffer from the parsimony of the state; or, if they are in the private sector, have personal experience of the hierarchical and undemocratic nature of the work process, and who may well feel that it does not give sufficient weight to their capacities. Many such people have tended to gravitate towards left parties, and they have played an important role in grassroots activism. Their numerical growth suggests that their influence will also become greater in the coming years, and as parties of the Left continue to undergo a process of what might be called 'petty bourgeoisification'.

As for the bourgeoisie, there have always been some members of

[14] See e.g. S. Hellman, 'The PCI's alliance strategy and the case of the middle classes', in *Communism in France and Italy*, eds D. L. M. Blackmer and S. Tarrow (Princeton University Press, Princeton, N.J., and London, 1975).
[15] A. Nove, *Socialism, Economics and Development* (Unwin Hyman, London, 1986), p. 4.

it who have been drawn to movements of reform and renewal, and also to revolutionary and insurrectionary parties; and such people, like members of the petty bourgeoisie, have also played an important, indeed a leading, role in the life of left parties. Traditionally, those parties have served as an important avenue of political and social advancement for members of both the petty bourgeoisie and the bourgeoisie; and it is from their ranks that the upper strata of social democratic parties have been drawn.

These, then, are the constituencies which have been, and remain, available for reforming purposes. How radical these reforming purposes are likely to be is of course a crucial question. But much of the answer, as noted, depends on the agencies which seek to bring the members of this constituency together.

2

'Agencies', in relation to the Left, has for the last hundred years mainly meant political parties. Other organizations – notably trade unions and also cooperative societies, single-issue associations and movements – have played their part in expressing demands associated with the Left, but it is parties which have mainly been expected to articulate the purposes of the Left and to make it a powerful and effective presence on the political scene.

In the twentieth century, two types of such parties have dominated the life and the politics of the Left: social democratic parties on the one hand, and Communist parties (after 1917) on the other. It was these parties (much more so social democratic parties than Communist ones) which achieved a mass membership in many countries, and received the support at the polls of a considerable part, sometimes a majority, of the electorate. Both social democratic and Communist parties, but particularly the latter, attracted an extraordinary degree of devotion and loyalty from their members – what might well be called a fetishism of the party.[16] This is one of the remarkable

[16] Trotsky, under strong attack after Lenin's death by what was then the 'triumvirate' of Stalin, Zinoviev and Bukharin, was driven to indulge in such fetishism with the fateful remark: 'Comrades, none of us wants to be or can be right against the party. In the last analysis, the party is always right, because the party is the sole historical instrument that the working class possesses for the solution of its fundamental tasks': 'Speech to the Thirteenth Congress, May

phenomena of the epoch – that secular institutions like Communist parties should have elicited the kind of attachment which was more commonly associated with religion – and the sentiments that were expressed towards Communist parties under Stalinist control often did have a quasi-religious tone.

Most Communist parties have now gone, or have greatly changed; and the kind of allegiance which was once given to them is part of a history which is unlikely ever to be repeated. Social democratic parties never attracted the same kind of fetishism of the party; and such allegiance as they now elicit is for the most part highly instrumental and contingent. In fact, parties, for many people on the Left, have come to be viewed with great scepticism and suspicion as inherently authoritarian, bureaucratic, manipulative, unprincipled, and plagued, so it is often said, by a fatal bias towards a working-class constituency which is shrinking and which has in any case long ceased to be a reliable basis of support. In the same vein, parties of the Left have been taxed with electoral opportunism, with sexism and racism, with a marked 'statist' bias, and with a deep-seated hostility to any grassroots activism which they were not able to keep under strict control.

Before considering this further, we must note the conclusion which many people on the Left have drawn from this indictment, namely that any real hope for the advancement of progressive causes in capitalist society rests with new social movements rather than parties. For, it is claimed, it is these movements, concerned with feminism, racism, ecology, peace, sexual orientation, the defence of civic and welfare rights, constitutional reform, participatory politics, and other causes, which have been the source of new ideas, new forms of organization, new political styles, and which have displayed a vitality and effectiveness far greater than that of the traditional parties of the Left. It is these movements which have pushed major issues

26, 1924', in L. Trotsky, *The Challenge of the Left Opposition (1923–1925)* (Pathfinder Press, New York, 1975), p. 161. Yet it was also Trotsky who, a short while earlier, had said: 'out of the party with passive obedience, with mechanical leveling by the authorities, with suppression of personality, with servility, with careerism! A Bolshevik is not merely a disciplined person; he is a person who in each case and on each question forges a firm opinion of his own and defends it courageously and independently not only against his enemies but inside his own party': 'The new course', in ibid., p. 127. It was of course the former formulation which came to dominate the life of the Bolshevik Party under Stalinism.

high on the political agenda, and forced parties and governments at least to take these issues seriously. As the editors of a volume of essays on new social movements put it, these movements 'represent a qualitatively new aspect of contemporary democratic politics'.[17] In support of such claims, women point to the degree to which the defence of women's rights has become part of the political culture; how much black movements in the United States and elsewhere have placed racism on the defensive; how effective ecological movements have been in increasing consciousness of the dangers which the neglect of ecological needs poses to humankind.

The advocates of new social movements do not claim that they have achieved their purposes; but they do claim to have imposed the issues which concern them upon the political cultures of their countries, and to have gained some significant concessions from their governments.

Justified though these claims are, they should not obscure the limitations, in socialist terms, of new social movements. The feminist movement has mounted a formidable challenge to a crucial aspect of the social order, namely the pervasive domination of men and the discrimination exercised against women. The struggle against male domination and discrimination has profoundly transformative implications for the social order. But these transformations, even if they could be realized to the full in a capitalist context, would not, as noted earlier, fundamentally alter the existing structures of capitalist power. They would effect a certain feminization of these structures; but it is only a minority of the feminist movement which seeks to go beyond this, and which sees feminism as requiring close alliance with parties engaged in the struggle for socialist advance, but without surrender of independence.

Similar considerations apply to all other new social movements. Black movements, for instance, include people – a majority – who seek an end to the discrimination which a white society exercises against black people, but their critique of that society tends to be narrowly focused on this aspect of it. Here too, it is a minority which is committed to positions that situate racism in a larger context and is willing to work in, or with, parties and groupings of the Left. New social movements naturally focus on the single, specific

[17]   R. J. Dalton and M. Kuechler (eds), *Challenging the Political Order* (Polity Press, Cambridge, 1990), p. 10.

issues which are of greatest concern to them, and this is precisely why they have proved so attractive to many people on the Left who no longer believe that a comprehensive challenge is possible or effective, and who therefore want to concentrate on issues that are more 'practical' and which seem more likely to yield more immediate results.

This move away from comprehensive schemes of social renewal is well in tune with post-modernist strictures against 'universalism' and with the stress on difference and specificity and the shunning of class as a dangerously 'totalizing' and 'totalitarian' label. New social movements, explicitly or not, tend to affirm their non-class or multi-class vocation, often even their 'non-partisan' character.

Nevertheless, activists in new social movements have usually been moved by issues which have constituted a challenge to the thinking and practice of parties of the Left; and they have thereby made a genuine contribution to left politics, by forcing upon left parties questions which they had in an earlier epoch tended to relegate to the periphery of their concerns, or to ignore altogether. As such, these movements must constitute an important element of the coalition of forces which has to be constructed on the Left. Kate Soper notes about ecology that 'just as socialism can only hope to remain a radical and benign pressure for social change if it takes on the ecological dimension, so the ecological concern will remain largely ineffective . . . if it is not associated in a very integral way with many traditional socialist demands, such as assaulting the global stranglehold of multinational capital'; and this, she also notes, requires a 'red–green synthesis'.[18] The same goes for other movements as well. The notion of coalition is crucial here. For it acknowledges the very large fact that no single organization of the Left will ever again be able to claim to represent all movements of protest and pressure, as Communist parties (and, less emphatically, social democratic parties as well) once did. Coalition means alliance of different forces, with negotiation and compromise between them as an essential condition of advance and success.

To return to parties of the Left, it is clear that many of the accusations made against them are quite justified. Above all, they

---

[18] K. Soper, 'Greening Prometheus: Marxism and ecology', in *Socialism and the Limits of Liberalism*, ed. P. Osborne (Verso, London and New York, 1991), p. 271.

have been marked by a lack of genuine democracy, based on the
wish to insulate leaders from challenge from within their ranks.
In the case of Communist parties, this was ensured by the principle
of 'democratic centralism' and the insistence on 'unity', however
spurious. In social democratic parties, undemocratic practices were
required in order to protect leaders from their radical followers.
How far oligarchic tendencies in parties of the Left can be overcome
is an open question. But however this may be, parties of the Left do
remain of primary importance as a potential, if not an actual, instrument of socialist advance. The qualification is necessary in order to
take account of all their present deficiencies. But the qualification
does not invalidate the point that the Left does need parties if it is
to be a force capable of being an effective and successful presence
on the political scene, and of mounting a serious challenge to the
existing structures of power.

The experience of the United States shows well enough how dis-
advantageous the absence of a serious party of the Left has been for
the labour movement and the Left in general. The United States has
produced many movements of reform which have forced concessions
from the system. Democratic administrations have, ever since the
New Deal, prided themselves on their reforming achievements; and
the Democratic Party has often been seen as a social democratic
party in fact if not in name. In reality, it has been a thoroughly
bourgeois party, wholly dedicated to 'free enterprise', but with a
very modest bias towards state intervention and social reform which
has enabled it to enlist the support of a large working-class constituency. It is also worth recalling that the American Communist Party
was able, in the thirties and up to the end of World War II, to play
an opposition role out of all proportion to its relatively small size.
No doubt this was due to the Great Depression, to the attraction of
the Soviet Union with which the Party was then proudly linked, and
to the successes of fascism, of which the Soviet Union appeared to
be the only real opponent. The Party's influence rapidly waned with
the onset of the Cold War.

Since then, the absence of a substantial party that was not wholly
dedicated to 'free enterprise' and (up to very recently) the waging of
the Cold War has left a vast hole at the centre of the American
political culture, and has produced a narrowing of the scope of
American politics which has been deeply detrimental to the vast
majority of the American people. Even though social democratic
parties have not been very keen, particularly in recent years, to

affirm a socialist vocation, it is only in the United States (and backward and repressive regimes like Saudi Arabia) that the word 'socialism' has been expunged from the political vocabulary, save as a term of abuse. Indeed, it is only in the United States that the word 'liberal' has, more recently, suffered the same fate. These are tokens of the massive political hegemony exercised by conservative forces, and of the success they have had in warding off a serious challenge to them, in the realm of political discourse and in the practice of politics.

In dictatorships where party life is confined to the ruling party, and where other parties live a precarious existence or are altogether suppressed, an opening may occur for small groups of people, outside any party structure, to engage in armed struggle and seize power: Fidel Castro's small band of men and women who began the process of revolution in Cuba is a good example of such non-party initiatives. Even in capitalist democracies, movements started by relatively small numbers of people can, in given circumstances, achieve remarkable effects and, further, cause a great deal of destabilization: this was demonstrated in the United States by the civil rights movement and the opposition to the war in Vietnam, and in still more dramatic fashion in France in May 1968, when students detonated a conflagration which brought the regime to the brink of collapse. But the 'May events' were not a revolution; and if the Gaullist regime had collapsed, power would have passed to politicians from traditional parties, none of whom (certainly not the Communist Party) had any intention of making a revolution. This is not to under-estimate the significance of such events, but only to note that in countries where major parties are solidly established, other groupings tend to wane when the issues which brought them to the fore disappear or lose their mobilizing force. Even small parties of the Left, on the other hand, are not nearly so dependent on particular circumstances; and, if they can escape from sectarian isolation, they can make a contribution to the dissemination of socialist ideas and to the waging of ongoing struggles.

3

To speak of parties of the Left nowadays is to speak above all of social democratic parties. For it is these which have tended to dominate the political scene on the Left throughout this century. Mass

Communist parties in France and Italy overshadowed social democratic ones in the post-war decades, but the crisis which has gripped Communist parties everywhere has meant that they have not been able to take advantage of the deep troubles which have beset social democratic parties in recent years. In any case, Communist parties have long undergone a process of 'social democratization', a point that will be taken up in a moment.

There is little doubt that social democratic parties will for the foreseeable future remain the main political force on the Left, or at least a factor of major importance. It is possible that in some cases, most obviously the Italian one, social democratic parties have been so discredited by their involvement in corruption that their chances of regaining effective strength may be problematic. But for the most part, their crises, however real, have not crippled them. As Perry Anderson notes, 'in 1974–5 there were Social Democratic Premiers in Bonn, Vienna, London, Brussels, The Hague, Copenhagen, Oslo, Stockholm and Helsinki';[19] 'by the early eighties', he also notes, 'as conservative regimes ruled the roost in London, Brussels, Amsterdam, Rome and Copenhagen, there were Social Democratic Premiers in Paris, Rome, Madrid, Lisbon and Athens.'[20] Similarly, Przeworski and Sprague note that

> between 1944 and 1978 four socialist parties obtained, on the average, between 40 and 50 per cent of the vote: in Austria, Norway, the UK and Sweden . . . The Left as a whole – socialist parties, communist parties, and other left-wing groups combined – saw its average vote slightly exceed 50 per cent in Sweden and Norway. In most other countries, the share of the total left hovered between 40 and 50 per cent.[21]

Social democratic fortunes generally suffered a marked decline in the eighties and in the early nineties, but where social democratic parties have achieved a solid implantation, they are most unlikely to cease being major players in the politics of advanced capitalism, sometimes in government, alone or in coalition, or in opposition.

The integration of social democratic parties into the political system was a lengthy process, which received a strong impetus in 1914 with social democratic support for bourgeois governments in the

[19]   P. Anderson, 'The light of Europe', in *English Questions* (Verso, London and New York, 1992), p. 309.
[20]   Ibid., p. 314.
[21]   Przeworski and Sprague, *Paper Stones*, p. 29.

waging of war. With World War II, these parties, like the Swedish Social Democratic Party before them, truly became 'parties of government'. In that capacity, they did achieve much by way of reform; and they were greatly helped in this by the boom conditions which prevailed in the post-war decades. With the end of the boom, on the other hand, social democratic governments became, however reluctantly, the managers of policies of retrenchment, cuts in public expenditure, the erosion of social services; and this mainly affected their wage-earning constituencies, without gaining them support elsewhere. Crisis conditions presented social democratic leaders with a challenge they were unable to meet: to adopt different policies would have led them into hazardous paths, with uncertain results, and against fierce opposition at home and abroad. Nor in any case were plausible and realistic alternative programmes readily available. It was much easier to choose policies of retrenchment. The trouble with this, however, is that it rendered much less credible the claim that social democratic parties were a real alternative to their conservative opponents.

Nevertheless, much of the future of the Left hinges on the question of whether there is any prospect that these parties might move towards more radical positions. The temptation, based on solid evidence, is to answer with a resounding negative, and to say that any expectation of social democratic parties being more than, at best, parties of mild reform, circumstances permitting, is a dangerous illusion. An important item in such a verdict is the fact that capitalist democracy gives social democratic leaders, both in parties and in trade unions, a powerful interest in working the system, in showing themselves to be moderate, responsible, and 'realistic'. Inevitably, this turns them into strong opponents of people on their left and leads them to wage war against them.

Against this, there are a number of different factors to be taken into account. One of the most important of these is the end of the Cold War, which has lifted the immense burden it had placed on the Left ever since 1945. Social democratic leaders had played a major role in the containment of left militancy in the inter-war years, particularly when it was Communist-inspired or led. This role became ever more pronounced after World War II; and it turned social democratic parties into invaluable allies of conservative parties. On all major issues, notably over foreign policy and defence, there existed in fact a fundamental consensus between social democratic leaders and their conservative opponents.[22] The Communist bogey was a most valuable weapon in the hands of social democratic leaders. Its elimination does not mean that their struggle against critics on the Left is now over; but it removes from the reckoning an argument against left critics that was used to great effect. 'Trotskyite' and other derogatory labels do not have quite the charge which 'Communist' and 'fellow traveller' once had.

The significance of the disappearance of Communism can hardly be over-estimated in other relevant respects as well. For ever since the coming into being of Communist parties after the Bolshevik Revolution, an unbridgeable gulf had existed between social democracy and Communism, and had meant among other things that many of the most militant activists in labour movements, who had opted for membership of Communist parties, were, wherever possible, effectively kept at arm's length from the bulk of labour movements; and this was greatly accentuated with the Cold War and the harassment of Communist parties, not least by social democratic labour leaders, which was one of its features. The division between social democratic and Communist parties was responsible for some catastrophic outcomes in the inter-war years, nowhere more so than in Germany, where the implacable enmity between Communists and social democrats played a major role in facilitating the access of the Nazis to power. Divisions between Left and Right in labour and socialist movements remain, but with nothing like the *institutionalized* intensity that previously existed.

However, by far the most important factor which is bound to affect social democratic parties is the failure of 'market economies' to tackle effectively a vast range of massive problems, from unemployment to the deterioration of public and collective services. The notion of 'crisis' in this context is somewhat misleading, in so far as it conjures up some immediate and dramatic episode or event in the economic or political realm, or in both. Such 'crises' are a common occurrence in all capitalist countries, but seldom threaten the regime itself. What is at issue here is a different sort of 'crisis', namely the

---

[22] The consensus also applied to the bitter and bloody struggle against movements of colonial liberation in former colonial possessions; and this struggle too was waged against 'Communism'. The French Socialist Party in particular was implicated after World War II in the savage wars waged by the Fourth Republic in Algeria and Indochina; but other social democratic parties in colonial countries, for instance the Labour Party in Britain, were also involved in such wars.

deterioration of the 'quality of life' for the mass of the people, and not only the most deprived, with a parallel and related weakening in the cohesion of political parties, and a consequent deterioration in the workings of the political system. This is the prospect facing capitalist democracies, and it poses an obvious challenge to the 'moderate' positions which social democratic leaders have adopted.

They may well wish to respond to the challenge by seeking to adopt even more 'moderate' positions; but they are then also likely to face considerable resistance on the Left. Social democratic parties have always been arenas of struggle between 'moderate' leaders and their left critics. This struggle has usually resulted in the victory of the leaders, though not without concessions having to be made to their opponents. The victory of leaders is explained by their control of the party apparatus; by the support which they have usually received from the majority of equally 'moderate' trade union leaders; by the divisions and uncertainties in the ranks of their challengers; by the use, already noted, of the dreaded accusation of Communist 'fellow travelling' against the critics, and the fear of the critics of being so labelled; by the support of a majority of their grassroots followers, who put a very high premium on loyalty to the leaders; and, not least, by the virulent denunciation of their left-wing opponents by bitterly anti-left newspapers.

Social democratic parties will remain arenas of struggle. But in conditions of economic, social and political malaise, with a political system unable to cope with evident ills like mass unemployment, deteriorating social and collective services, and general insecurity, the Left, in these parties and outside, may in future be able to exercise a greater degree of influence than it has in the past. Even on the most optimistic reckoning, this can hardly be taken to mean that social democratic parties will easily be turned into an unequivocal force for socialist advance; but they might come, to put it no higher, to be rather more open to radical policies than has traditionally been the case. The key factor in determining this is the manifold failure of the system, and the social and political repercussions of that failure. Because of it, eruptions of militancy from many independent groups over specific issues and grievances, without reference to or help from social democratic parties, will undoubtedly occur, and may well produce concessions from governments; and the pressure exercised by such groups is a crucial part of the democratic process. But more than this is required to make possible real and sustained advances in the direction of socialist democracy. Ultimately, the best that the Left can hope for in the relevant future in advanced capitalist countries (and for that matter elsewhere as well) is the strengthening of left reformism as a current of thought and policy in social democratic parties. The outlook for left reformism is at present rather bleak; but this does not detract from the crucial proposition that it will for some time to come constitute the best hope for the advancement of radical policies.

This too has very large implications. For it means, in this instance too, that a government in which left reformist purposes were predominant would be marked by continuities as well as discontinuities; in other words, it would not represent a total break with past experience, yet would involve a transcendence of that experience. This also means that such a government would be able to work with, and even include, people who were somewhere to the right of left social democracy, and also people who were to the left of it. Left social democracy, in this sense, represents a position around which at least some other currents on the left spectrum could rally, without surrendering their distinctive positions. Quite clearly, there will always be people on the right and on the left of left reformism who will choose to express their commitments in their own ways and in their own separate formations; and what happens to social democratic parties must to a large extent depend on the state of the Left outside them.

4

In this respect, it may be useful to look briefly at the past role of Communist parties.

Following the Bolshevik Revolution of October 1917 and the formation of the Third International in 1919, the Communist parties fostered by the International emerged in the countries of developed capitalism as the main opposition on the Left to social democracy. Their revolutionary credentials were vouched for by their membership of the Third International and their subscription to its '21 conditions'.[23] They also distinguished themselves from all other

---

[23] Including such items as the dictatorship of the proletariat, the unrelenting struggle against all forms of 'reformism', the combination of legal and illegal work, and undeviating acceptance of all the decisions of the Executive Committee of the International.

movements, particularly 'reformist' ones, by their violent hostility towards them, sentiments that were richly reciprocated; and their revolutionary vocation was in some ways confirmed by the harassment and persecution to which their members were subjected by the bourgeois state.

From the mid-thirties onwards, however, with the adoption of the Popular Front strategy, Communist parties became in effect the main representatives on the Left of left reformism. This evolution was obscured by their continued verbal adherence to Marxism-Leninism and to revolutionary rhetoric; by their unswerving defence of all the twists and turns of Soviet foreign (and internal) policies; by the internal exile this defence occasionally imposed upon them – for instance, their acceptance in 1939 of the 'line', until 1941 and the German invasion of the Soviet Union, that the war was an imperialist war; by their support of the Soviet Union in the Cold War; and by the harassment and persecution to which I have referred. With the invasion of the Soviet Union, the 'line' changed, and Communists played a major role in the resistance to Nazi occupation, and emerged from the war greatly strengthened.

Their strength in the immediate post-war years was largely used to help in a reconstruction of what was in effect the old order. This corresponded well both to Stalin's wishes and to the inclinations of Communist leaders in the countries of advanced capitalism. Immediately after the war, Communist ministers were members of bourgeois coalitions in France, Italy, Belgium, Austria, Denmark, Norway, Luxemburg, Finland and Iceland. After their expulsion from office at the onset of the Cold War, they remained essentially reform-oriented parties, different from social democratic parties in terms of their sharper and more radical programmes of reform, and their willingness to resort to extra-parliamentary agitation and action; of their opposition to the colonial and foreign policies of their governments;[24] and also of their continued subservience to the Soviet Union until the late fifties. These differences did not prevent them from being integrated, as far as they were allowed, into the political system, or from being fully involved in electoral competition.

[24] The French Communist Party after World War II, with Communist ministers in government, did vote for special powers demanded by the government to wage war against liberation movements, but these were lapses, however scandalous, in what was otherwise a sustained opposition to the colonial and foreign policies of successive French governments.

In the seventies, their subscription to what was called Eurocommunism confirmed the trend towards their 'social democratization', with the full acceptance of the parliamentary system, political pluralism, and the belief in an advance towards socialism by constitutional means. However, they too fell victim to the decline of the Left, much aggravated in their case by the general crisis of Communism in the eighties. By then, the French Communist Party, after its period of minority and very junior partnership in government from 1981 to 1985, was in steep decline; and the Italian Communist Party sought to achieve a more 'modern' identity by giving itself the innocuous name of the Party of the Democratic Left. Other Communist parties were involved in a similar process, or were actually dissolving themselves.

This decline easily leads to a great under-estimation of the importance which Communist parties once had in the life of the Left. For good or ill, it was these parties which constituted the main source of extra-parliamentary activism on behalf of progressive causes, and which did so out of all proportion to the number of their members; and it was also they which were the main source of socialist propaganda and education. The propaganda and education were marred by Stalinist deformations and a dogmatic rendering of Marxism. But Communist Party members, and many others, were nevertheless inducted into a mode of analysis – class analysis – which was a genuine alternative 'world view', and which provided them with a powerful 'counter-hegemonic' armature against the integrative propaganda of conservative forces.

On this score, the decline of Communist parties, for all their weaknesses and derelictions, has been a real impoverishment for the Left. But however it is judged, that whole experience belongs to an historical moment which is irrevocably gone. Communist parties or ex-Communist parties, in such countries as France and Italy, and elsewhere as well, will continue to play a role on the Left, with programmes of more or less radical reform. But they are unlikely to be the powerful pole of attraction that they once were to men and women seeking convincing agencies of commitment on the Left.

Where Communist parties have been dissolved, or have changed their name and moved away from their previous commitments, some at least of their former members have sought new political homes in existing formations or in new ones. This has already happened in a number of countries, notably in Italy, and will no doubt happen elsewhere as well.

The emergence of new socialist parties in many countries is one of the notable features of the present time. Most of them are small but they do have a place on the Left, and their membership and influence may well grow in the coming years. Indeed, their growth is essential if the Left is to prosper. For their strength as independent organizations of the Left is a condition for the affirmation (or the reaffirmation) of an unequivocal socialist presence, in intellectual, moral and political terms, in the national culture. These new parties of the Left do not share the perspectives of the parties of the 'revolutionary Left', of which more in a moment. They are 'reformist' parties, but their reformism has a radical edge which social democratic parties at present lack. They are not, in most cases, likely to supplant these parties, but they can act as a spur and a challenge to them.

In addition to these parties, there are green parties and other political formations which are part of a new 'New Left'. What this portends is the coming into being of alliances between groups whose differences, which are real, are not such as to create a solid wall between them, for they all share a common revulsion from capitalist values and all that goes with them.

It may seem somewhat eccentric to ask if any of this is relevant to the United States. In fact, it is not eccentric, for the same considerations which have provoked endless debate in, say, Britain, about whether socialists should or should not work in the Labour Party, or whether they should seek alternatives to it, have also preoccupied the American Left for a very long time in relation to the Democratic Party. In strict electoral terms, what might be called the reforming side of the American political scene has since World War II been virtually monopolized by the Democratic Party; and however sceptical people on the Left may be (quite rightly) about the reforming propensities and promises of a Democratic President, the assumption of the presidency by a Democrat nevertheless tends to reduce the inclination to build anything beyond the Democratic Party.

The 'old Left' was virtually destroyed in the late forties and early fifties. But various movements from then onwards, such as the civil rights movement, the opposition to the Vietnam War, the feminist movement, the green movements and the Rainbow Coalition have shown well enough that there is life on the Left outside the Democratic Party. Nor, despite all its manifest weaknesses and failings, would it be right to ignore the enduring importance of the trade union movement as a pressure group.[25]

It is of course impossible to say how the many disparate movements which are now part of the left spectrum in the United States will choose to act out their aspirations, and whether any coherent formation on the left of the Democratic Party will come into being. Attempts are being made in that direction; but whether they succeed or fail, it is at least important to note that the vitality of this left side of the spectrum shows how false is the idea of the United States as a nation wholly steeped in fundamental conformity. As was said earlier, capitalist hegemony is a massive reality. But the obvious strength of profoundly reactionary forces should not occlude the existence of significant opposition forces at work in American society; nor the fact that these forces can only derive advantage from the end of the Cold War, and from a strong and widespread sense that the United States is no longer able to meet the expectations generated by the belief in the 'American dream'. Indeed, the American dream has long turned into a nightmare for countless numbers of people in the inner cities, since their conditions make a bitter mockery of the notion of 'welfare capitalism'. How this will play itself out in political terms is one of the great unanswered questions of American politics.

5

Revolutionary socialism, in the strong sense of the term 'revolutionary', has, since the twenties, been mainly represented by a variety of

[25] See e.g. T. B. Edsall, *The New Politics of Inequality* (W. W. Norton, New York and London, 1984): 'Organised labor remains the major institution in theory most capable of pressing the interests of the working and lower-middle classes. The potential scope for this representation goes far beyond the demand for higher wages, extending to participation in the formulation of government policies concerning taxation, the distribution of wealth and income, health care, disability compensation, employment safety, education, vocational training – the list covers the entire spectrum of possible government activity' (p. 142). The trade union movement has suffered further weakenening since this was written; but not so as to invalidate the point being made.

groupings and sects, deriving their inspiration from Leninism and particularly from Leon Trotsky's life and thought.[26]

For present purposes, the main features of revolutionary Marxism may be divided into four related parts. First, there is the expectation that, sooner or later, the contradictions of capitalism will become so acute as to create a revolutionary situation leading to the overthrow of the existing regime by the working class under the leadership of a revolutionary party able to seize the opportunity presented by the situation. Secondly, there is the insistence that, in Marx's own words in *The Civil War in France* (1871), 'the working class cannot simply lay hold of the ready-made state machinery, and wield it for its own purposes', but that it must 'smash' that machinery and replace it with a state of an entirely new type, subject to genuine popular power, and well on the way to virtual disintegration.[27] Thirdly, and following from the second point, there is the insistence that, though reforms must be fought for, a radical transformation of the social order cannot be achieved by way of measures of reforms alone, that the ruling class will not abandon its positions without unremitting and, if need be, violent resistance, and that a major confrontation between revolutionary and reactionary forces is therefore inevitable. Fourthly, an important feature of Trotskyism is the notion that 'socialism in one country' is a nonsense and that revolution must be conceived on a global scale, with revolution in one country or in one continent detonating revolutionary upheavals elsewhere.

As a movement, Trotskyism has done very poorly almost everywhere. Trotskyist parties and groups have generally been very small in numbers, and extremely prone to splits, with bitter accusations and counter-accusations of deviation and betrayal levelled by the warring factions against each other. What Freud, in a different context, once called 'the narcissism of small differences' certainly applies to them.

From the early twenties until fairly recently, 'Trotskyism' was a term of virulent abuse by the Communist Left, and beyond it as well;

---

[26] For a convenient presentation of the perspectives of the most notable of these currents, the Fourth International, see E. Mandel, *Revolutionary Marxism Today* (New Left Books, London, 1979).

[27] K. Marx, *The Civil War in France*, in Marx and Engels, *Collected Works*, vol. 22, p. 328. What is involved is described at length in the pamphlet and in greater detail in V. I. Lenin, *The State and Revolution* (1917), in *Selected Works* (Lawrence and Wishart, London, 1969).

it is even today used by much of the Left as a term of abuse, and its adherents are berated as sectarian, opportunistic, and living in a self-made ghetto. To most people on the Left, Trotskyism has seemed to be an accumulation of slogans, with no bearing on reality.

Many of these charges are justified. But the propositions which are at the core of Trotskyism, and which I have noted above, do not warrant the instant dismissal which they are commonly given; in fact, they present a significant challenge to anyone seriously concerned with the advance of socialism.

It is, to begin with, a very 'utopian' socialist who does not take seriously the insistence that a gradual, constitutional and peaceful transition to socialism is an extremely problematic enterprise, simply because dominant classes are bound to fight hard to defend a social order which they believe to be the best attainable, and to try and defeat any attempt to dislodge them from the positions which that social order affords them. Nor would dominant classes be short of substantial support in other classes. This was the theme of Harold Laski's writings in the thirties, and he was no Trotskyist but an exceptionally percipient member of the Labour Party;[28] and there were of course many socialists in other countries outside the Trotskyist ranks who explored the same theme. For people who believe that socialism is dead, the question has ceased to have any meaning. For people who take a more sensible view, and are concerned with the advance of socialism, it is or ought to be at the centre of their thinking.

The real question, however, is not whether dominant classes and their allies in other classes would seek to resist socialist change: this may be taken for granted. The real question is how well they would be able to do so, which itself greatly depends on what a socialist government and movement would do about it. This will be taken further in chapter 6.

Secondly, there is the very large question of the state. As noted earlier, the notion that the state apparatus needs to be 'smashed' was formulated by Marx, taken up by Lenin and adopted by Trotskyism. Marx's idea, and Lenin's, was that the 'smashed' bourgeois state would be replaced by one of an entirely different kind,

---

[28]   For a recent discussion of Laski's writings on this theme in the thirties, see M. Newman, *Harold Laski: a political biography* (Macmillan, Basingstoke and London, 1993), and I. Kramnick and and B. Sheerman, *Harold Laski: a life on the Left* (Hamish Hamilton, London, 1993).

which would no longer be quite a state, in that its functions would have been largely taken over by the people.

In fact, a very real state is essential if socialism is to be advanced. It is of course the purpose of socialism to transform the state in democratic directions; but once socialists have rejected the idea that the state can be 'smashed', or that it can very soon begin to 'wither away', a host of problems arises. For a socialist government is then enmeshed in the coils of the old state, and will not find it easy, as we shall see presently, to free itself from them. Means have to be found to combine state power and popular power. This is a much more complex task than socialists have been willing to admit.

Other problems are implicit in the revolutionary (or insurrectionary) position. One of them is that the 'scenario' envisaged by Trotskyist groups of a revolutionary upheaval led to victory by a 'vanguard' party is nowhere remotely on the cards. I have already noted that the crises which afflict capitalism do produce violent eruptions; but this is not to be confused with a 'revolutionary situation' in which, in countries with a capitalist democratic regime, a majority of the population, or even a substantial minority, would support the overthrow of the regime under the leadership of a revolutionary party. It is possible to argue that what does not seem likely today will become reality tomorrow, or the day after, or the day after that. But where other avenues of radical change do not seem to be altogether blocked, as in the case of a dictatorship, it is these avenues which will be chosen rather than the insurrectionary one. Of course, matters must present themselves altogether differently where a ruling class is prepared – and able – to abolish democratic forms altogether. Even then, however, the outcome of a successful struggle against an authoritarian regime would in all probability be the coming into being of a very real state.

There is also the critical fact that where revolutions do occur, the result is not likely to be the establishment of a regime of popular power. The best that can be hoped for is a regime embodying at least some of the features of constitutional democracy; and this is an advance indeed when compared with dictatorial regimes. On the other hand, the more violent the upheaval, and the more prolonged the period of civil strife, the more likely is the outcome to be dictatorship. This is not to preclude the necessity of revolution where other possibilities do not exist. But where they do exist, revolutionaries have no option but to explore them.

As for 'socialism in one country', it is quite true that no such thing can be 'achieved'. But once the notion of socialism as an achieved state has been rejected, and socialism is seen as an objective involving a permanent striving, the point loses much of its strength: it is possible for a socialist government to *advance* the process, without waiting for world revolution. On the other hand, it is obvious that the more socialist governments come to power and move in the same direction, the greater the chances of cooperation, mutual help, and easing of the process.

For all its theoretical and practical weaknesses and flaws, insurrectionary socialism will remain a visible and vocal part of the Left, however much the rest of the Left may dislike it. The very marginality to which it is doomed is one factor among others which will continue to attract some people, for whom anything less marginal is itself a matter of deep suspicion.

6

This brief survey of the state of the Left suggests a twofold conclusion. At one level, there is a more vigorous life on the Left, understood broadly, than would be surmised from what is said about it: the notion of populations steeped in an apathetic unconcern for anything other than consumption is a gross misrepresentation. On all sides in capitalist societies, there is, on the contrary, a lively, often a militant, assertion of demands and rights, not least from people who not so long ago were hardly visible on the political scene – women, black people, gays and lesbians, the greens, the disabled, the young, the old. Nor have wage-earners and their unions ceased to make demands and assert rights, even if levels of strike activity declined in the eighties and beyond.

This must not be taken to signify any great interest on the part of the mass of the population of capitalist democracies in any specific socialist alternative to the present. On the contrary, there is a great deal of suspicion of any such alternative, derived in part from the experience of Communist regimes, which are often thought to represent what socialism really means. There is also the failure of social democratic governments to offer a clear alternative to conservatism, to which has to be added the corruption which in many countries has come to be associated with parties of the Left as well as the

Right. An explanation of popular indifference or hostility to the notion of socialism, in whatever version, must also include the failure of the mass organizations of the Left, notably social democratic parties, to press the case for it. From the seventies onwards, the Right was left in virtual command of the ideological terrain, with most of the Left unable or unwilling to engage in 'counter-hegemonic' struggles.

This, given the manifest failures of 'neo-liberalism', is already beginning to change; and, while a great deal of suspicion attaches to socialism as a word and as a doctrine, there does exist a great deal of support for demands which socialism encompasses, and which constitute a challenge to conservative ideology and practice – demands relating to welfare, public services, rights, democracy, fairness, justice, humane behaviour. Such demands and socialism are at present firmly dissociated. The problem for socialists is to show and make acceptable the link between them, and to explain that radical demands, for democratization, for equal rights for all, for the creation of communities of citizens, can only very partially be met, if they can be met at all, within the existing structures of power and privilege, and why their fulfilment requires the kind of comprehensive transformation which socialism signifies – yet to do this without in any way belittling the importance and value of the struggles which are conducted for immediate and limited reforms.

This 'counter-hegemonic' task is a collective endeavour, in the pursuit of which intellectuals can make an important contribution. There is a misguided notion in some parts of the Left that to say this is an 'elitist' attribution of a 'privileged' role to intellectuals. It is in fact no more than a recognition, based on abundant evidence, that intellectuals, on the Right and on the Left, can make a difference by articulating ideas which greatly influence political practice. This is not a matter of intellectuals, in the famous proposition of Kautsky so greatly admired by Lenin, 'bringing socialism to the proletariat from outside', but of helping to clear a path in the jungle constituted by contemporary reality. This is always needed; but it is particularly needed at a time when a multitude of new problems, in a world in the grip of extraordinary change, present themselves and require elucidation and resolution if advance is to be achieved.

It is now fashionable to say that Marxism has very little if anything to contribute to this enterprise – indeed that it a barrier to clear thinking. This is a great mistake. A distinction needs to be made between two aspects of Marx's thought. One of them is a vision of socialism and communism, which has never been surpassed, but which is a projection into a far-distant future. The other is the class analysis which is at the core of Marxism. This Marxism remains of incomparable value for the understanding of class societies and their conflicts, notwithstanding the refinements it requires in the light of developments in the world since Marx. Socialists who deprive themselves of its help are thereby greatly impoverished.

The coming to power of left-wing governments, armed with programmes of radical reform, and determined to see them carried out, nowadays seems a very remote prospect, particularly in developed capitalist democracies. But it was noted earlier that capitalist democracies are already faced with pressure from below for the satisfaction of a great variety of demands and expectations which they are unable to meet, or can only meet very inadequately. In realms of crucial importance, such as health, education, the provision of work, security of employment, acceptable practices at the place of work, the treatment of the young and the old, the struggle against crime, and much else that has a decisive impact on the 'quality of life' of 'ordinary people', these societies function badly or very badly. The same is true, on a vastly larger scale, for all other countries as well.

The accumulation of grievances which this implies will in time bring about, on the basis of strong popular support at the polls and beyond, the accession to power of governments of the Left pledged to carry out measures of radical reform and renewal throughout the social order. To dismiss this as mere fantasy is very short-sighted.

What then are the tasks and the problems that such governments would confront? To ask this is not an exercise in idle speculation. Much of the value of the question lies in the fact that it is only by probing what these tasks and problems would be that we are able to define what socialist advance actually means, and how it is to be achieved. Anything else amounts to little more than the spinning of a web of wishes, with little or no concern for immediate and concrete circumstances. It is not very difficult to outline in the abstract what an ideal socialist society would look like. It seems to me much more useful to discuss socialist purposes in the light of the real conditions their advancement would be most likely to confront. This is what I seek to do in the next chapter.

6

The Politics of Survival

1

The assumption was made at the end of the last chapter that a government pledged to a programme of radical, 'structural' reform, and determined to carry out its pledges, would in time come to power; and that it would come to power within the bounds of the existing constitutional system, that is to say by way of a general election in which a party of the Left, or a coalition of such parties, had won a majority of votes and a majority of seats in the legislative assembly.

I have suggested earlier that, while such a prospect may seem rather remote at the present time, there are good grounds for thinking that it is in fact rooted in concrete circumstances, and in the eventual will of a majority to change them. This involves a process of political evolution, of uncertain duration, in which political parties and other 'counter-hegemonic' forces have an indispensable role to play. As Gramsci said a long time ago, the counting of votes is 'the final ceremony of a long process'.[1]

Any such counting of votes, it was at one time firmly believed by revolutionary socialists, would be forcibly prevented by a coup from the Right if there was any likelihood of a government seriously committed to radical change coming to power. An example of such

[1] A. Gramsci, *Prison Notebooks* (International Publishers, New York, 1971), p. 193.

a preventive move occurred in Greece in 1967 when a colonels' coup anticipated elections which seemed likely to result in the coming to power of a government committed, not to socialist renewal, but to mild reform. Greece, however, was not a country with a solid capitalist democratic regime. Even so, revolutionaries have argued, reactionary forces, threatened with a loss of power, in circumstances of great political tension and polarization, after a prolonged period of political degradation, would be likely to consider seriously all possible means to avert an election outcome deemed to be utterly detrimental to 'the national interest'.

This possibility cannot be dismissed. But in countries with well-established democratic forms, and a strong tradition of constitutional rule, a preventive coup would be rather unlikely, first because it would be difficult to organize with any real expectation of success, and secondly because the consequences of failure could be the strengthening of the forces which the plotters were seeking to defeat. The Left would by definition have achieved considerable popular support before an attempt at a right-wing coup, and its response to any such attempt could easily assume explosive forms.

The cases of Salvador Allende in Chile in 1970 and of François Mitterand in France in 1981 illustrate the point that the real problem for the Left, within the constitutional framework of capitalist democracy, is not so much its accession to power by constitutional means, but rather what happens after it gets there. In the presidential election of 4 September 1970, Allende, benefiting from a split in conservative ranks, obtained 36.3 per cent of the votes, on a programme of extensive public ownership and a considerable democratization of the structure of power. There was some plotting by military men, encouraged by the United States, to prevent Allende from being voted into office by the Chilean Congress on 24 October, but this came to nothing and he was duly installed as president, though not before the constitutionally minded commander-in-chief, René Schneider, had been assassinated. In neither the Chamber of Deputies nor the Senate, however, did the Popular Unity government have a majority. This relative lack of support in the legislature was of great importance in itself, as the history of the Allende government was to show; but it was also of crucial importance in a different sense, in that it reflected less than massive support in the country. How much popular support a government bent on radical reform requires at the start if it is to have a real chance of success is not a matter of precise numbers; but it is fair to say that it does require a large and solid degree of such support, and the greater and more solid the support, the better the prospects. The achievement of that support clearly requires that a socialist party or parties should have previously been able to convince as large a number of the non-committed electors as possible that the election of a socialist government would be of advantage to them.

For his part, Mitterand was elected to the presidency in May 1981 as the candidate of a revived Left which included the Communist Party, and with a 'common programme' of radical change, including a considerable amount of public ownership.[2] Nor did the Left only win the presidency: it also achieved a very comfortable majority in the elections for the Chamber of Deputies. There was never any question of a preventive coup. In this particular context, the notion appears slightly ridiculous.

An electoral campaign in which a party or coalition of parties with a radical programme seemed a possible winner would no doubt be extremely bitter, with even more smears and scare-mongering than usual by conservative forces,[3] and some violence as well. But the chances are that, having won, a government of the Left would be able to assume office, and face an opposition resigned for the time being (at least as far as traditional conservative leaders were concerned) to wage a war of attrition against it, with the hope of bringing it down before too long without stepping outside the constitutional bounds.

On the other hand, if the government did begin to implement its commitments, *and* continued to enjoy popular support, there would be people in the opposition who would come to think that it must be destabilized and brought down by whatever means were required. It was after the Popular Unity Government in Chile obtained 44 per cent of the votes in local elections in March 1973 that plotting for

---

[2] The Left's 'programmatic statements from the 1972 Socialist–Communist Common Program onwards, all promised serious changes of a kind that had hardly been advocated, let alone practised, for decades in any advanced society': G. Ross, S. Hoffman and M. Malzacher, *The Mitterand Experiment: continuity and change in modern France* (Polity Press, Oxford), p. 5. The Socialist Party's own electoral manifesto of January 1981 was 'one of the most radical documents from a serious contender for power in Western politics' (ibid.).

[3] What lies in store for left parties in this connection is well illustrated by the daily diet of anti-Labour hysteria directed against a most moderate Labour Party by a reactionary tabloid press in the British general election of April 1992.

the overthrow of the government became really serious, and culminated in the military coup of September and the installation of the Pinochet dictatorship.

It is also worth noting that a coup does not necessarily mean that all constitutional forms need be abolished. The accession of General de Gaulle to the presidency of France in 1958, as a result of a military coup in Algeria (then a French possession) against the Fourth Republic, occurred within the bounds, more or less, of the French constitution.[4] In Brazil in 1964, the overthrow of the legitimate government of President Goulart and the establishment of military rule left Congress in being, though with reduced legislative powers. 'Simply by meeting regularly and uninterruptedly, the legislature produced, among the relevant populace and elites,' R. A. Pakenham notes, 'a wider and deeper sense of the government's moral right to rule than would otherwise obtain.'[5] In other words, there are many ways, depending on the country, in which an opposition could seek to bring about by unconstitutional means the demise of a government bent on radical change, and mask the reality of what had been done by maintaining some outward constitutional forms; and there are always conservative politicians and other notables available to help maintain the fiction of constitutionalism.

Here again, it may seem idle to ask how far such considerations are relevant to the United States, since the likelihood of the election in the foreseeable future of a president and Congress seriously committed to radical policies involving the erosion of corporate power and strongly redistributive measures must appear to be rather remote. The appearance, however, may be deceptive. For the United States is a capitalist country which, like other capitalist countries, is beset by a whole series of major problems; and while this offers opportunities to the Right, it would, as was suggested in the previous chapter, also strengthen demands for change. The election of President Clinton in 1992 on the slogan of 'change' may not portend much radical reform, but it does suggest that unresolved and obtrusive issues, with the train of insecurity, violence and malaise which they produce, could in time bring to power an administration and a Congress intent on the implementation of more radical policies than

[4] See e.g. J. Lacouture, *De Gaulle: the ruler, 1945–1970* (Harvill, London, 1991).
[5] R. A. Pakenham, 'Legislature and political development', in *Legislatures*, ed. P. Norton (Oxford University Press, Oxford, 1990), p. 87.

now seems possible. If this were to occur, the considerations which apply to the tasks of a reforming government elsewhere would also apply in the United States, with the even greater certainty that a serious attempt to implement a radical programme would encounter fierce, unremitting opposition in a country where corporate power and private wealth have for so long been immune from any such challenge.

As a general rule, it is quite certain that any left government in a capitalist democracy would be involved from the start in a struggle with a variety of conservative forces over most aspects of its policies. It is, in this perspective, remarkable that so much writing on socialism by writers on the Left should take little or no account of this struggle, and of what its consequences must be for the way the government proceeds. Thus, one of the most interesting works on socialist construction in recent years, Alec Nove's *The Economics of Feasible Socialism* (1983),[6] envisages the socialization of a large part of the economy without reference to the resistance this would engender and the additional problems of implementation this resistance would create. Similarly, one of the editors of a book of essays on *Market Socialism* (1989) writes that, under a socialist government, 'all productive enterprises would have to be transformed into self-managed firms and a system of holding companies created to administer the social capital.'[7] Again, what obstacles such an endeavour would have to surmount in the face of the opposition it would inevitably encounter, and what it would mean for the government, would seem to deserve at least some discussion, of which there is none. This points to a general failure on the part of many writers on the Left to take seriously the existence of a formidable structure of power in capitalist democratic regimes, and the lengths to which people will go in order to preserve it. To ignore this allows any amount of model construction; but the construction, however attractive, lacks any basis in reality. Revolutionaries may have tended to under-estimate what is possible within the compass of capitalist democracy; but social democrats have tended to be blind to the

---

[6]   A. Nove, *The Economics of Feasible Socialism* (George Allen and Unwin, London, 1983).
[7]   S. Estrin, 'Workers' cooperatives: their merits and limitations', in *Market Socialism*, eds J. Le Grand and S. Estrin (Clarendon Press, Oxford, 1989), p. 191.

severity of the struggle which major advances in the transformation of the social order in progressive directions must entail. Of course, all such warnings can be airily dismissed as left-wing paranoia, but this is to fly in the face of extensive experience.

Nor is the issue only one of economic reforms. It is also a question of the changes which a socialist government would want to introduce in other parts of the structure of power in the state and in society, in line with its ultimate objectives; these changes are also certain to be seen by opponents as profoundly subversive and as an intolerable threat to their idea of a good society. There is, in relation to reform, a crucial point to be made, namely that, as the Austrian socialist leader Otto Bauer noted long ago, it is not only revolution which dominant classes fear, but an accumulation of reforms which substantially reduce their predominance, even if that predominance is not thereby fundamentally challenged. Writing in 1936, after the crushing of 'Red Vienna', Bauer wrote that

> in reality fascism did not triumph at the moment when the bourgeoisie was threatened by the proletarian revolution: it triumphed when the proletariat had long been weakened and forced on the defensive, when the revolutionary flood had abated. The capitalists and the large land-owners did not entrust the fascist hordes with the power of the state so as to protect themselves against a threatening proletarian revolution, but so as to depress the wages, to destroy the social gains of the working class, to eradicate the trade unions and the positions of power gained by the working class; not to suppress revolutionary socialism, but to destroy the gains of reformist socialism.[8]

In the same vein, Paul Preston notes in relation to the Spanish Civil War that

> the origin of the conflict has to be sought not in extremist attempts to overthrow society but in reformist efforts to ameliorate the daily living conditions of the most wretched members of society . . . The achievements of reformist socialism at a time of economic crisis are as likely as all-out revolutionism to provoke attempts to impose a fascist or corporatist state.[9]

[8] Quoted, save for the sub-sentence at the end, by F. L. Carsten in 'Interpretations of fascism', in *Fascism: a readers' guide*, ed. W. Laqueur (Wildwood House, London, 1976), p. 420. The quotation is from O. Bauer, 'Der Faschismus', in *Otto Bauer, Herbert Marcuse, Arthur Rosenberg et al – Faschismus und Kapitalismus*, ed. W. Abendroth (Europäische Verlaganstalt, Frankfurt, and Europa Verlag, Vienna, 1968), pp. 153–4.
[9] P. Preston, *The Coming of the Spanish Civil War* (Methuen, London, 1983), p. xiii.

It is unnecessary to invoke the resort to fascism to see how valid the point is that dominant classes do resent an accumulation of reforms which tilt the balance of power and privilege some way against them. The Thatcher 'counter-revolution' in Britain in the eighties was not fascism in any sense. But there was by 1979 a strong sense, particularly in the middle and upper classes, that something like a soft counter-revolution was necessary (though this is not what it was ever called) in order to erode if not to destroy the gains which the working class had made in previous decades, to reduce if not to eradicate the power of trade unions and the positions of influence gained by trade union leaders,[10] and thus to make Britain 'governable' again. The 'winter of discontent' of 1978/79, with the strikes of public sector workers, greatly fuelled the resentments that had been accumulated, and the strikes were bitterly denounced not only by an hysterical tabloid press, but also by leading figures in the labour movement. A general sense was thus created that the trade unions were 'out of control' and that the strikers were guilty of monstrous indifference to the sufferings they were inflicting upon the 'general public'. Nothing of course was made of the fact that the strikes were provoked by the Labour government's imposition of a ceiling of five per cent on wage increases for public service employees, a measure which was later agreed to have been misconceived.

By 1979, the Labour government, which had lacked an overall majority, had long been in a state of virtual paralysis, and the labour movement at large was greatly divided. The government was duly defeated at the general election of 1979 and the 'counter-revolution' could proceed within the accommodating framework (at least for a Conservative government) of the British constitution: nothing more dramatic in constitutional terms was required. Methods of achieving what is wanted differ greatly according to place and circumstance; but the purpose itself is common to all dominant classes and those who act on their behalf.

The opposition which a committed radical government would encounter, and the problems it would in any case confront in the implementation of its policies, must sooner rather than later face it

[10] Save for privatization, the government's most persistent effort was directed at the weakening of trade unions: no less than five pieces of legislation were enacted for the purpose. Further legislation to the same purpose has also been enacted by the Major government.

with a fundamental choice – either to retreat, or to press on, and if the latter, how to proceed.

The history of social democratic governments has repeatedly involved such fateful choices. For it is after the first year or two of their coming to office after a major electoral success that the going gets harder, with the opposition recovered from its demoralization following electoral defeat and with a new energy to obstruct the government. In the first years, a government pledged to radical reform is carried forward by its victory at the polls; and the record suggests that, in its early days, a reforming government can achieve a great deal, as was the case with the Labour government in Britain between 1945 and 1947, and with the socialist government in France in 1981–82. It is after this first stage that a choice has to be made whether to continue with the programme or pause, which means in effect retreat. In 1948 in Britain, for instance, the Labour government elected in 1945 had to decide whether to move further on the path it had mapped out then, or to 'consolidate'. In the light of its ideological inclinations, and the difficulties which it confronted, there was not much doubt that it would opt for 'consolidation'.[11] But this *was* a choice, consciously made.

Similarly, President Mitterand, after a first year of serious reform,[12] found himself faced with a deteriorating balance of payments and had to make a choice between 'austerity' and 'retrenchment' on the one hand, and measures advocated by some members of the government, such as leaving the European Monetary System, setting up temporary import restrictions, and promoting investment and modernization, on the other. Mitterand chose the former course, with the suspension of wage indexation agreements and the introduction of a four-month wage freeze.[13]

[11] On this, see e.g. R. Miliband, *Parliamentary Socialism* (Merlin Press, London, 1973, 2nd edn), ch. IX, section 3.
[12] In addition to social legislation, such as a fifth week of holidays with pay, an extension of trade union rights, the abolition of the death penalty, the government embarked on an extensive programme of nationalization: 'Five major industrial groups in electrical and electronic engineering and chemicals were taken over, together with the two largest steel groups (already effectively controlled by the government since 1978), 39 banks (taking the share of banking in state hands from 60 to 90 per cent), two important financial holding companies and a major firm in each of aircraft, computers, telecommunications and pharmaceuticals.' P. Armstrong, A. Glyn and J. Harrison, *Capitalism since 1945* (Blackwell, Oxford, 1991, 2nd edn), pp. 331–2.
[13] Ibid., p. 327. 'This', the authors observe, 'was the first suspension of collective bargaining in France since 1950.'

It is of course impossible to tell whether alternative policies would have succeeded, but the notion that circumstances imperatively imposed one set of policies and actions upon reluctant governments, and that there was no other choice, is spurious. There is always a choice to be made. Whether a different choice from the one decided upon would be beneficial or catastrophic cannot be known but only surmised; and it is certainly true that it is much easier to opt for retreat rather than advance. Retreat eases pressure on the government, whereas advance involves further confrontation with powerful forces. Retreat means in effect the adoption of policies which meet with the approval of these forces, and is usually followed by defeat at the polls because of the disaffection in the working class which the policies adopted engender.

2

Before discussing in detail what kind of opposition a government committed to fundamental reform will encounter, we must note two factors which have a considerable bearing on the issue.

One of them, to take up again a point made in the last chapter, is how well prepared the ground has been in the years before the government's accession to office for the reforms it wishes to undertake; how much, in other words, its philosophy and its policies have come to be part, again in Gramsci's terms, of 'the common sense of the epoch', at least for a large part of the population; and how much in consequence the vote which brings it to office is not only a vote against hitherto governing parties, but a positive vote for what the government proposes.

Secondly, there is also the crucial question of the government's whole approach to its tasks. What is at issue here is of fundamental importance. For it concerns the degree to which the government is able – or willing – to combine determination on the one hand with flexibility on the other – a determination not to be deflected from its basic commitments, but a readiness to seek agreement beyond its own ranks in the immediate application of its policies. The obvious danger is that any such readiness may create problems within its own fold, and be taken as a token of weakness by its opponents. This is why demonstrated determination of purpose on the basic programme is essential even as flexibility is shown in relation to its application. The advantage of this relative flexibility is that the

opposition may well be weakened as a result of it, with some at least
of its elements being willing to consider a measure of cooperation
with the government. In any case, a government coming to office
within the constitutional system cannot well afford to adopt a different approach. A revolutionary upheaval, and the 'smashing of the
state apparatus' as part of the upheaval, obviously preclude any
kind of conciliatory approach: the achievement of office by way of
the electoral process imperatively demands it. An important reason
for this is that the combination of determination and flexibility may
bring over to the government's side large numbers of people who
had hitherto been suspicious of it, and who would be swayed by its
willingness to listen and take account of legitimate uncertainties and
complaints. This support from hitherto uncommitted people is obviously worth a great deal, both in immediate terms and also for the
government's future electoral prospects.

However conciliatory a socialist government newly come to power
might seek to be, it would still be confronted with intense opposition from the Right so long as it remained committed to radical
reform: opposition from inside the state; from conservative forces in
society; and from external sources. The three are likely to be closely
linked; but they are best discussed in turn.

A newly elected socialist government occupies one specific part of
the state system, the executive part, and is also likely to be supported by a majority in the legislature. Without such support, as
noted earlier, its task becomes virtually impossible: minority
governments, unable to rely on solid legislative support (and strong
popular support as well), are in trouble from the start. But the
support of a legislative majority still leaves the government with a
state apparatus, much of which, most notably in its upper echelons,
cannot be expected to share the dispositions and purposes of the
government, and some of whose personnel must be reckoned to be
deeply hostile to them. No doubt the election of a socialist government
on the basis of wide popular support would mean that the views and
policies of the Left had also gained the support of a great many
professional people, including people in the upper levels of the state
system. This is what had happened in France at the time of the
election of Mitterand to the presidency in 1981. But extensive
government intervention in economic life has always been widely
accepted in France, and welcomed by 'technocrats' with a very

pronounced 'sense of the state'. Even in countries with no such strong tradition, it could be expected that, as was once said about judges of the Supreme Court of the United States, a fair number of men and women in powerful positions in the state apparatus would 'follow the election returns' and serve the government, whatever reservations they might have about its policies.

With the dissemination of the ideas of the Left in the social order prior to the government's election, the picture of a state apparatus implacably committed from the start to the destruction of the government is clearly false. Some people in the top echelons of the administrative branch of the state apparatus would no doubt regard the government and its policies as disastrously mistaken and worse than mistaken. Some others would be more or less enthusiastic supporters; and the majority would probably be mildly or highly sceptical about the government's programme, but willing to go along with it and even to help its implementation.

This distribution of supporters and opponents would be very different in the various branches of the state. In the judiciary, for instance, the number of people really sympathetic to the government might be fairly small; and the number of such people could be reckoned to be even smaller in the upper reaches of the police, military and intelligence. But it would be wrong to single out these branches as exceptional: in all branches, there would be enough people strongly opposed to the government to create a problem.

In the same context, the government would have to reckon with the bitter opposition of the bourgeois parties in the legislature, even though this, assuming the government had a majority, would be much less troublesome than opposition elsewhere. Again, the government would also face opposition from units of local and regional government under the control of opposition parties.

As time went on, and as the government showed that it was resolved to implement its policies, some parts of the opposition might seek compromise and accept, however reluctantly, many of the changes which the government was introducing. Some of the opposition, on the other hand, would harden. Some top civil servants would be increasingly concerned to 'limit the damage' which their political masters were, as they saw it, inflicting upon the nation; and they would see it as their duty to urge more 'reasonable' policies, meaning in fact the erosion or abandonment of major items in the government's programme. Some judges, and perhaps many, would use their considerable powers in cases brought before them to render adverse judgements in regard to contentious issues of policy, with the conviction that they were doing so in the name of the law and common sense. A reforming government would inevitably intervene in economic and social life in ways which challenged the rights of property and entrenched privilege. It would do so under legal provisions; but many judges would consider it their duty to do whatever they could to resist the challenge, guided as they would be by the conviction that they were defending fundamental rights.

Members of the military and intelligence establishment would almost certainly view the government as embarked on courses which constituted a menace to the 'national interest', particularly as these courses affected their own domain; and they would naturally also take it as their duty to do all they could to defeat these policies. There is abundant evidence in all advanced capitalist countries that intelligence agencies constitute a world of their own, with such minimal control as to amount in effect to virtual independence in their day-to-day activities. For the United States, F. J. Donner speaks of 'the scope and intensity' of 'the secret war waged continuously for over fifty years against all shades of dissenting politics by the domestic intelligence community'.[14]

This is true of intelligence agencies everywhere else. But this 'secret war' has not only been waged against private citizens: it has also been waged against ministers and governments. Many members of intelligence agencies view the world outside through spectacles tinted with patriotic paranoia. It is through such spectacles that Harold Wilson, when he was prime minister, was taken by members of the security services to be an agent of the KGB; and his premiership was accordingly the target of a sustained smear campaign.[15] In the United States, J. Edgar Hoover, who headed the FBI for 48 years, had established a vast and secret record of information, much of it of a damaging sexual nature, on public officials, from presidents downwards, and this was extensively used, all, needless to say, in the name of security and the national interest. With the end of the Cold War and the end of the 'Soviet threat', socialist governments could not well be accused of being witting or unwitting tools of the Kremlin, but they could all the same be accused of seeking to reproduce,

[14] F. J. Donner, *The Age of Surveillance* (Knopf, New York, 1980), p. xii.
[15] See e.g. D. Leigh, *The Wilson Plot* (Heinemann, London, 1988), and S. Dorril and R. Ramsey, *Smear: Wilson and the secret state* (Fourth Estate, London, 1991).

against all reason, the system which had so disastrously failed in Communist countries, and thus to constitute a deadly menace to the public good.

It is not difficult to imagine how compelling members of intelligence agencies would find the notion that it was their duty to weaken a hated government; and the very attempt to reform these agencies would itself be construed as yet another proof of the government's perverse and unpatriotic intentions.[16] These agencies have close connections with members of conservative parties, with newspaper proprietors, editors and journalists, and other people who occupy influential positions in society; and the government would have to be prepared to confront a concerted effort to weaken it by way of black propaganda, forged documents and other devices. Local intelligence agencies are also part of an international network; and they could count on the help of foreign intelligence and other agencies.

The attempt by a socialist government to bring intelligence agencies under its strict control would provide an early – and crucial – test of its determination. This, however, would be part of a much larger enterprise, namely a considerable renewal of much of the top echelons of the state personnel. It is inconceivable that such a government would be able to advance its purposes if it could not rely on the strong support of the people at the top levels of the state apparatus. What would be required of them is not subscription to a narrowly defined 'world view'. It would be, as it has always been in capitalist regimes, a rough agreement with the fundamentals of the existing social order. This is quite compatible with disagreement on many aspects of policy. No government can function effectively if key personnel in the uppermost reaches of the state apparatus are actively opposed to the whole thrust of government policy. Unless such people are replaced, failure and paralysis must ensue. The question is not 'Is he one of us?', but, much more inclusively, 'Is he (or she) one of *them*?', that is to say someone with strong conservative or reactionary views. The guiding principle, in other words, is not 'Anyone who is not for us is against us', but rather 'Anyone who is not against us is for us.'

The changes that need to be made would be easier to achieve in

[16] After President Kennedy's election in 1960, 'almost everything on the Kennedy agenda Hoover perceived as a threat – not only to the nation, as in the case of the president's alleged softness on domestic Communism, but to Hoover and the Bureau itself': A. G. Theoharis and J. S. Cox, *The Boss* (Harrap, London, 1989), p. 327.

some branches of the state than in others. Senior civil servants can be replaced or moved. The problem is greater in the case of senior police, military and intelligence personnel. But it is a problem that would imperatively need to be overcome. Senior judges also pose a problem. As noted in an earlier chapter, a socialist government would need to appoint to judicial positions men and women of progressive disposition. The cries of outrage which this would provoke would be entirely synthetic. For implicit political criteria also govern the appointment of senior judges – or for that matter less senior ones – in capitalist democracies; and it is no accident that left-wing judges are extremely rare in these political systems. The spectrum extends from the utterly reactionary to the mildly liberal, and very seldom beyond it: a senior judge with socialist inclinations in these systems is almost a contradiction in terms. A socialist government would have to ensure that this ceased to be true; and that the spectrum came to take account of a changed climate of thought in the country.

3

Opposition within the state to a government set on radical change would of course be matched by opposition outside the state, in society at large. The most visible opposition would be that of conservative leaders in legislative bodies. But much more important opposition work would be done outside these bodies. As noted earlier in relation to the intelligence agencies, all leading conservative politicians are part of networks of association with influential people in many different walks of life, not only at home but abroad; and many of them would want to use their connections to the detriment of the government. This is one point where the skilful conduct of affairs by the government could well divide the opposition and deter some of its leaders from dubious enterprises.

An important role of a different kind would also be played by conservative parties in the country. They would be centres of propaganda throughout the length and breadth of the land; and they would also be centres of conservative activism, by way of meetings, demonstrations etc.; and this would also be true of a variety of associations, clubs and other organizations, all part of the 'earthworks' of civil society, and concerned in one way or another, and with varying degrees of virulence, to deplore, denounce and oppose what the government was doing, and persuade as many people as possible of the wickedness of its ways. Many organizations have been able to count on considerable financial help from conservative foundations and other agencies in the United States and elsewhere in the past;[17] and this help would be forthcoming all the more generously to sustain the struggle against a government plainly moved by evil intentions. It is instructive in this respect to recall the setting up of a secret organization by NATO in Italy at the height of the Cold War, named Gladio, with tentacles in other countries, whose task was to fight 'Communism' and its establishment in Italy and France, by whatever means were deemed necessary, including terrorism. Notwithstanding the end of the Cold War, such organizations, under different sponsorship, could be expected to come into being wherever a socialist government had been installed and was proceeding with its programme.

Churches would no doubt be divided in their attitude, but many members of the clergy could confidently be expected to oppose the 'divisive' courses on which the government was engaged, and to urge greater 'moderation' upon it, in effect meaning retreat from its purposes. On the other hand, it is worth stressing that a good deal has changed in religious institutions in the last few decades and that a socialist government could expect a real measure of support from the clergy, particularly at the lower levels of the church.

A good deal further to the right of all these voices of opposition, there would be neo-fascist groups whose members (and everybody else) would be encouraged by their leaders to view the government as involved in a conspiracy against the integrity of the nation. A socialist government would obviously be concerned to do its utmost to protect ethnic and other minorities from discrimination and attack. This alone would be sufficient to lead neo-fascist groups to denounce it as being in thrall to foreigners, blacks and Jews. Resort to violent action would readily be seen as a legitimate response to it, with attacks on left activists, officials and ministers, and with the occasional, or more than occasional, fire-bombing of the buildings of left parties, or of government buildings, or of immigrant hostels. Nor would neo-fascist and terrorist groups be lacking in recruits.

---

[17] Note in this connection the financial and other help which the neo-fascist National Front in France has received from the Reverend Moon's Unification Church (*Le Monde*, 8 February 1991), and the help which right-wing propaganda organizations in Britain have received from the strongly conservative American Heritage Foundation.

Already, with the growth of neo-fascist movements in Western Europe, acts of violence are committed on a daily basis by members of such movements, and others, against black people, Arabs, Jews, immigrant workers, refugees and other minorities; and the coming into being of a radical government would greatly enhance their propensity to violent activism.

As already noted in chapter 3, it cannot be assumed that all conservative politicians would be implacably opposed to such groups: in circumstances in which a left government was proceeding with the implementation of its programme, many such politicians, while formally disapproving of violent language and actions, would find some virtue in many of the views of neo-fascist groups, and would attribute their more indefensible actions to the alleged provocation presented by a government bent on national ruin. Here too, there is plenty to go on: the experience of many countries shows well how respectable politicians of the Right can come to be sympathetic to, and even to collaborate with, people whom they would shun in 'normal' circumstances.

The majority of newspapers could also be relied on to be highly critical of the government, with a daily exposure of its alleged failings and derelictions, and with dire warnings of the catastrophic pass to which its doctrinaire measures were bringing the country. On a less elevated plane, readers of the gutter press would be served with a daily ration of smears against ministers, officials and anyone else involved with the government. Nor would the 'quality press' be above such attacks; and the views, sentiments and denunciations issuing from conservative sources would be echoed wherever else in other media it was possible to place them. There would be nothing much new in all this: such propaganda is the normal output of conservative agencies against the Left, and is also directed at very 'moderate' social democratic leaders and parties when occasion demands, as it does at the time of a general election, or when any kind of left government is in office. The difference would lie in the heightened virulence that would be directed at a genuinely radical government and all its works.

In short, the coming to power of such a government is bound to create a situation in which all parts of society are increasingly drawn into taking one side or the other, with factories, offices, schools, universities, churches becoming arenas of struggle between Right and Left. A radical government is bound by its very nature to pursue policies which are to a greater or lesser degree resented and offensive to people whose privileged position in society, in terms of power, wealth, income, opportunities etc., are being seriously challenged, and who genuinely believe that any such challenge spells ruin for the country at large; and the same people would no doubt be able to count on the support of large numbers of people who had no privileged position, but who had been persuaded that the government was bent on courses that were dangerous and evil.

As in the case of the personnel of the state apparatus, it would be a mistake to view the whole of the business world as implacably and unanimously opposed to the government. At least initially, there would probably be a number of people in the industrial, financial and commercial world who would be prepared to wait and see, and some would even be willing to cooperate with the government. It is in this area that the point made earlier about the government's approach to the implementation of its policies is most relevant. Two deeply contradictory pulls would here be at work. On the one hand, the government would want very early on to introduce some of the measures to which it was committed and which would be viewed adversely by the 'business community' at home and abroad. On the other hand, the government would also want as much cooperation from business as it was possible to obtain.

The will by the government to seek and achieve cooperation from business would in any case be forced upon it by the fact that it had come to office in an environment dominated by corporate power. The immediate escape from that domination would be the equivalent, in economic terms, of 'smashing the state apparatus', namely the nationalization at a stroke of the main means of economic activity, and the wholesale dismissal of the people who had hitherto run the private sector, or at least the dismissal of anybody who was not clearly in favour of what was being done. Such an immediate transformation is not possible in the conditions envisaged here. Nor for that matter would it be in the least desirable if it were possible, since it would spell economic dislocation on a grand scale. This means in effect that the government would continue, for a certain period of time, to operate in the context of an economy in which capitalist enterprise played a major role. It also means, among other things, allowing firms an adequate rate of profit, and indeed helping them to achieve it.

To say this goes against the grain, but is inexorably inscribed in the actual situation a radical government would face, and cannot be altered by rhetoric. What makes it somewhat more palatable is that it need not deflect a socialist government from beginning the process of change to which it was committed. Capitalism, as was noted in an earlier chapter, comes in different shapes: in some countries, its freedom of action is more strongly constrained, in others less. A socialist government would need to constrain it in many crucial areas. Also, a socialist government would have to make it very clear that, if there was to be any kind of partnership between business and the government, it was the government that would be the senior partner. Its firmness would be an important factor in determining how far opposition to its purposes and policies would go.

The fact remains that much, even most, of the business world would be unhappy with the coming to power of a radical government, to put it no higher, and its unhappiness and hostility would most probably grow as time went on and the government continued on its course. Its hostility would assume different forms – vocal opposition, strongly expressed throughout the media, to what the government was doing or proposing to do; the attempt to circumvent, or even to disregard and evade, government regulations and controls; an investment strike explained by 'lack of business confidence'; the closing down of plants owned by foreign-owned multinational corporations; and speculation against the currency.

Even more important than this internal opposition are the constraints imposed upon national governments by the globalization of capital and the influence of powerful foreign governments and international institutions like the World Bank and the International Monetary Fund. How a socialist government would deal with this is considered in the next section.

4

Many people in recent years have taken the view that a socialist government would face an impossible task, given the ever growing integration of national economies into the world economy. This, and the formidable pressures it generates upon national economies, so it is claimed, make 'socialism in one country' even more utopian than it was in earlier days. 'Integration has gone so far', Susan Strange writes in this vein, 'that the establishment of a "pure" socialist state is no longer feasible.'[18]

This is one more reason why so many people on the Left have come to settle for cautious reform within a capitalist social order and have given up as wholly unrealistic any thought of going beyond it. This is, in effect, to accept the notion that this social order does for all relevant purposes represent the 'end of history': for it to be otherwise, and for capitalism to be transcended, there would, in this perspective, need to occur a more or less simultaneous eruption of socialist revolution in a number of major countries, with the consequent coming into being of a genuinely 'new world order', wholly different from the present one.

This is a fantasy. But it is also possible that the defeatism implicit, from a socialist point of view, in the acceptance of this notion, namely that liberal capitalism in an interdependent world economy is the best that can be hoped for, is based on far too pessimistic a view of the space which integration would leave to a socialist government determined to meet its commitment to radical reform. I have discussed this in chapter 4, and will discuss it further in the course of this chapter. But it is also important to be clear as to what a socialist government would seek to achieve in the early stages of its existence, and even for some time beyond. For what is at issue is *not* the achievement of socialism in one country, let alone the establishment of a 'pure' socialist state, but rather the initial steps in a process extending over a long period of time, and moving progressively in the direction of socialist goals. This clearly involves a sustained attack on the inegalitarian and undemocratic features which mark the existing social order, and, correspondingly, the redistribution of resources and power in favour of the vast majority which has hitherto formed the subordinate and disadvantaged part of the social order. It is short-sighted to take for granted that the present predominance of neo-liberal orthodoxies will last into the indefinite future, and that labour, socialist and other left movements will not gain (or regain) much greater strength in many capitalist countries than they have at present. It is also possible that a new international organization of the socialist Left might come into being, and establish a real presence on the international scene, which is beyond the

[18] S. Strange, *Casino Capitalism* (Blackwell, Oxford, 1986), p. 92.

capacity of the present Socialist International. An effective international organization of the socialist Left is badly needed; and so are international organizations of specific groups on the Left, among them intellectuals committed to socialist objectives.

By the time a socialist government seriously committed to radical reform comes to power in an advanced capitalist country, or anywhere else for that matter, the chances are that the international climate would be rather more favourable to the kind of interventionist policies which it would wish to pursue, with hostile governments and agencies at least less able to do much by way of opposition to such policies. The coming to power of a socialist government in one country would quite probably itself be a token of a more general shift of opinion in the advanced capitalist world. The present balance of forces in countries which are important players on the world scene would then have shifted, and would have created strong opposition by labour and left movements in these countries to policies directed against a radical government.

This would represent a major change in the character of world affairs since World War II. The world economy was largely shaped in the post-war years by the United States, and by its bias in favour of free trade, save where this did not suit its interests.[19] But American economic power has declined, and this, with the multitude of ills which plagues the United States, and the disappearance of the 'Soviet threat', is certain to make more and more Americans demand that their government should concentrate on domestic affairs rather than seek to police the world. This means that the United States will find it more difficult to assume the role of world gendarme which, as we noted in chapter 1, it played in the post-war decades; and this would be particularly the case in relation to governments legitimated at the polls in capitalist democracies. So too could it be expected that the power of international agencies such as the International Monetary Fund and the World Bank, closely linked as this power has been with that of the United States, would also decline. Nor would other major capitalist powers, such as Germany and Japan, be able to replace the United States in the role it had assumed after

[19]   The United States, one writer notes, 'suspended free trade principles whenever these were not in its economic interests': M. Hudson, *Global Fracture: the new international economic order* (Harper and Row, New York and London, 1977), p. 135. This has remained the pattern ever since this was written. Other countries do the same where they can.

1945. That role was then given plausibility and strength by the belief that the United States was, by virtue of its historic commitment to democracy, the natural standard-bearer of democratic forces against totalitarianism. Other countries would not easily appear in this light.

This is by no means to under-estimate the enduring importance of capitalist hegemony on a global scale, or how real will long remain what is in effect class struggle on an international scale; it is only to say that this hegemony will be much less assured in the future than it is at present, and therefore less able to prevent attempts at radical reform. No doubt some countries, notably in the 'developing world', are more vulnerable to pressure and blackmail than others; and left internationalism must nowadays largely be taken to mean support for reforming governments anywhere in the world, and opposition to the efforts of capitalist governments and agencies to deflect them from their endeavours or to destabilize them.

The fact of class struggle on an international scale inexorably points to the need for a socialist government to preserve as large a measure of independence as is possible. Notwithstanding the globalization of capital and the ever greater economic interdependence of nations, the nation-state must remain for the foreseeable future the crucial point of reference for the Left. This is not a matter of clinging to an 'obsolete' notion of sovereignty but simply to assert the right of a government seeking to carry out a programme of radical social re-newal not to be stopped from doing so by external forces. Such a government would clearly need to impose various measures, includ-ing exchange and carefully selected import controls, to protect its eco-nomy; and it would need to reject the constraints which the General Agreement on Tariffs and Trade seeks to impose upon governments.

A member country of the European Union would face the particu-lar problems associated with membership of an organization committed to 'neo-liberal' policies, only marginally qualified by the provisions of the Social Chapter. This too might change over time, but that cannot be relied on. One of the chosen instruments to advance these policies is the proposed European Central Bank and a common currency. This exemplifies the wish that animates the leaders of the Union to free the banking system from the 'interference' of politicians. As Bernard Cassen has aptly noted, 'the Central Bank, as the real economic and financial government of Europe, unelected, deliberat-ing behind closed doors, "in complete independence" in regard to national governments and parliaments, to the European Parliament and public opinion, will dispose of a degree of power which no national central bank (not even the Bundesbank) now enjoys in Europe.'[20]

Left integrationists readily agree that the European Union is marked by a considerable 'democratic deficit', but argue that the Left should therefore seek to increase the powers of the European Parliament. This is fine, but it is extremely doubtful whether that body could come to exercise a strong control over the European Commission or the Council of Ministers, and to exercise it for left purposes.

Left parties cannot retreat into a national bunker; and a socialist government would not leave the Union of its own volition, but would rather seek to find allies in its attempts to overcome unacceptable constraints. Its general aim would be to loosen integration in favour, at most, of arrangements which would leave a socialist government with the greatest possible degree of autonomous decision-making in economic and all other fields of policy. There are conservatives who advocate loose arrangements on narrow nationalist grounds. Socialists should advocate such arrangements on very different grounds, and should be committed to an internationalism based on solidarity with all left forces in the world. It will be time enough to consider closer connections when socialist governments exist in many countries: until this happens, the Left cannot accept integration into a 'union' whose members are actively opposed to the kind of fundamental transformation which it is the purpose of a left government to achieve. This is not to under-estimate in any way the importance of the globalization of capital or the internationalization of economic life. It is simply to say that socialists cannot accept a parallel political internationalization which, for the present and the immediate future, is bound to place intolerable constraints on the purposes they seek to advance.

5

For a socialist government to survive and prosper, certain conditions would have to be met. The very first is that the government itself

---

[20] B. Cassen, 'Au nom de l'orthodoxie monetaire', *Le Monde Diplomatique* (June 1992), p. 6.

should remain united. For whether the government is a coalition or not, it would be bound to be composed of men and women representing different positions in regard to its general strategy. It is one of the few firm laws of political life that any left government (or party or movement) will include three groups of people: those pressing for quick advance and uncompromising defiance of opposition; those inclined to dangerous concessions; and those inclined to a pragmatic view about the best course to adopt in the particular circumstances. In other words, there is always to be found a division between left, right and centre. This division is greatly exacerbated in a time of acute crisis. The crucial question is whether the government is able to maintain a degree of unity and coherence sufficient to proceed with its tasks.

One of the major concerns of the government would be to maintain and extend its support in the country. Nothing is more important than this. A remarkable feature of the history of the Left since the coming of universal suffrage is that a considerable part of its 'natural' constituency in the wage-earning population, and in the lower middle class, has chosen for a variety of reasons not to support parties of the Left. There is here a great reserve of potential popular support which these parties need to attract. This constituency of non-supporters is in any case part of that vast majority of the population whose place in society the government would be most concerned to enhance. Here too, however, the government would have to be mindful of the fact that the wage-earning population, or the lower middle class, is not a monolithic bloc; and one of the government's difficult tasks in its exercise of statecraft would be to strike a balance among the diverse claims which would be produced from within these classes.

Social democratic governments have traditionally been willing to go very far in sacrificing the interests of all sections of the wage-earning population with policies of 'austerity' and 'retrenchment'. Notwithstanding glib talk of 'equality of sacrifice', 'austerity', in practice, has always meant austerity for the working class, with unemployment, the reduction in public expenditure for collective and social services, a wage freeze, the curtailment of social benefits, and all the familiar train of measures which form part of such policies. A socialist government, on the contrary, would be absolutely determined from the start to make a real improvement in the conditions of life of the great majority, by way of visible advances in the provision of collective services and by tackling as a matter of the utmost urgency the most obvious blights on society – unemployment, deprivation, homelessness and so on. The government would bring to this task the same spirit that moves governments in relation to war. Even minor wars, not to speak of major ones, produce an extraordinary deployment of resources which were said to be unavailable for peaceful purposes. For the Falklands/Malvinas expedition in 1981, billions of pounds which had not been available for health, education, housing and transport were suddenly found to exist after all. So too did the United States government, which did not have the resources to save the inner cities from continuing degradation, find it possible to send half a million soldiers across the globe to expel Iraq from Kuwait; and to embark on the so-called Strategic Defence Initiative, also known as Star Wars, costing billions upon billions of dollars, dreamt up by President Ronald Reagan, and now widely recognized to have been a hare-brained scheme. The same determination which moves bourgeois governments to deploy resources for miltary purposes would move a socialist government to wage war against intolerable conditions at home.

Such a war would entail financial burdens; a socialist government would see to it that the greatest part of the burden would fall upon those best able to bear it. This is not a matter of vindictiveness towards corporations and higher income groups, but a matter of fairness and genuine 'equality of sacrifice'.

The focus so far in this chapter has been on what a socialist *government* would need to do in order to survive. This is not due to a 'statist' or 'centralist' bias, but to the fact that it is the government's own actions which would in large measure determine its chances of success. It is on the other hand quite certain that a crucial element in its determination of policy and action would depend on the support it enjoyed *and* on the pressure to which it was subjected from groups concerned with the advancement of its programme. That pressure is a key element in the total picture. It is, however, upon the government that would inevitably fall the ultimate responsibility for deciding what to do and how to do it at any particular time. It would certainly be engaged in the widest possible process of consultation prior to decisions being made; and it would also be acting on a firm mandate from the party or parties which it represented. This is an essential part of the democratic process which the government was pledged to follow, and which it would want to enrich by widening as far as possible the opportunities for effective participation by anyone willing to help. In the end, though, and however elaborate and thorough the democratic process and the pressure from below that had gone into the making of policy, major decisions would have to be entrusted to the people in charge of the executive power.

Among the organizations upon whose cooperation the government would have to rely are trade unions. For all the fulminations of politicians and newspapers against trade union power, that power, in relation to government policy, and particularly in comparison with the power of capital, has really been quite small – with the exception of Sweden under a social democratic regime. The notion has been fostered that British trade unions in the sixties and seventies had Labour governments under their thumb. In fact, what is most notable about those years is how much trade unions sought to cooperate with the government, usually on the government's own terms. The idea that the trade unions then, or at any other time, had 'too much power' is part of a distortion of reality, one of whose purposes is to obscure the power of capital. The country where this is most evident is the United States, where the unions have been painted as a 'special interest', a formulation which has a faintly sinister ring, and which carries the implication of selfishness, greed, and indifference to the public good, vices from which corporate power, not being a 'special interest', is absolved. But while the United States leads the way in this distortion, Britain and other countries do not lag far behind.

This is not to say that trade unions are free from vices. In particular, they tend to share the oligarchic tendencies of all large organizations, with structures of power which inhibit and stifle democratic participation. The democratization of society would clearly include greater democracy in the organization of trade unions. Changes in their organization and mode of operation are in any case necessary in the light of the changes which have occurred in recent decades in the nature of work and the composition of the labour force, with part-time working and casualization making trade union organization much more difficult than in the 'Fordist' era. A socialist government would acknowledge that trade unions are an essential means of defence and redress for wage-earners and other employees, and that

this is even more true now than it was in the past, given the propensity of employers to use the new conditions of work to deny their
employees the benefits in regard to health, security and conditions of
work which had earlier been achieved. A socialist government would
seek to strengthen trade unions, help them widen their membership,
and make them effective, though autonomous, partners in the enterprise in which the government was engaged.

The government would also have to rely on the support of left
parties and other associations. Left parties need to fulfil a number
of roles. They would need to explain and defend the policies being
pursued; and they would constitute a visible local representation of
the government's purposes. In every locality, parties would need to
be centres of activity and persuasion. On the other hand, the party
and its activists would be a vital channel of information about currents of thought and feeling at the grass roots; and they would also
serve as a constant and critical reminder of what the most dedicated
supporters of the government expected from it.

A close partnership would need to be forged between government
and activists, of a kind that would replicate the partnership, referred
to earlier, between government and business; and this would represent a continuation, in different circumstances, of the partnership
which had been established between activists and party leaders in
opposition. In Marxist thought, 'dual power' has always been taken
to mean an adversary relation between a revolutionary movement
operating in a revolutionary situation, and a bourgeois government
under challenge from that movement. It is, however, possible to
think of dual power in different terms: as a partnership between a
socialist government on the one hand and a variety of grassroots
agencies on the other.

In no way would activists be mere servants of the government. On
the contrary, they would have an organized life of their own, and
they would affirm their presence on the scene as they saw fit. No
doubt there would be cooperation with the centre, but it would be
a cooperation marked by a high degree of autonomy at the periphery. This would be one instance of democracy at the grass roots,
with self-organization and self-initiative as guiding principles. Such
grass roots democracy would no doubt create a certain tension between the partners, with many activists most probably pressing for
more radical advances than the government would favour. These
differences of perspective are inevitable, with the government

burdened with the knowledge of the vastness of the task which it had undertaken, and very conscious of how arduous was the path it was treading; and with activists equally conscious of how much needed to be done that had not yet been done, and impatient with delays in the implementation of the programme. I noted earlier that tension between leaders in government (and in opposition) and activists, or large numbers of activists, has traditionally been the result not simply of different locations in the process of change, but of deep differences in *ideology*, with a very wide gap separating leaders and activists on this score. It may be assumed that the partnership between them, based upon a genuine democratic process and a far greater unity of purpose than had been the case hitherto, would greatly attenuate the strains between leaders and the grass roots.

One of the activists' main tasks, as noted, would be to explain and defend the government's policies and actions, and to counter the opposition's propaganda. But much would also have to be done from the centre: the government itself would need to use all the resources at its command for the purpose. It would in this connection have to follow the example of conservative governments and engage in its own massive and sustained campaign of persuasion, distinguished, however, from the similar exercises of its opponents by its commitment to truthfulness. One of its concerns in this field would be to support the flowering of a left press which, though independent and critical, would have a distinct bias in its favour.

6

All that has been said here about a socialist government's prospects of survival and success is based on an assumption which is bound to be unwelcome to socialists: the assumption, already made in chapter 3, that in a first period, necessarily of uncertain duration, the executive power in the state would need to be very strong. This clearly runs counter to the very pronounced anti-statist bias which has dominated the thinking of most of the Left in recent decades. This is an understandable recoil from the experience of Communist regimes, where the state, or the party-state, ruthlessly dominated society; and it also rests on a strong and healthy belief that the state is in any case a likely source of arbitrary, bureaucratic and undemocratic deformations, and that socialism pre-eminently means the reappropriation by society of powers alienated to the state, with a steady and drastic reduction of state power. This of course has also been a fundamental theme of classical Marxism, and forms part of the 'anarchist' side of Marxist thought.

The problem – and it is a problem – is that a strong executive power is an absolutely essential, though not a sufficient, condition for the government to survive at all, and for it to do what it is committed to do. Notions of popular power as a *substitute* for a strong executive simply do not match up to the tasks which a radical government would face. What agency but the state has the power to tackle the multiple blights of capitalism – exploitation of workers and consumers, ecological vandalism, impoverished social services, inner city decay, racial, gender and ethnic discrimination, gross inequality in every sphere of life, and so much else that is part of a capitalist social order? Related to this, what agency other than the state can lead the drive towards a different, egalitarian and democratic, kind of society?

The fact is that executive power *can* be used to advance progressive purposes. The history of capitalism itself shows this to be the case: a radical government and the state under radical control would be needed to do infinitely better what the capitalist state has reluctantly and grudgingly been forced to do over the years.

A strong executive power would be essential if a socialist government was to endure and make progress. For it could not otherwise cope with the emergencies that it would almost certainly face. In conditions of acute crisis, a radical government would need to be armed with the kind of powers which have always been at the disposal of bourgeois governments in times of crisis, and of which so little is made in orthodox descriptions of liberal democracy.[21] These powers are remarkably extensive, even in peacetime, and in circumstances which bourgeois governments declare to constitute an emergency. In wartime, they are truly extraordinary, and include virtually unlimited powers over persons and property. It would be an odd logic for people on the Left to wish to deny to a left government some at least of the powers which bourgeois governments commonly use in a state of emergency. These powers have usually

[21] For a notable exception, see C. L. Rossiter, *Constitutional Dictatorship: crisis government in modern democracies* (Princeton University Press, Princeton, N.J., 1967).

been deployed by these governments to defeat strikers and to harass and subdue parts of the Left. A radical government would use them to do whatever was required to deal with the emergency, and also to cope with the unlawful actions, often of a violent nature, which some parts of the opposition would undertake.

The notion that special powers might have to be invoked, however legitimately, by a socialist government does greatly jar. The use of special powers is habit forming, and leads to a style of rule which, pushed far enough, must spell a drastic erosion, or even the abrogation, of democratic forms.

As was also noted earlier, this, however, is by no means inevitable. Thus, it cannot be said that, for all the vast and discretionary powers which they have wielded in emergency situations (or situations declared to be such), bourgeois governments moved from capitalist democracy to authoritarianism. Democratic forms remained, even though their functioning was severely curtailed. Civic freedoms were subjected to definite limitations, but were not wholly abrogated. These limitations can be endured where the majority of the population supports what the government is doing, or does not actively oppose it. This has generally been the case in states of emergency proclaimed by bourgeois governments, particularly in wartime. Where this support is lacking, and where there is strong opposition, the imposition of a state of emergency is likely to exacerbate the crisis and produce conditions not far removed from civil war. What this means for a socialist government is that it imperatively needs the support of a substantial part of the population for what it is doing, and this is particularly so if it does need to invoke emergency powers. In any case, these powers would need to be carefully limited in time, subject to careful legislative scrutiny, and renewable only where a strong case had been made for their renewal.

All governments, when hard pressed, are tempted to behave in arbitrary ways; and a socialist government, faced with a multitude of grave problems, would also be subject to that temptation. This is why effective constraints upon the exercise of power are essential. But it is as well to be clear that the realization of a programme designed to transform the social order in democratic and egalitarian directions requires, as an essential condition, that the government be equipped with adequate power. It is only where that condition is met that a socialist government would be able to proceed with the reforms to which it was committed.

7

Prospects

1

The liberation from capital is nowhere on the agenda of politics. The 'new world order' will for a long time to come be a capital-dominated world order, run by corporate power and by governments acting, as far as circumstances permit, on its behalf; and this gloomy prospect applies as much to ex-Communist countries and the countries of Asia, Africa and Latin America as to the countries of advanced capitalism.

In the latter, the domination of capital is as well assured as it has ever been. Governments come and go; political crises of every kind are a frequent occurrence; revelations of corruption in high places are common; the political system is viewed with great cynicism; economic woes abound and social problems multiply; unemployment on a massive scale is a stubborn fact; crime is on the increase and so, relatedly, is the spread of drugs; and neither single governments nor governments acting in concert are able to make much difference. But this leaves the rule of capital unimpaired and virtually unchallenged; no social democratic party is nowadays concerned to mount a serious challenge to that rule. As for conservative governments, their policies are designed to strengthen capital, not to weaken it. For some time to come, this will remain the underlying reality for the countries of the advanced capitalist world.

One important capitalist country whose future in the next few years remains very unsettled is South Africa. But it would be a very optimistic socialist who could believe that a government dominated by the African National Congress would be able to begin in earnest the implementation of a socialist programme. This is not to say that such a government would not constitute great progress; but it is most unlikely that an ANC-dominated government could do more than extract from South African capitalism enough revenue to ensure real advances in housing, education, health, transport and other services for the black population: in other words, to turn South African capitalism into something approximating to the welfare capitalism that has hitherto been reserved for whites. That would be an advance indeed, so much so that even this may prove far too optimistic, given all the difficulties and resistances it would encounter from an entrenched and powerful white minority. If it does prove too optimistic, the gulf between a 'moderate' ANC leadership and radicals in the townships will widen, with disastrous consequences. In any case, the chances are that South Africa will long remain in the capitalist fold.

As noted in a previous chapter, ex-Communist countries are now in a process of transition towards capitalism, a process strongly encouraged by the United States and other Western powers, and by international institutions like the IMF and the World Bank. Not that much encouragement is really needed: former members of the Communist *nomenklatura* and a new generation of 'Thermidorians', including entrepreneurs on the margin of legality, or actually well beyond it, are eagerly exploiting the opportunities which a chaotic economy and improvised privatization afford them. The process is still at its beginnings, but it may confidently be expected to spread much further. One of its features is the implantation of multinational companies in strategic sectors of the economy. As everywhere else, the larger interests of the countries in which they are implanted are of no concern to these firms; all they naturally want is the maximization of their own profits, whatever negative effects this may have on the cities and regions where they are (temporarily) located. Governments newly converted to 'free enterprise' are unlikely to provide any effective counterweight to them.

The wild capitalism which is being established in ex-Communist countries will need to be backed by regimes able to serve the new bourgeoisie and to contain and repress the discontent which the process generates. This means that, alongside weak democratic forms,

which need to be maintained, not least for international public relations purposes, these regimes are likely to exhibit strong repressive
features, and seek to gain support by demagogic appeals to a nationalism deeply tinged with ethnic racism. It is also quite possible that,
where governments find themselves in the grip of intractable problems and are subjected to great pressure from below, the full authoritarian option will be taken up, of course in the name of the
defence of democracy.

China remains a Communist country in name because it is ruled
by a monopolistic Communist Party, which continues to proclaim
its commitment to 'socialism'. But it is the same Communist Party
which is presiding over a frantic drive to extend the 'market economy'
and to affirm the values which the formula embodies. Private enterprise still represents a small fraction of industrial capacity, but has
spread to the land, where the overwhelming majority of the Chinese
population still lives. On present trends, it seems likely that private
enterprise will come to dominate all sectors of economic life. How
this will affect the regime is an open question; but its transformation
from a dictatorship with strong Stalinist features to anything resembling socialist democracy is a long way off. For the present, it remains
a resolutely repressive regime in which any form of dissent is savagely
dealt with.

Whether the Castro regime in beleaguered Cuba can overcome its
present difficulties is very uncertain. If it does, it may well shed the
negative features which have so greatly helped its enemies to obscure
its achievements. In the face of unrelenting American harassment,
its survival as a country committed to socialist purposes would be
a major gain for the Left everywhere.

As for the dictatorship of Kim Il-Sung in North Korea, it merely
serves as a grim reminder of how extreme a caricature of socialism
Communist regimes can be. In this case, it would seem that the
demise of the regime can at best be followed by a capitalist regime
patterned on South Korea.

In the 'third world', it is quite clear that where economic development occurs, it will be under capitalist auspices, with Western
capital much involved in the process. In the fifties and sixties, there
was much talk of African socialism and Arab socialism, and there
was also much hope that countries in Latin America might seek to
emulate the victory of Fidel Castro in Cuba. So too was there much

hope on the Left that Maoism would turn China into a beacon for socialists everywhere. All this proved illusory – the product of a will to believe rather than sober analysis. Also, such hopes as had been placed in the 'Marxist-Leninist' regimes of Angola and Mozambique have long vanished. A major reason for this, but not the only one, is the war which the governments of both countries have had to wage with anti-government forces supported by the United States, South Africa and Israel.

India too, after its liberation from British rule, generated hopes that it might move in socialist directions. This has also proved illusory: India, for all the rhetoric that was once common among its leaders, is a solidly capitalist state, and will long remain so.

In the decades following World War II, governments in Asia, Africa and Latin America were able to engage in a balancing act between the United States and the Soviet Union, and exact some advantages from the rivalry of the two 'super-powers'. Now that this has gone, governments in the 'third world' have accepted the hegemonic role of the West and adapted their economic and social policies to it. The price for not doing so is beyond their capacity and their will.

2

All this should be a matter of great rejoicing on the Right, as it is a matter of distress and despair on the Left. But after a short burst of triumphalism following the fall of the Berlin Wall and the disintegration of the Communist world, there is in fact very little rejoicing on the Right. For it is quite obvious that the 'new world order' is in fact an immense disorder, with which capitalist powers are unable to cope. Far from being in the least attenuated, the woes of the world grow ever more pronounced and painful. The threat of nuclear annihilation by war between the 'super-powers' has gone, but nuclear proliferation makes a 'local' nuclear war more rather than less likely in the years ahead. To this must now be added such issues as ecological disaster, the population explosion, the growth of mega-cities in which a decent life for the majority cannot be had, and the perpetuation and growth of poverty, deprivation and destitution on a global scale.

This situation, as I have noted in previous chapters, provides an extremely fertile terrain for the growth of what I have called pathological deformations of many kinds. Demagogues and charlatans peddling their poisonous wares abound; and the message they peddle is one of ethnic and religious exclusion and hatred. This is not confined to any particular part of the world. It affects the rich and stable societies of the West as well as the rest of the world. In the United States in particular, a noxious breed of televangelists preaches a deeply reactionary brand of Christian fundamentalism; and others, of a secular cast of mind, find audiences for their own reactionary politics. Anti-communism is no longer as effective as it was; but there are other enemies in plenty to be denounced. As the inner cities continue to fester and plunge ever deeper into hopelessness punctuated by violence, so does racism gain new strength, with insistent calls for the strengthening of the state's repressive apparatus.

In Western Europe too, immigrants have become the scapegoat for the ills of society, and are the target of gangs bent on violence and murder. Immigrants and other minorities, particularly black people and Jews, serve a very useful purpose: hatred of them provides many people with an identity largely based on exclusion. Increasingly, neo-fascist groups like Le Pen's Front National in France or the Republikaner in Germany gain electoral respectability. On the outer fringe, violent people nostalgic for Nazism form networks spread across Europe; and terrorism is part of their mode of political intervention.

Christian fundamentalism is matched by Islamic and Jewish (and in India Hindu) fundamentalism. In Israel, religious zealotry is linked to a rabid nationalism whose common basis is the rejection, however hopeless in the long run, of any notion of Palestinian statehood. Islamic fundamentalism, and Hindu fundamentalism as well, feed on the discontents produced by the failure of corrupt governments to do anything much, or anything at all, for the people they rule. In many cases, it is also an expression of a nationalism which feels threatened by Western hegemony. In any case, it too spreads a message of intolerance and exclusion.

Everywhere, ethnic and national racism is on the march, and delivers its daily dose of cruelty, violence and murder. In any twenty-four-hour period, as surely as the movement of the planets, countless men, women and children across the globe are doomed to meet a violent end. Nor is there any reason to think that this will not go on for a long time to come.

3

This catalogue of horrors and miseries could easily be extended; and it raises again the question whether what has been said in the preceding chapters about the possibility of radical improvements in the human condition under an entirely different social order is not a rather ridiculous illusion, a construction of a utopia which can have no basis in reality. Does not the state of the world seem to confirm a post-modernist view of life which Shakespeare put in the mouth of Macbeth – 'a tale told by an idiot, full of sound and fury, signifying nothing'?

To take this view, and to be overwhelmed by the evil stalking the earth, is to miss a great deal which points away from pessimism and despair. For it is essential to bring into the picture the fact that it is a *minority* which is susceptible to the pathological deformations I have noted *and* which is prompted to act upon them. Again and again, we find that it is a minority which is vocal in the affirmation of exclusion, intolerance and hatred, and which performs murderous deeds. As I have also noted in an earlier chapter, the great mass of people in all countries may acquiesce in what is done in their name, and may even support it, or turn away with unease or silent reprobation. But to ascribe to the vast majority the cast of mind which impels criminal behaviour and to charge that majority with guilt for the crimes committed by the minority is a dangerous and debilitating mistake: for it unjustly condemns whole populations, and it enhances the belief that nothing much is possible by way of progress.

Also, in addition to a reactionary minority and a more or less passive and acquiescent majority, there is a third element in play, namely a minority which actively *opposes* racism, xenophobia, antisemitism, fundamentalist intolerance and other such evils, often at considerable risk. In essence, the shape of things to come largely depends on which of the two minorities will be able to win the battle for the 'hearts and minds' of the larger part of the population.

On this score, the prospects are not nearly as sombre as is often made out. The reason for saying this lies quite simply in the nature of capitalism and in its failures. Much has been said about this in these pages in relation to advanced capitalism. But the point applies with even greater force in relation to countries where life tends to be far more nasty, poor, brutish and short. The majority of people in the world live in countries where a wild capitalism prevails, where welfare provision is minimal or non-existent, where drinking water is a luxury denied to masses of people and where sanitary conditions are appalling, where unemployment affects much of the population, where vast numbers of children are put to work at the age of six or seven, where rates of infant mortality are horrendous, where child prostitution is common, and so forth at sickening length. At the same time, in the same countries, men of power in the state and in society have it as their main concern to maintain and reinforce a system which gives them and the local bourgeoisie a life of ease and comfort and luxury; and where they speak of reform, it is always on condition that this should not endanger the prevailing social order. In this, they can rely on the support of Western governments and international institutions.

Such a situation cannot endure. It simply makes no sense to believe that men and women who *know*, because of the revolution in communications, that there is a different life to be lived will not in time seek to achieve a different and better life. Already, tyrannical regimes have been overthrown by popular explosion; and where elections have been forced upon tyrannical rulers, majorities have taken advantage of the opportunity to throw them out; and in countries of the ex-Communist world, elections demonstrate that, while people do not want to return to the old regime, neither do they want the wild capitalism which is being imposed upon them. I noted in an earlier chapter that change in the political system and the advent of 'democracy' do not change the social order; but the demand that it too should be radically changed is certain to come into focus, as indeed it already has in many countries. The specific demands and the forms of struggle which they generate will vary greatly from country to country: there is no single 'model' of progressive or revolutionary change. But everywhere, there are common goals and aspirations, of the kind I have sought to describe and define here – for democratic forms where they are denied, and for more democratic forms where they are no more than a screen for oligarchic rule; for the achievement of a social order in which improvements in the condition of the most deprived – often a majority of the population – is the prime concern of governments; for the subordination of the economy to meeting social needs. In all countries, there are people, in numbers large or small, who are moved by the vision of a new social order in which democracy, egalitarianism and cooperation – the essential values of socialism – would be the prevailing principles of social organization. It is in the growth in their numbers and in the success of their struggles that lies the best hope for humankind.

Index